D1196622

ment in the works of Hawthorne and Poe. Irving, in contrast, created a lighter, often humorous branch of the Gothic, balancing its terrors with a fundamentally rational viewpoint.

The Gothic mode has too often been denigrated by critics. Here, through his exploration of its antecedents and his analysis of both major and minor Gothic writers, Mr. Ringe brilliantly elucidates the growth and flowering of an important branch of American literary expression.

Donald A. Ringe, professor of English at the University of Kentucky, is the author of books on James Fenimore Cooper and Charles Brockden Brown, and of *The Pictorial Mode: Space and Time in the Art of Bryant, Irving, and Cooper.*

AMERICAN GOTHIC

Imagination and Reason
in Nineteenth-Century Fiction

DONALD A. RINGE

THE UNIVERSITY PRESS OF KENTUCKY

Copyright © 1982 by The University Press of Kentucky

Scholarly publisher for the Commonwealth,
serving Berea College, Centre College of Kentucky,
Eastern Kentucky University, The Filson Club,
Georgetown College, Kentucky Historical Society,
Kentucky State University, Morehead State University,
Murray State University, Northern Kentucky University,
Transylvania University, University of Kentucky,
University of Louisville, and Western Kentucky University.

Editorial and Sales Offices: Lexington, Kentucky 40506

Library of Congress Cataloging in Publication Data

Ringe, Donald A.
   American Gothic.

   Bibliography: p.
   Includes index.
   1. American fiction—19th century—History and
criticism.   2. Gothic revival (Literature)   3. American
literature—European influences.   4. European literature—History and criticism.   I. Title
PS374.G68R5   813'.0872'09   82-4877
ISBN 0-8131-1464-0   AACR2

CONTENTS

"Imagination is the queen of darkness; night the season of her despotism. But daylight, by presenting a thousand objects to the eye, the hearing, and the touch, restores the empire of the senses, and, from being the sport of fancy, we become the slaves of realities."

—*Paulding*

813.0872
R58a

PREFACE

Although the Gothic mode has seldom been accorded much respect by literary critics, it has elicited a remarkable amount of scholarly commentary. Books on the Gothic abound. Edith Birkhead's *The Tale of Terror* (1921), Eino Railo's *The Haunted Castle* (1927), Montague Summers's *The Gothic Quest* (1938), Devendra P. Varma's *The Gothic Flame* (1957), and most recently Elizabeth Mac Andrew's *The Gothic Tradition in Fiction* (1979) are all devoted to a discussion of the mode. They detail its history, especially as it developed in Europe, and discuss its characteristic subject matter and themes. None of these books, however, provides an extended discussion of the Gothic mode in the United States, nor is this deficiency corrected by those symposia that devote all or part of their attention to American books and writers: the two issues that *ESQ* devoted to the American Gothic in 1972; *The Gothic Imagination,* a collection of essays edited by G.R. Thompson in 1974; and the Gothic issue of *Studies in the Literary Imagination,* edited by Robert D. Jacobs, that also appeared in 1974. These collections contain interesting and informative essays on the American Gothic, but they present no sustained treatment of its development.

This book is intended to fill the need for such a study. Its purpose is two-fold: to show that a distinctively American mode developed out of the British and German roots, and to demonstrate that the Gothic, far from being the puerile form it has so frequently been considered, became, in the hands of the Americans, a suitable vehicle for the development of serious themes. To establish the relation between the European and American Gothic, I have selected for discussion British and German works that Americans were likely to have read at the time the mode was developing in the United States. With only a few exceptions, they are novels and tales which, it can be demonstrated, were imported into the United States or were reprinted here. Each contributed in some degree to the development of an American taste for Gothic fiction and helped

86-17577

 PUBLIC LIBRARY OF NASHVILLE & DAVIDSON COUNTY

to form a tradition on which American writers could draw for their own tales and romances. The British and German works are discussed, therefore, not for themselves alone, but for what they can contribute to an understanding of the American mode.

Some of the British and German works were ephemeral. Few people today recall *Count Roderic's Castle, The Haunted Priory, Netley Abbey, Horrid Mysteries,* or even such extremely popular novels as Regina Maria Roche's *The Children of the Abbey.* Others have attained a respectable position in the history of fiction: Ann Radcliffe's *The Mysteries of Udolpho* and *The Italian,* Matthew Gregory Lewis's *The Monk,* Friedrich von Schiller's *The Ghost-Seer,* and the novels of William Godwin. Still others must be considered important works in their own right: the major romances of Sir Walter Scott, Charles Robert Maturin's *Melmoth the Wanderer,* and the romantic tales of Ludwig Tieck and E.T.A. Hoffmann. Popular tale or masterpiece, each must be included here for the influence it may have had on the Gothic mode in the United States. In selecting American works, on the other hand, I have included only those tales and romances which have a substantial claim to literary value. I have thus excluded so sleazy and sensational a book as George Lippard's *The Monks of Monk Hall* (1844).

Certain other self-imposed limitations should also be noted. The Gothic mode is difficult to define. Its roots go well back into the Renaissance, its subject matter is varied, and it appears in several genres. To keep the line of development clear, I have accepted the established view that dates its inception from the appearance of Horace Walpole's *The Castle of Otranto* in 1764, and I have focused attention almost exclusively on its use in fiction. Knowledgeable students of American literature will recall that Philip Freneau published a Gothic poem, "The House of Night," as early as 1779, and that William Dunlap wrote and produced Gothic drama: *Fontainville Abbey* (1795), an adaptation of Ann Radcliffe's *The Romance of the Forest;* and *The Mysterious Monk* (1796), later revised as *Ribbemont; or, the Feudal Baron* (1803). But none of these works was so important or so influential as the novels of Charles Brockden Brown, who established the mode in the United States and gave it its form and tone. Since the American Gothic developed most originally and most surely in his and subsequent fiction, it seemed best to treat the mode in terms of that genre.

In the course of this study, I have incurred a number of debts that should be acknowledged here. I am especially grateful to the University of Kentucky for a sabbatical leave in the fall of 1978 and for my appointment as University Research Professor in 1979–1980, which afforded me large blocks of time to work on this and another major project. I would also like to thank Professor Paul G. Blount and the Department of English at Georgia State University in Atlanta for permission to reprint, as a major part of chapter 5, an article that appeared in *Studies in the Literary Imagination* in the spring of 1974. It has been slightly revised to fit the present context. Finally, I must, once again, acknowledge a long-standing debt to my wife for creating, over the years, the kind of atmosphere in which scholarly work becomes possible.

ONE

Introduction

When, in December 1859, Nathaniel Hawthorne wrote the preface to his new romance, *The Marble Faun,* he considered the problem he had faced as an American author. He had recently spent a year and a half in Italy, where he had written an early draft of the book, and he had lingered in England throughout the summer and fall while he brought it to completion. Now, the work done, he tried to estimate the value of the material he had used in this, his first major work laid in a foreign country. Italy, he believed, was chiefly useful to him as a kind of fanciful world where "actualities would not be so terribly insisted upon, as they are, and needs must be, in America." The writer of fiction in the United States confronts a difficulty known only to those who have tried to practice the craft. The "common-place prosperity" of American society, the "broad and simple daylight" in which everything occurs, deny the writer those elements most appropriate to romance, the shadow and mystery and sense of gloomy wrong that the crumbling ruins of Italy so strongly suggest. Years must pass, Hawthorne concludes, "before romance-writers may find congenial and easily handled themes" in American society.[1]

Some thirty years before, James Fenimore Cooper had made a similar observation. He too had been living in Europe, first in Paris, where he had settled in July 1826, and then in London, where he had moved toward the end of February 1828 to complete and publish his *Notions of the Americans.* That book, designed to explain American institutions to a European audience, contains a section on American writing in which Cooper voices a complaint much like Hawthorne's: American literature suffers from a poverty of materials. There are "no obscure fictions for the writer of romance," no dark passages in the annals of the country that he might treat with the freedom of imagination that his craft demands. Everything is illuminated with the light of truth and judged on the principles of common sense. Cooper knew, of course, that successful American fiction had been written, and he mentions Charles Brockden

Brown's *Wieland* as having left an indelible impression on his mind. But Brown had "curbed his talents by as few allusions as possible to actual society." Though he produced a fiction "distinguished for power and comprehensiveness of thought," his success derived from the fact that he drew so little upon the distinctive realities of American life.[2]

Not every American writer agreed with Cooper and Hawthorne. James Kirke Paulding, for one, refused to accept the belief that the history and traditional lore of America afforded few materials for romantic fiction. America was admittedly devoid of those elements of the mysterious and obscure that Hawthorne and Cooper allude to—elements that Paulding associates with the ghosts and goblins of the Gothic tradition in Europe—but he did not consider such elements appropriate for American fiction. He believed, rather, that American romancers should concentrate on the world of actuality, depicting real-life adventures and presenting all circumstances as arising from natural causes. The characters must, of course, exhibit American traits and the events must take place in a native setting, but such distinctively American qualities must be so blended with the generally known aspects of human character and experience as to produce a kind of fiction that departs from reality only insofar as the events of the narration did not actually happen "in precisely the same train, and to the same number of persons, as are exhibited and associated in the relation." In this way, the American writer might create "those higher works of imagination, which may be called Rational Fictions."[3]

Paulding's critical stance, so markedly different from that of Hawthorne and Cooper, was without question the orthodox one of the time. Americans were, after all, children of the eighteenth century. Priding themselves on having established "a new order of the ages,"[4] they hardly looked for their origins beyond the inception of the American Revolution, and they revered as founding fathers men such as Franklin and Jefferson, themselves the embodiment of Enlightenment principles, who had helped create a government based upon them. Americans were thoroughly imbued with eighteenth-century thought. They shared a common belief in the primary value of reason, the absurdity of mythology, and the danger of superstition. They dismissed ghosts, goblins, and witches as the relics of a more credulous age and were proud of the fact that American society had been formed when such phenomena were no longer credited and tales of superstition had been relegated to the nursery. Paulding's espousal of literary realism, therefore—his insistence upon the depiction of American actuality in his fiction—is the natural concomitant of the pervasive rationalism of his day. Most Americans would have considered his opinions common sense.

The conditions of American life also contributed to this attitude. To build a new socety, develop a thriving economy, and open the wilderness to settlement required on the part of the first generation of independent Americans a pragmatic rationalism and a concern with material reality that their descendants have never lost. Most of their time and energy went to practical matters as the eastern seaboard developed in the closing years of the eighteenth century and the westward movement began. Within a generation, large parts of the Northwest Territory and the Old Southwest were settled, and a solid band of new states stretched to the Mississippi and even into the trans-Mississippi West. It has often been said, and it bears repeating, that a people engaged in so vast an enterprise had little time to engage in such impractical pursuits as literature and the arts. It should be noted as well, however, that the bent of mind they developed predisposed them to a literary realism when they did turn their attention, as people always do, to creating a literature. If their writing was to reflect the national experience, it would have to be based on a fundamental rationalism and to depict realistically the actualities of American life.

Contemporary critical thinking, based on the Common Sense theories of the Scottish realists, provided a powerful reinforcement for this view. The Scottish school had arisen in the eighteenth century in reaction against two important developments in British philosophy, the idealism of George Berkeley and the skepticism of David Hume, both of whom had located reality, not in the external world, but in the mind of the perceiver. The Scots, on their part, accepted the physical world as objectively real and ultimately knowable by human beings, who could perceive the world as it is—the objects themselves—through impressions and sensations. Their views soon spread to America. Lord Kames and Hugh Blair early influenced both Franklin and Jefferson, and as the eighteenth century waned, Common Sense philosophy was introduced into American colleges, whose graduates quickly carried it across the country. In the early nineteenth century, such well known Scots as

Thomas Reid, James Beattie, Dugald Stewart, and Archibald Alison
were widely read by educated Americans, their opinions were discussed
in the journals, and their principles were applied to the criticism of literature. By Paulding's time, Scottish philosophy had become the dominant mode of thought in America.[5]

Scottish realism had a profound effect on the development of American fiction. It provided a justification for those who opposed novels as a
literary form and argued against the reading of fiction. Because a novel
is only an imagined reality, as opposed to the true actuality of God's creation, and because the novelist is only a fallible human being, his fictions
must always be inferior to the reality he tries to imitate. Therefore,
those who spend a great deal of time reading novels instead of mingling
in the normal affairs of the world incur the danger of acquiring a distorted vision of reality. In reaction against so powerful an argument as
this, most American novelists in the 1790s and early 1800s claimed that
their works were based on fact. Susanna Rowson called her *Charlotte
Temple* (1791) "A Tale of Truth," and others were quick to assert that
their novels were "Founded on Incidents in Real Life" or "Founded on
Recent Facts." In their prefaces, too, the authors insisted upon the authenticity of their fictions, in one breath acknowledging the danger of
novel reading and in another reassuring their readers that the particular
work before them was an accurate depiction of reality.[6]

Even after the prejudice against fiction had somewhat abated, American novelists clung to the realistic mode and critics were quick to praise
those novels which accurately depicted the American scene. In a review
of Catharine Maria Sedgwick's *A New-England Tale* (1822) in *The Literary and Scientific Repository, and Critical Review,* the anonymous critic
(possibly James Fenimore Cooper) notes that the author's intent was
"to give a descriptive sketch of some prevailing characteristics of New-
England," and he praises her book for its accurate illustration of "American society and manners." Though writers, he goes on to say, often
discuss such broad aspects of the American experience as politics, learn-
ing, and religion, "our domestic manners, the social and the moral influences, which operate in retirement, and in common intercourse, and
the multitude of local peculiarities, which form our distinctive features
upon the many peopled earth, have very seldom been happily exhibited
in our literature." He especially welcomes *A New-England Tale,* therefore, because it serves as a kind of history: not that which records "stat-

utes, and battles, and party chronicles," but that which tells us "what manner of men" these people "were, in their domestic affections, and retired deportment."[7]

The reviewer of Sedgwick's novel was well aware that such a realistic depiction of common life was not the highest form of literary expression, but only the one most easily understood and appreciated by the average reader. "The delight of pure imagination," he writes, "the transportation of ourselves beyond our own bounded vision and existence to the past and the distant, into scenes of splendor, and into conditions which fancy has devised, and fancy only could sustain or enjoy, are among the rarest pleasures that the reader of fiction tastes." But, though he does "not distrust that the enchantment thus produced is among the liveliest enjoyments of the fanciful mind," he doubts "whether the susceptibility of this excitement is universal, whether it is a healthful employment of the mind, and whether it is a source of so sweet, so complacent, or so deep emotions, as the other more frequent and familiar exercise of imagination, which is afforded by those who never soar to 'the highest heavens of invention.'" Only "the most cultivated and exalted minds" can experience "in their strongest power" the works of imaginative genius.[8]

In this passage, Sedgwick's reviewer is reflecting to some extent the fundamental distrust of the imagination implicit in the Common Sense position, a distrust that had far-reaching effects on American art. To the Scottish philosophers, the imagination was a deceptive faculty. If not kept firmly under the control of reason, it could make the observer misperceive actuality and even see things that were not really there. Since the unbridled imagination could be so seriously at fault in establishing one's relation with the external world, it was likewise to be distrusted when it created the possible worlds of fiction. Such a view was not at all incompatible with the fundamental rationalism that nineteenth-century Americans inherited from the Enlightenment, and it was perfectly consistent with the work-a-day attitudes of those whose main business in life was the settlement and development of the American continent, but it placed a heavy burden on the creative artist in that it seriously limited him in the use of that faculty most necessary for the creation of a substantial literature. The burden fell most heavily on writers of fiction. It placed them in the position of merely reporting the commonplace realities of the material world.

If James Kirke Paulding accepted the limitations placed on the novelist by the Common Sense realists, other American writers in the early nineteenth century chafed under the restraints. For decades the same refrain appears in both fiction and criticism: the rationalistic foundations of American thought are a serious hindrance not only to the writing but also to the enjoyment of fiction. William Cullen Bryant voiced just such an opinion in 1825 at the beginning of one of his short stories, "A Pennsylvanian Legend," a tale which describes the encounter of a young man with a wood spirit. Bryant knew he was violating the critical bias of the time by recounting such a story, and he tries to blunt objections with the following introduction: "Is the world to become altogether philosophical and rational? Are we to believe nothing that we cannot account for from natural causes? Are tales of supernatural warnings, of the interposition and visible appearance of disembodied spirits, to be laughed out of countenance and forgotten? . . . Alas! we shall soon learn to believe that the material world is the only world, and that the things which are the objects of our external senses are the only things which have an existence."

Such a view, Bryant believes, would have unfortunate consequences for readers of fiction. Should the philosophers carry their theories too far, they will destroy "one of the highest pleasures" people can enjoy: the "deep sense of delight" which one may take in tales of the supernatural. People enjoy them, Bryant thinks, because they have heard them since childhood. "A dread of supernatural visitations, awakened in our tender years, keeps possession of the mind like an instinct, and bids defiance to the attempts of reason to dislodge it." Such tales, in other words, appeal to the imagination, and though the phenomena they describe may have no referents in the actual world, the pleasure one takes in the stories is no less real. Indeed, Bryant would like to see some area of life left free from the relentless rationalism of the everyday world, a place where the imagination might still have room to play. "You are welcome," he tells the philosophers, "to explode such [mental] delusions as are hurtful, but leave us, I pray you, a few of such as are harmless; leave us, at least, those which are interesting to our hearts, without making us forget our love and duty to our fellow creatures."[9]

Some fourteen years later, Edgar Allan Poe attacked the problem of American rationalism in even stronger language. Reviewing the Baron de la Motte Fouqué's *Undine* (1818), a tale of water sprites, in *Burton's*

Gentleman's Magazine for September 1839, Poe welcomes the republication of Fouqué's little romance "in the very teeth of our anti-romantic national character," and he calls on "every lover of literature . . . to speak out, and speak boldly, against the untenable prejudices which have so long and so unopposedly enthralled us." *Undine* is precisely the kind of romance that Americans are "too prone to discredit," and Poe uses the occasion to make what headway he can "against that evil genius of mere matter-of-fact, whose grovelling and degrading assumptions are so happily set forth in the pert little query of Monsieur Casimir Périer— '*A quoi un poète est-il bon?*'" To accomplish his purpose, Poe stresses those qualities of the book that are not likely to be appreciated by the average American reader: its intense beauty and "the exquisite *management of imagination*" in its handling of the supernatural beings.[10] These are the qualities that Poe would like to see more widely exhibited and appreciated in American fiction.

As late as 1845, twenty years after the appearance of Bryant's story, William Gilmore Simms was still voicing a similar complaint. At the very beginning of "Grayling; or, 'Murder Will Out,'" the first tale in *The Wigwam and the Cabin,* the youthful narrator makes a familiar observation: "The world has become monstrous matter-of-fact in latter days. . . . The materialists have it all their own way." As a result, "our story-tellers are so resolute to deal in the real, the actual only, that they venture on no subjects the details of which are not equally vulgar and susceptible of proof." Even the children are affected by the rationalistic prejudices of the times. Instead of believing the tales told by his grandmother, "the little urchin, eight years old, . . . now stands up stoutly for" the new opinions: "He believes in every 'ology' but pneumatology. 'Faust' and the 'Old Woman of Berkeley' move his derision only, and he would laugh incredulously, if he dared, at the Witch of Endor. The whole armoury of modern reasoning is on his side; and, however he may admit at seasons that belief can scarcely be counted a matter of will, he yet puts his veto on all sorts of credulity."[11]

Like Bryant before him, Simms employs this means to introduce a tale of the supernatural, but unlike his predecessor he uses the story to make a telling comment on the intellectual issue. The narrator recounts a tale he has heard from his grandmother, who believes it implicitly. Shortly after the Revolution a traveler on his way to Charleston is robbed and brutally slain. The following night his ghost appears to a young friend, reveals the name of the murderer, and gives the information needed to apprehend him. The friend does as the ghost instructs him, the body is found, and the murderer is brought to justice. Because the narrator is inclined to believe that the ghost was real, his rationalist father tries to explain it away. That explanation, however, involves so complicated a set of assumptions about the way in which the mind could generate such a perception that the youth cannot accept it. He continues instead "to believe in the ghost, and, with [his] grandmother, to reject the philosophy" because, he concludes, "it was more easy to believe the one than to comprehend the other."[12] Simms's point is clear. The marvelous takes a stronger hold on the mind than any explanation the rationalist can offer.

It is also a source of great pleasure for readers of fiction. Simms's narrator is not alone in enjoying tales of the supernatural. Despite the realistic predilections of the theorists of fiction, American readers in general seem to have read with delight tales of ghosts and specters. Paulding himself takes notice of the phenomenon in his essay on "National Literature." "It is not the least of incongruities," he writes, "that in an age which boasts of having by its scientific discoveries dissipated almost all the materials of superstition, some of the most popular fictions should be founded upon a superstition which is now become entirely ridiculous, even among the ignorant."[13] Paulding does not consider that the very stress on realism may have created a hunger for a different type of fiction, and that Gothic romances, popular in England since the 1790s, may well have helped satisfy the craving for something more imaginative than the commonplace actualities of American life. Be that as it may, it is certain that American writers from Brown to Hawthorne were so strongly influenced by the contemporary vogue of the Gothic as to create an American branch of the mode.

But American writers did not find it easy to write Gothic fiction. The received opinion of the times, as Paulding correctly notes, rejected ghosts and goblins as objectively real creatures, explaining them away as the chimeras of a diseased, or at least disturbed, imagination. Writers of fiction were faced, therefore, with two equally unsatisfactory courses of action: to give full play to the imagination and write a fiction that, on its very basis, was necessarily suspect, or to concentrate on the unimaginative commonplaces of actuality. Neither extreme would work. As Paulding puts it in *Westward Ho!* (1832): "Imagination is the queen of darkness; night the season of her despotism. But daylight, by presenting a thousand objects to the eye, the hearing, and the touch, restores the empire of the senses, and, from being the sport of fancy, we become the slaves of realities."[14] Both fancy and reality tyrannize over the mind and lead to unsatisfactory consequences. American writers of fiction had, therefore, to walk the thin line between the two extremes, basing their works, as Simms puts it, on unstrained probability—the real, or the seemingly real—and using the marvelous only with great discretion.[15]

That all of them—Paulding included—introduce the marvelous into their novels and tales clearly indicates both the strength of popular demand and the felt need of the writers to allow some play for the imagination in their fiction. That they did not fully trust the imagination, however, but saw it most often as a delusive faculty that could lead the mind astray, also shows that Common Sense principles remained a potent force in American art—a force that none of them could escape completely. Each, of course, devised his own solution to the problem. Some, like Paulding, unshaken in their rationalism, treated the strange and marvelous as merely the products of an aberrant imagination. Others gave fuller play to the fancy. Hawthorne established a middle ground between the real and the imaginary where most of his fictions take place, and Poe created at least the appearance of a completely imagined reality. No two are quite alike in the strategies they employ, nor do they all use the Gothic mode for the same purposes, yet each finds a special place for it in his fiction: to express his vision of reality and to communicate his particular themes.

The study of the Gothic mode in America must therefore take into account the many variations worked on it by our native writers. We cannot examine only the works of Brown, Irving, Poe, and Hawthorne as the leading writers of Gothic fiction in the United States. Though they are without question the most important ones and have for that reason attracted the most attention from those who have been in any way concerned with Gothic fiction, other writers must also be included and the interrelations among them well established if we are to understand fully the pervasive influence of Gothicism in American fiction. We must recognize that even philosophical realists such as Paulding and John Pendleton Kennedy could not escape its touch, and that even those writers who were deeply committed to the use of native materials—historical and frontier romancers such as Cooper, Simms, and Robert

Montgomery Bird—introduced the mode into their fiction and sometimes transformed it in interesting ways. Even such early romantics as Washington Allston, Richard Henry Dana, Sr., and the eccentric John Neal cannot be excluded. Each of these writers added something of value to the American Gothic mode, and, in their handling of the marvelous, contributed to the development of the literary imagination in America.

Because the Gothic mode flourished for over sixty years both here and abroad, changing and developing as each new group of writers appeared, we must do more than merely observe the differences in technique and meaning among the various American authors. We also need to examine the historical development that took place from one writer to another, and determine the various influences, both native and foreign, that over a period of years were exerted on all of them. No matter how nationalistic American literary theorists may have been in the early nineteenth century, no matter how strongly they called for a native American literature independent of foreign models, a flood of books from Europe reached these shores each year, the reading public devoured them, and the writers read them as well. It is idle to speak of American Gothic, then, as if it were something completely distinct from its European counterpart. As long as works by such influential writers as Ann Radcliffe, Friedrich von Schiller, William Godwin, Charles Robert Maturin, Sir Walter Scott, Ludwig Tieck, and E.T.A. Hoffmann were imported and read, they must be included in any serious study of the American branch of the mode.

This does not mean that the American Gothic should be considered only an appendage to the European mode, or that such a study need focus on the transformations that the European elements underwent when placed in an American setting. We recognize, of course, that Donatello's tower in Hawthorne's *The Marble Faun* and the many grotesquely decorated rooms in Poe's most effective tales are all latter-day manifestations of what Eino Railo calls the Haunted Castle.[16] So too do some of the characters that appear in the works of Hawthorne, Poe, and other American writers of Gothic fiction derive from the criminal monk, the Wandering Jew, the ghosts and demonic beings, and other Gothic figures that Railo also presents as significant elements in the European mode. To examine the American Gothic solely in terms of these sources, however, may lead the critic to conclude that American writers used such Gothic materials for much the same purposes as the British and German writers from whom they derived them—a conclusion that can only obscure the significant accomplishments of the Americans, who, adapting the mode to their individual ends, turned it into an appropriate vehicle for the expression of their most important themes.

On the other hand, to approach the American Gothic from the assumptions of twentieth-century psychology can be equally misleading. That Gothic writers both here and abroad probed the dark and irrational side of the human psyche goes without saying, and the psychological implications of their fiction contributed, no doubt, to the discovery of the unconscious mind. But it does not necessarily follow that their works must be interpreted in terms of one or another of the intellectual systems that have evolved from that discovery—Freudian, Jungian, or some combination of the two.[17] Such interpretations always distort the works they treat, emphasizing only those aspects that fit the systems, and minimizing, ignoring, or perhaps simply failing to perceive those which run counter to the preconceived theory. Worse, they blind us to what the authors themselves were trying to do. We cannot hear what the writer himself is saying through the overwhelming noise of the message that the critic imposes upon him.[18] Such psychological studies of the Gothic mode may have their interest and significance, but they usually tell us more about the critic himself than about the works he professes to discuss.

Our first responsibility to any writer is to listen to him attentively and try to understand what he is saying. We must, as Henry James insisted, grant him his *donnée*.[19] We may agree or disagree with him, think him a genius or a fool, or believe him to be a great or mediocre artist, but we must not violate his integrity by turning him into a mirror image of our own minds. Since he speaks to us from a different time and place, we must lay aside our modern preconceptions and, insofar as we are able, perform an act of historical imagination. We must try to understand the milieu in which he lived and wrote, the ideas that were current in his time, the books he read, and the way he viewed his intellectual, social, and physical environment. When we turn to his works, we must try to perceive how he made those materials his own and used them to present his individual themes. The process must be inductive. If the author's works are read with sufficient knowledge of his life and times and in the proper spirit of critical humility, they will yield the meanings he sought to express through them.

To understand a literary movement, moreover, we must expand the process to include not only individual writers but also the interrelations that develop among them over a period of years. For the American Gothic, we must begin in England in the late eighteenth century, review the British and German Gothic romances that Americans imported and read over the ensuing decades, and determine the role they played in the development of American Gothicism. As the years passed and increasing numbers of Gothic tales and romances were produced, the lines of influence became increasingly complex. Most of these writers knew each other's works, absorbed the books that came from Great Britain and Germany, and fell, consciously or unconsciously, under the influence of what they read. All accepted to some degree the critical assumptions of their time, yet most reacted against the limitations that the critical theory placed upon them. All, finally, acceded in one way or another to the popular demand for the marvelous in fiction. Working apart—yet, in another sense, also working together—they created a version of the Gothic mode which, without denying its European roots, became in time recognizably American.

TWO

Early Gothic Imports

The publication of Charles Brockden Brown's *Wieland* in September 1798 marked the beginning of American Gothic fiction, for in that book and in those he published the following year, especially *Ormond* and *Edgar Huntly*, he established a mode that has had a vigorous life in American literature. Brown was a serious writer and wrote his fiction for highly serious purposes. His intent was not to titillate but to raise important intellectual issues, and his fiction, like that of Edgar Allan Poe and Nathaniel Hawthorne after him, employs the Gothic mode because it is well adapted to the themes he wished to express. American scholars are right, therefore, in stressing the importance of Brown. Seen from the point of view of a later age, his works were seminal. The mental aberrations of Theodore and Clara Wieland and of Edgar Huntly pointed ahead to similar psychological phenomena in the works of Poe; the problem of perception that so many of his characters face is much like that in the tales and romances of Hawthorne; and his strong affirmation of the use of American materials links him to practically all the American writers who came after him in the early nineteenth century.

But this is not the only point of view from which Brown should be seen. *Wieland*, after all, did not mark the beginning of Gothic fiction in America. It appeared, rather, just at the time when a flood of Gothic novels imported from England was beginning to crest, and he added in 1798 but one more book—albeit by an American—to the steady stream of British and German romances that had been filling the bookstores and circulating libraries of the United States for a number of years. Royall Tyler was probably right when he observed in his preface to *The Algerine Captive* (1797) that the reading taste of Americans had altered in a very few years, that works of amusement had supplanted those of instruction, and that the tales of Mrs. Radcliffe were sending both dairy maid and hired hand into such agreeable states of terror "that they were both afraid to sleep alone."[1] The book catalogues that survive from that time provide ample evidence of the popularity of fiction—and especially of Gothic fiction—in the 1790s in America. Appearing in these lists for the first time around 1793, the Gothic titles increased year by year until at the end of the century they represented a substantial part of the offerings.[2]

The pattern is not difficult to trace despite the fragmentary evidence that has come down to us. Of the first three books written by Ann Radcliffe, the third, *The Romance of the Forest* (1791), established her reputation in England. Within two years of its publication, both it and *A Sicilian Romance* (1790) were available in Boston, and her first novel, *The Castles of Athlin and Dunbayne* (1789) was listed in Salem in 1794. Thereafter her works appeared in American catalogues the year after their first publication: *The Mysteries of Udolpho* (1794) in Philadelphia in 1795, and *The Italian* (1797) in Baltimore and Boston in 1798.[3] More important, there is hardly a surviving catalogue that does not include at least one or two of her works. At least six catalogues printed between 1795 and 1797 offered her three major novels available by that time, and three—in Boston (1798) and New York and Philadelphia (1799)—listed all five. Indeed, Hocquet Caritat's 1799 catalogue listed them all with an asterisk to indicate that they were available for both circulation and sale. One may assume from this evidence that in the major intellectual centers of the United States, Radcliffe's work became increasingly available as the decade wore on.

Ann Radcliffe's novels, however, formed only a minor part of the British importations. Other works by well known writers—Horace Walpole's *The Castle of Otranto* (1764), Clara Reeve's *The Old English Baron* (1777), and Sophia Lee's *The Recess* (1785)—began to appear in the book catalogues around the same time as hers, and recent works by Charlotte Smith—most notably *The Old Manor House* (1793) and *Montalbert* (1795)—were listed for the first time in 1795 and 1796 respectively. Charlotte Smith was probably as well known as Ann Radcliffe, and some of her earlier novels—*Emmeline* (1788) and *Ethelinde* (1789)—also appeared in the listings. Even Matthew Gregory Lewis's notorious romance *The Monk* (1796) appeared occasionally in the catalogues of 1798 and 1799, and the evidence suggests that it may have been present in both its original and its expurgated forms. Entitled *The Monk* in its first three editions, the book was vigorously attacked for the lustful and blasphemous passages it contains. The expurgated fourth edition, called *Ambrosio*, was published in 1798. Hence the appearance of the romance under both titles and starred in Caritat's catalogue of 1799 would seem to indicate that both versions were available in his bookstore and could be borrowed or bought.

A number of German romances, translated into English and published in Great Britain in the mid-1790s, were also offered by American booksellers as soon as they could be imported.[4] Christiane Naubert's *Herman of Unna* (1794), Friedrich von Schiller's *The Ghost-Seer* (1795), and Cajetan Tschink's *The Victim of Magical Delusion* (1795) were all in America by the latter year. *Herman of Unna* appeared in a book catalogue for 1795, and the other two were immediately reprinted in their entirety in the *New-York Weekly Magazine*, Schiller's work from August to November of the same year, and Tschink's from December 1795 to April 1797. Both turned up as well in the book catalogues of several succeeding years. Other German novels, though apparently less well known, were also imported. Karl Kahlert's *The Necromancer* (1794) and Karl Grosse's *Horrid Mysteries* (1797), two books that have attracted attention because of their inclusion in Jane Austen's list of "horrid" novels in *Northanger Abbey* (1818), were occasionally offered. Indeed, Grosse's work was translated twice—first as *The Genius* (1796) and then as *Horrid Mysteries* in the following year—and both titles, as well as *The Dagger* (1795), another novel by Grosse, appeared in Hocquet Caritat's catalogue for 1799.

In addition to all these novels, there were many other books which, though largely forgotten today, were read by Americans in the closing years of the eighteenth century. Many were from the Minerva Press, that source of so much popular fiction in England,[5] and several seem to have had a vigorous life in this country. *Count Roderic's Castle* (1794), Stephen Cullen's *The Haunted Priory* (1794), and Richard Warner's *Netley Abbey* (1795) appeared year after year in the catalogues, and by the end of the decade Americans were being offered such works as Regina Maria Roche's *The Children of the Abbey* (1796) and *Clermont* (1798), Eliza Parsons's *The Mysterious Warning* (1796), Francis Lathom's *The Midnight Bell* (1798), and Eleanor Sleath's *The Orphan of the Rhine* (1798). Except for those by Cullen and Lathom, all were Minerva Press books, and four—*Clermont, The Mysterious Warning, The Midnight Bell,* and *The Orphan of the Rhine*—were in the Northanger canon. These lists do not by any means exhaust the Gothic novels that were brought into this country, but little would be gained by extending them to greater length. These are the books that have some claim to our attention, and they form a cross-section of the kind of Gothic fiction that was available to Americans in the 1790s.

The popularity of Gothic fiction in America is further indicated by the number of American editions of these works.[6] Three of Ann Radcliffe's books—*A Sicilian Romance, The Romance of the Forest,* and *The Mysteries of Udolpho*—had American editions by 1795. *The Castles of Athlin and Dunbayne* followed in 1796 and *The Italian,* with two editions, in 1797, the year of its English publication. Schiller's *The Ghost-Seer* (1796) was apparently the only German romance to achieve publication in book form on this side of the Atlantic, and Lewis's *The Monk,* reprinted from the fourth, expurgated edition and entitled *Ambrosio,* was published in Boston in 1799.[7] Of the second line of British novels, Clara Reeve's *The Old English Baron* (1797), Charlotte Smith's *Montalbert* (1795), and Regina Maria Roche's *The Children of the Abbey* (1798) achieved American publication; and four now forgotten books, Stephen Cullen's *The Haunted Priory* (1794), *Count Roderic's Castle* (1795), Ann Yearsley's *The Royal Captives* (1795), and Richard Warner's *Netley Abbey* (1796), were also published. The number of American imprints was perhaps small, but the titles are significant in that they indicate what the publishers thought would attract American buyers.

The American magazines of the time provide additional evidence of the interest in the Gothic. An occasional ghostly tale appeared in them, and translations of at least three poems by Gottfried August Bürger, whose specter ballads became internationally famous, were also printed.[8] Excerpts from such popular novels as *Herman of Unna, The Ghost-Seer, The Italian,* and *The Children of the Abbey*—usually passages which exploit the interest in the frightening or the mysterious—were printed from time to time, and one short-lived periodical, *The American Monthly Review; or, Literary Journal,* published in one year (1795) reviews of such popular books as *The Royal Captives, The Necromancer, Count Roderic's Castle, The Count of Hoensdern, The Abbey of St. Asaph,* and *The Castle of Ollada.*[9] By the end of the decade, moreover, some accounts appeared of the two main Gothic writers of the age. Lewis, as one might expect, was accorded some credit for the literary merit of his work but was severely censured for its morality. Radcliffe, on the other hand, though criticized for the number and minuteness of her landscape descriptions and the repetitiousness of her Gothic effects, was nonetheless praised for her "power of painting the terrible and the mysterious."[10]

Yet when all is said and done, perhaps the best testimony to the popularity of the Gothic in America during the 1790s was the appearance of parodies on the form, for one does not parody what is not well known. In the *New-York Weekly Magazine* for 1796, there was a brief paragraph called "The Apparition," which seems to make fun of a passage in *The Mysteries of Udolpho*. There Emily St. Aubert, wrought up to a pitch of excitement by her imagination, shrieks in terror when something moves in the room and brushes against her, only to discover that it is Manchon, her dog. In the magazine version, the shiny-eyed monster that comes through the creaking door and terrifies the insomniac huddling in bed turns out to be "Poor Pussey Cat."[11] Two years later, in the Philadelphia *Weekly Magazine,* there appeared "A Receipt for a Modern Romance." The usual ingredients are specified: the ruined castle; old retainers; ghostly legends; and the inevitable journey of the heroine through a trapdoor to a cell, a chapel, and a subterraneous passage where she perceives some frightening phenomenon. The author, called "Anti-Ghost," concludes:

> A novel now, says Will, is nothing more
> Than an old castle, and a creaking door:
> A distant hovel,
> Clanking of chains, a gallery, a light,
> Old armour, and a phantom all in white—
> And there's a novel.[12]

If we recall that this receipt appeared in June 1798, just three months before the publication of *Wieland* and right at the time when the flood of Gothic fiction from abroad was beginning to approach its crest, we will understand something of the cultural environment from which Brown's book emerged. Unlike the modern critic, American readers in that day did not approach the book with vague memories of Walpole, Radcliffe, and Lewis, or with assumptions about the Gothic mode derived almost exclusively from their works. Those who opposed the entire genre would probably have passed it by as but one more example of a wornout form, while those who relished the mode would have seen it, no doubt unconsciously, in terms of a much more complex literary milieu than the modern critic, no matter how persevering, can ever quite reconstruct. They lived with the books over a period of several years; we read them in the library. Nonetheless, we must attempt to understand the Gothic mode as it developed during the 1790s and was imported into America. In no other way can we fully perceive what the works of Charles Brockden Brown and the major writers who followed him are really all about.

Such a discussion must begin with Horace Walpole's *The Castle of Otranto* (1764), a book that so firmly established the Gothic genre that the basic elements have been repeated by writers both skilled and unskilled throughout the two centuries since its first publication. The castle, the cave, the subterranean labyrinth, the extinguished lamp, the hollow groan—all appear in *Otranto* with the emotive power that has long been recognized as indispensable to the evocation of Gothic terror. Indeed, if one were to treat the form only in terms of such external characteristics, he would be hard pressed to distinguish the book from the large number of imitations that have followed it. Yet the Gothic mode did develop, even in its earliest days. Though subsequent writers in England, Germany, and the United States freely employed its devices, they enlisted them in the service of widely divergent systems of thought and created a series of transmutations that must be retraced if we are to understand its later use. What the critic must do, therefore, is to turn his attention away from the external elements that quickly became so hackneyed, and focus upon the functions they were intended to serve and the meanings they were meant to embody.

The best place to start is with the most obvious characteristic of *The Castle of Otranto,* its unabashed supernaturalism. The book is filled with elements that strain credibility and defy explanation: a helmet so large that a man can be imprisoned beneath it, a sword so huge that a hundred men strain under its weight, a picture that comes down from the wall and walks in the room, a statue that bleeds three drops from its nose, and an immense ghost that ascends to heaven with a clap of thunder and disappears into a blaze of glory. Walpole claimed to be imitating the ancient romance, where "all was imagination and improbability," and he set the story in medieval Italy, partly at least to make such elements acceptable to his readers.[13] In the later years of the eighteenth century, however, only a few writers were willing to follow his lead in creating such extreme effects. Even Clara Reeve, his avowed imitator, objected to his use of such devices. In her preface to *The Old English Baron* (1777), she complains of Walpole's excesses. "The machinery is so violent," she writes, "that it destroys the effect it is intended to excite."[14]

She does not condemn the use of the supernatural, however. "We can conceive, and allow of, the appearance of a ghost," she goes on to say (p. 5), and she includes some elements of the supernatural in her own romance. So also do two writers of the 1790s: Stephen Cullen, whose *Haunted Priory* appeared in 1794, and Richard Warner, whose *Netley Abbey* was published in the following year. In *The Old English Baron,* the ghosts of Lord and Lady Lovel, whose child Edmund has been deprived of his inheritance, haunt part of their former castle, and two young men, enemies of Edmund, are terrorized by a ghost when they try to spend the night in the haunted apartment. In *The Haunted Priory,* Alphonso, the young hero, follows the ghost of a huge knight to a magnificently lighted church, which, after a series of strange occurrences, turns out the next morning to be only a moldering ruin. And in *Netley Abbey,* the ghost of old Sir Raymond appears three times in the course of the narrative to thwart the attempts of his murderer to destroy his children. Like *The Castle of Otranto,* these novels accept supernatural events as part of their fictive worlds.

To dismiss such elements as simply bizarre, however, would be to miss the point of these books, for in all of them the strange events are intimately connected with the basic theme: the restoration of order to a world in which a usurper has broken the natural line of descent and seized possessions that are not rightfully his. The legitimate heir is lost, he is thought to be dead, or he is not known to exist. Theodore is not recognized as the heir of Otranto because his grandfather, Alfonso, is believed to have died without issue; Edmund in *The Old English Baron* is thought to be a peasant's son; Alphonso, the true grandson of the Baron de Rayo in *The Haunted Priory,* is believed to be the son of the Baron's friend, Don Isidor, because the two boys were exchanged when they were infants and the Baron's supposed grandson has vanished; and young Sir Raymond in *Netley Abbey* is reported to have been killed in France. In such worlds of disrupted order the strange apparitions may serve a number of purposes: to reveal the truth of the usurpation, to identify the legitimate heir, and to help restore him to his rightful position in society.

In three books, the restoration is accomplished in rather sensational fashion. Because there is a prophecy "that *the Castle and Lordship of Otranto should pass from the present family whenever the real owner should be grown too large to inhabit it*" (p. 194), the appearance of a gigantic knight in a huge suit of armor clearly suggests that Manfred, the usurper's grandson, is about to be supplanted. Then, at the end of the book, the apparition of Alfonso, now "dilated to an immense magnitude" (p. 300), reveals the identity of Theodore and, by his spectacular ascension, convinces everyone that the revelation is not to be questioned. In a similar fashion, Edmund is revealed as the true heir in *The Old English Baron* when, on his return to the manor house to take formal possession of his inheritance, all of the doors miraculously fly open to admit him. And Alphonso, in *The Haunted Priory,* is led to a secret chamber by the ghost of the huge knight and is directed to a key which eventually opens the way to the cell of his imprisoned mother. Thereafter a series of explanations reveals him finally as the grandson and heir of the Baron de Rayo.

A less sensational device used for the same purpose is the prophetic dream.[15] Sir Philip Harclay, Edmund's friend and protector in *The Old English Baron,* dreams that the dead Lord Lovel summons him to his castle and reveals that the hope of his family rests on him. Edmund, in turn, dreams that a warrior and his lady appear by his bed and identify him as their child. The Baron de Rayo in *The Haunted Priory* dreams three times that he sees the bloody ghost of his son-in-law, Henry Gonsalvo, who exhorts him to find his lost child; and Edward de Villars in *Netley Abbey* has a complex dream of subterranean passages where he sees a dead knight, a girl praying, a dead monk, and a dying knight streaming with blood. In each of these dreams the characters receive true intimations of an unknown past or shadowy future. Sir Philip perceives that he is to serve some important purpose; Edmund suspects that his birth and lineage are different from what he has thought; the Baron not only learns that his lost grandson still lives, but also receives a commission from the grave to discover him; and Edward has seen unfolded in his sleep the whole dark mystery of Netley Abbey and its conclusion.

For all of these characters, then, the supernatural agents who invade their dreams and lead them to important discoveries are instruments of good divinely sent to restore the disrupted order of society. Though sources of terror for some, they are for the dispossessed young nobles and their friends the agents of Providence leading them to their ultimate happiness. Throughout *The Castle of Otranto,* indeed, Divine Providence guides the characters toward the restoration of order, a fact which they themselves recognize when, at the great revelation, they fall "prostrate on their faces, acknowledging the divine will" (p. 300). It is Providence, too, in *The Old English Baron,* that makes Sir Philip Harclay the protector of Edmund, that reveals to the young man the truth of his parentage, and that also makes him—like Edward de Villars in *Netley Abbey*—an instrument for the restoration of order. Finally, it is "the finger of Providence pointing out the way to some strange and momentous revelation"[16] that the Baron de Rayo thinks he perceives in the events which follow his first dream of Gonsalvo—an expectation that is fulfilled by subsequent events in *The Haunted Priory.* In the world of these romances, the Divine Will validates both the supernatural messenger and his message.

Though such frank supernaturalism is rather uncommon in British Gothic fiction of the 1790s, the theme introduced by Walpole continued to be developed by writers who eschewed his sensational effects. The restoration of the true heir to his ancestral possessions appears in Charlotte Smith's *The Old Manor House* (1793), and variations upon the theme occur in a number of other tales from Ann Radcliffe's *The Castles of Athlin and Dunbayne* (1789) to Francis Lathom's *The Midnight Bell* (1798). In Regina Maria Roche's *The Children of the Abbey* (1796), Amanda Fitzalan acquires the wealth and position that make her the proper match for Lord Mortimer only after her brother Oscar is restored to his rightful place as the Earl of Dunreath. And in Eleanor Sleath's *The Orphan of the Rhine* and Roche's *Clermont* (both 1798) there are double restorations. The hero and heroine in each have both been denied their rightful possessions, and in the working out of the plots both must be restored to their inheritances. All of these tales, however, differ from those of Walpole and his followers in that no dramatically striking supernatural events occur to bring about the accession of the true heir.

Most of the British romancers of the 1790s preferred to assign a material cause to even the strangest phenomena included in their books. The lights that move through deserted wings of castles in both Ann Radcliffe's *A Sicilian Romance* (1790) and Eliza Parsons's *The Castle of Wolfenbach* (1793) all have natural causes, and the ghosts that seem to haunt the chapel in *The Old Manor House* and the sealed off rooms in Chateau-le-Blanc in Radcliffe's *The Mysteries of Udolpho* (1794) are, respectively, smugglers and pirates who use the recesses of the buildings to conceal their illegal traffic.[17] The horrifying vision that Emily sees behind the veil in the Castle of Udolpho is only the wax image of a decaying corpse, and the strange voices that Ferdinand hears at crucial moments in Parsons's *The Mysterious Warning* (1796) are made by an old servant who is trying to help him. The list could be extended at length through the works of Roche, Lathom, and Sleath, but the pattern itself is clear. Though the writers go to great lengths to suggest the supernatural, they are all fundamentally rationalists who always anchor the main events of their books in the world of material reality.

The supernatural does not disappear completely, however. These writers, too, were firm believers in the providential doctrine and saw the hand of a just and benevolent God at work in the affairs of men. Because there is no limit to God's ability to act, it is certainly possible that, as Madame de Menon puts it in *A Sicilian Romance,* the spirits of departed persons may appear on earth, and if they do they are sent by God "for some very singular purposes."[18] Despite this concession, however, these writers choose not to employ the direct intervention of the Deity in the natural order of things. No ghosts appear to effect the Divine Will. It is, rather, in the timely arrival of a character at a crucial moment, or in the opportune natural occurrence—events that a later age is likely to dismiss as coincidence—that the Providence of God is most often seen. And it is only in the final resolution of the action, when the wicked, no matter how much they have prospered, are brought to justice, and the good, no matter how much they have suffered, are granted success and happiness, that, in the words of St. Julian in *Clermont,* "the ways of Providence are justified to man."[19]

Within this general pattern, however, some elements of the supernatural—true presentiments and prophetic dreams—occasionally appear, though usually placed in a psychological context that makes them at least ambiguous. Though a number of characters are disturbed by forebodings of evil, many of their fears prove groundless and must be attributed to natural feelings of anxiety. The presentiments of some of the heroines that their lovers are dead or that they will never see them again are clearly of this type. Other forebodings may be attributed to the same cause, or they may be interpreted as actual intimations of the future. St. Aubert, the father of Emily in *The Mysteries of Udolpho,* has a true presentiment of his wife's approaching death, and Valancourt's fears of

Montoni seem to Emily, after she has lived at Udolpho, to have been really prophetic. In *The Mysterious Warning,* Louisa feels a sure presentiment of all the evils that lie before her when she leaves the convent with her father, and in Radcliffe's *The Italian* (1797), Vivaldi feels "a shuddering presentiment of what [the] monk was preparing for him" when he and Schedoni meet near his mother's closet.[20] Startling though such feelings may be, nothing about them is necessarily supernatural.

A similar ambiguity pervades some of the seemingly prophetic dreams that occasionally appear. All of these writers were well aware that a person's state of mind could influence his dreams, and fear, guilt, and other kinds of emotional stress are all presented as causes of nightmares. But sometimes a truly prophetic element seems to appear in them. In *The Old Manor House,* for example, the conflict that Orlando feels between his love for Monimia and his duty to his family produces a nightmare in which his father seems to have died, yet still warns him away from Monimia and urges him to care for his mother and sisters. Though the dream can be interpreted as the logical projection of Orlando's fears, it truly forebodes his future troubles. In a similar fashion, Laurette in *The Orphan of the Rhine* prophetically dreams that she will be taken into a wood to be murdered and that Enrico, her lover, will follow her, but the dream is so general that it may also be attributed to her distraught imagination. In both of these books the characters' dreams are curious mixtures of the rational and the possibly supernatural. They are well motivated psychologically, but also contain presentiments that turn out to be true.[21]

The master of this device was Ann Radcliffe, whose prophetic dreams are placed in an even more carefully drawn psychological context. So deeply disturbed in mind is Adeline in *The Romance of the Forest* that she has a series of closely connected and terrifying dreams. She sees a dying chevalier in an ancient, desolate room, is almost dragged through the floor by him, is beckoned into a series of darkened chambers, and finally sees his bleeding corpse in the room where he died. The following day she finds a hidden door, penetrates to a room exactly like that in her dream, and finds a dusty manuscript. The eerie conditions under which she reads it, including the fleeting glimpse of a possible apparition, suggest to her mind that a supernatural power lies behind these events, and when she finally discovers that the manuscript was written by her murdered father, she considers the entire sequence providential. In *The Ital-*

ian, too, Vivaldi, imprisoned by the Inquisition, thinks about a shadowy monk he has repeatedly seen, only to dream of his presence in his cell, where he reveals his face. When Vivaldi awakens, the monk stands before him and, throwing back his cowl, reveals the countenance that Vivaldi saw for the first time in his nightmare.

In both of these dreams there is at least one detail that cannot be explained rationally: the prescience of Adeline in dreaming about a particular chamber before she has seen it, and that of Vivaldi in seeing the face of the monk in his dream before it is revealed to him in actuality. All other details can perhaps be explained as the workings of an overwrought mind. Adeline has heard rumors of a murder that is thought to have been committed in the abbey, and the ruined state of the building is enough to suggest the ancient rooms of her dreams. The apparition she sees may be merely the creation of her disturbed fancy, and her conclusion of direct supernatural intervention may be only a personal interpretation. In like manner, Vivaldi's arrest and imprisonment in the chambers of the Inquisition are enough to give him nightmares, and the shadowy monk has long troubled his mind. That he thinks of him, too, just before falling asleep makes even more reasonable his appearance in the dream. Both dreams are, of course, prophetic, but they are placed in so psychologically convincing a context that the reader is willing to accept the prophetic part as doing no real violence to the fundamentally rational world in which the dreams are imbedded.

By placing so much emphasis on the psychological state of their characters, Radcliffe, Smith, and their followers were able to maintain a rationalistic position, avoid the spectacularly supernatural, and still create a sense of terror. What they did was to internalize what Walpole, Reeve, and their followers presented as objectively real. From the point of view of the rationalists, it made no difference whether the sources of terror were real or not. What a character thought he perceived had the same effect on his mind as what was actually there. Pierre de la Motte, for example, fleeing from his creditors and the law in *The Romance of the Forest,* thinks at times that he hears the sounds of pursuit, or "the voices of his enemies" in each "murmur of the wind,"[22] and Emily St. Aubert, on her way to meet Barnadine on the ramparts of the Castle of Udolpho, is so deceived by patterns of light and shadow that she thinks she sees someone "in the distant obscurity of the perspective," and fear overtakes her.[23] Though all these perceptions have in fact no basis in reality, they affect the minds of the characters as much as if t

The relation, moreover, is reciprocal: the state of mind of
ter can also profoundly affect what he perceives. Specters of
are projected into the real world by the guilty minds of Sister Agnes in
The Mysteries of Udolpho, by Colonel Belgrave in *The Children of the Abbey,* and by Spalatro in *The Italian,* all of whom perceive frightening visions of people they have harmed. And, because they have listened to
tales of the supernatural told by the superstitious servants, both Emily in
The Mysteries of Udolpho and Madeline in *Clermont* are so infected with
terror that they misinterpret natural events as supernatural phenomena.
Emily is frightened by so simple an occurrence as the opening of a door,
and Madeline is terrified by the appearance of a man whom under other
circumstances she would immediately recognize as a friend. Most of the
terrors the characters feel, therefore, come from faulty perception. They
either perceive what is not objectively present or they misinterpret even
the commonplace elements of the everyday world, transforming them
into objects of terror. What is important in these books, then, is not so
much the Gothic effects themselves as the intellectual and emotional
sources of the characters' misapprehensions of reality.

The primary one is ignorance, the source of superstition. This is the
usual failing of the lower classes—all the serving maids and peasants in
these books, whose minds, imbued since childhood with tales of ghosts
and specters, never question the reality of supposed apparitions. It is a
failing not normally shared by the educated gentry, whose minds are
superior to it. Even Emily St. Aubert, for all her imaginary fears, is not
nearly so superstitious as her maid, Annette, and most of her terrors derive from quite different sources. Indeed, of all the heroes and heroines
in these books, only Monimia in *The Old Manor House* is thoroughly
superstitious, for she has been taught to believe in ghosts by her aunt,
who seeks thereby to maintain an influence over her. The effect of this
early education is to render Monimia terrified by perceptions for which
her rational lover, Orlando, seeks natural causes. He attempts to persuade her out of her fears, and her apprehensions decrease as her reason,
guided by him, teaches her that there is really "little to fear from the interposition of supernatural agency."[24] So deeply ingrained are her fears,
however, that only with great difficulty is she ever able to reason herself
out of them.

Yet under certain circumstances even the educated characters can ex-

perience superstitious fear and misinterpret the reality that presents itself
to their senses. Orlando himself feels a terror he is ashamed of when,
after a long absence, he returns to Rayland Hall, wanders through the
deserted rooms at dusk, hears a hollow gust of wind sweep through
them, and perceives as beckoning specters the figures that he knows full
well are portraits of his ancestors. Though his mind, too, is above superstition, Ferdinand in *A Sicilian Romance* also experiences fear when,
locked in a dungeon, he hears a sound and recalls the story of a ghost
that is said to haunt the castle. And Rosalie in Smith's *Montalbert* (1795)
goes through a terrifying experience when she attempts to escape from
the castle in which she is imprisoned. To unlock a door for her rescuers,
she must go to the lower apartments where the ghost of a murdered
knight is supposed to walk. When, on the appointed night, she ventures down into them to unbolt the door, the sound of voices and a loud
crushing noise send her in terrified flight back up to her room, unaware
that her rescuers have arrived much earlier than expected and have broken down the door to effect her escape.

For each of these characters—and for many others—the condition of
their immediate surroundings and their physical and mental states cause
their imaginations to distort the evidence of their senses and create a
world that has little basis in reality. Fear, dread, sorrow, passion, anxiety, or even fatigue can reduce the power of reason; light, shadow, and
sound, especially in strange or suggestive surroundings, can stimulate
the imagination; and the overwrought mind may leap to a conclusion
that the unfettered understanding would probably not accept. This is
the reason why Adeline in *The Romance of the Forest* thinks she hears the
word "Here!" as she contemplates the chambers where the author of
the manuscript suffered; and why Emily in *The Mysteries of Udolpho*
thinks she sees the ghost of her father in his chair when she returns to
her home, La Vallée, after his death and walks through the rooms so
closely associated with his memory. Both of the girls are in highly emotional states, they find themselves alone in dimly lighted rooms where
the senses are easily deceived, and they soon become the victims of their
distempered imaginations.

What all of these books suggest, therefore, is the danger inherent in
the uncontrolled imagination, especially in those who have, for whatever reason, a predilection for perceiving the marvelous. As Schedoni
tells Vivaldi toward the close of *The Italian*, "what ardent imagination

ever was contented to trust to plain reasoning, or to the evidence of the senses? It may not willingly confine itself to the dull truths of this earth, but, eager to expand its faculties, to fill its capacity, and to experience its own peculiar delights, soars after new wonders into a world of its own!" (pp. 397-98). That world is, of course, not always one of terror. Under certain conditions, the imagination can also lead the mind to visions of beauty and delight, or even to the contemplation of the Deity. Under others, it can make it the abject slave of superstition. The delusive imagination makes Monimia afraid to enter the chapel in *The Old Manor House,* it makes Adeline fearful of looking into a mirror lest she see an apparition there, and it sends Emily shrieking from the haunted rooms in Chateau-le-Blanc when a face appears from beneath a black pall. When reason is subdued, the imagination assumes complete sway.

In all the major characters reason is finally placed once more in control, terror is banished from their minds, and the world of actuality is perceived once again for what it is. Though a few presentiments and prophetic dreams may occur, that world has little room for ghosts and apparitions. Unlike Walpole, Reeve, and their followers, who present supernatural phenomena as objectively real elements in the divine order of things, Radcliffe, Smith, and the other rationalists deliberately avoid the use of supernatural beings. They emphasize instead the powers of the unrestrained imagination to create deceptive appearances or to misapprehend reality. For this reason, it is imprecise to distinguish between these groups of writers, as so many critics have done, in terms of the "unexplained" and the "explained" supernatural. It is not so much that Radcliffe, Smith, and the others "explain" the supernatural in their works, as that they create a fictive world in which apparently supernatural phenomena are all revealed as merely delusive appearances. The world is rationally ordered and operates by natural law. It is only in the minds of men that frightening apparitions—the phantoms of the imagination—appear.

That this was the dominant view in British Gothic fiction during the 1790s is well evidenced by the large number of books written in imitation of Ann Radcliffe and Charlotte Smith that fell from the presses and filled the circulating libraries. An occasional novel like those by Stephen Cullen or Richard Warner might appear, but the vast majority of Gothic books presented supernatural phenomena as mental delusion. The one memorable exception is the notorious romance by Matthew

Gregory Lewis, *The Monk* (1796), a book that rivals *The Castle of Otranto* in its openly avowed supernaturalism. Lewis was well acquainted with both types of the British Gothic. While still a student at Oxford, he had begun a romance modeled upon *Otranto,* and he had read and admired *The Mysteries of Udolpho* before he began his own sensational book. Lewis had also spent some time in Germany, had learned the German language, and was strongly influenced by the literature of horror which he had encountered in that country. So diverse, indeed, were the sources of his inspiration that Lewis created a book at once related to, yet markedly different from, the kind of Gothic romance that others had been writing before him.

Despite its sensational aspects, *The Monk* bears some resemblance to the novels of Radcliffe and Smith. A number of the characters maintain the rationalistic attitudes that pervade such works as *The Mysteries of Udolpho* and *The Old Manor House,* and, like the heroines of those books, some fall under the sway of imaginary fears. Lorenzo de Medina, for example, scoffs at the idea of ghosts as "ridiculous in the extreme," and, while protecting a group of frightened nuns in the vaults of the convent, he tells them their fears of the dead are "puerile and groundless," the result of superstition.[25] Antonia, on the other hand, the object of Lorenzo's affection and of the monk Ambrosio's lust, is, like Monimia, especially susceptible to imaginary terrors because of the ghostly tales she heard as a child, and she continues to be affected by superstitious fear no matter how often she learns that her terrors have only a "natural and insignificant cause" (p. 309). Even Ambrosio himself does not escape such fear. Though assured that a specter Antonia has seen is "a mere creation of fancy," he feels "a certain mysterious horror" when alone in a room supposedly haunted, and he finds it hard to dismiss his "absurd terrors" (pp. 326, 328).

But if Lewis sometimes employs a psychology of terror much like that of the popular ladies, he introduces as well some entirely new elements of the supernatural. The story of the Bleeding Nun, which Lewis probably derived from the German of Musäus,[26] is a good example. One night in every five years, she is supposed to walk the halls and pass through the gates of Lindenberg Castle, and the time for the apparition is approaching just when Don Raymond and Agnes decide to elope. They dismiss the story as mere superstition, and, by disguising herself as the Bleeding Nun, Agnes hopes to impose on the credulity of others, who, if they see her, will be too terrified to block her escape to the waiting carriage of her lover. The Bleeding Nun, however, turns out to be real. It is she who enters the carriage instead of Agnes, and when Don Raymond departs from the castle, he is taken on a wild specter ride, is dropped next morning a great distance away, and is haunted night after night by the horrible specter he has carried away with him. There is no escape for Don Raymond until a mysterious stranger, later revealed as the Wandering Jew, arrives to exorcise her.

Nor is this all. As the action of *The Monk* develops, a strain of diabolism appears which, muted at first, comes at last to dominate the story completely. About halfway through the book, Matilda, who has entered the monastery disguised as a novice and has seduced Ambrosio, begins to use sorcery to gain her own and Ambrosio's ends. At first she acts offstage to cure herself of poisoning, but later, in full view of the monk, she summons Lucifer to provide Ambrosio with a talisman by means of which he can open locked doors and so approach Antonia, the intended victim of his lust. When he fails in his attempt to possess her, moreover, Matilda provides him with the means to entrap and rape the unfortunate girl, and after his arrest and trial, with a way to summon Lucifer again to free him from prison. Only after Ambrosio has lost his soul irretrievably does he learn that Matilda was all along an evil spirit sent to tempt him. The novel ends, then, with the monk totally in the power of Lucifer, who promptly destroys him. Carried high in the air by the demon, the shrieking monk is dropped to earth, where his mangled body lies until washed away by a flood.

Lewis had clearly made some significant additions to the English Gothic mode. Though books like *The Castle of Otranto* and *The Old English Baron* had long before employed supernatural beings, both Horace Walpole and Clara Reeve had made their apparitions the instruments of Divine Providence to restore the innocent to their rightful inheritance. Lewis, on the other hand, makes his major ones diabolic and the deliberate instruments of the monk's perdition. He also includes some aspects of the horrible that his predecessors avoided. The death, decay, and putrescence that pervade the vaults where Agnes and Antonia are imprisoned are a far cry from the corpse made of wax that frightens Emily St. Aubert in the Castle of Udolpho,[27] and the cold kiss that the specter of the Bleeding Nun plants each night on the lips of Don Raymond suggests an element of horror that can never be attained through the use of such imaginary ghosts as those that appear in *The Old Manor House* or *The Mysteries of Udolpho*. Sensational—indeed, even puerile—though *The Monk* may sometimes be in its sexual fantasies, it adds some important material to British Gothic fiction and opens the way for a new kind of demonic horror.

Although the supernatural elements that Lewis includes in *The Monk* are of the kind usually associated with the German Gothic—where indeed Lewis had found them—the German romances that appeared in English during the 1790s contain no specter nuns or compacts with the devil. Products of the Enlightenment, these novels are, if anything, more thoroughly rationalistic than the romances written by Lewis's English contemporaries. The strange events and reputed ghosts that abound in these works are without exception either self-induced mental delusions or, more often, the result of deliberately planned deception. The specter riders that sweep wildly through the night in Karl Kahlert's *The Necromancer* (1794) are merely a band of robbers playing upon the superstition of the neighboring villagers in order to avoid detection, and the numerous ghosts and apparitions that appear with thunder, lightning, gusts of wind, and clouds of acrid smoke are all carefully produced magic tricks that rely on such common apparatus as trap doors, machinery, and magic lanterns—all operated by one or more confederates who assist the pretended sorcerer in his deceptions. Many of the effects are clever and seem to defy explanation, but even the most mysterious are eventually exposed as mere magical delusion.

Because the Gothic effects result from mechanical deception, the German romances are, on the whole, considerably less successful as ghost stories than are their English counterparts. They seldom create the sense of immediacy, the aura of impending terror, for which Radcliffe's romances are so justly famous, and they do not engage the reader so closely in the psychological experience of the characters. This is only to say, however, that the primary interest of the Germans lies elsewhere: not so much in frightening the reader or playing upon his emotions as in leading him to perceive the ease with which the protagonist can be ensnared by the deceivers and the serious consequences that can flow from such deliberate deception. It is enough, therefore, if the reader can believe that a character of the type depicted could indeed fall prey to the machinations of artful and dedicated jugglers. The reader need not him-

self accept the phenomena as objectively real nor be strongly
them. It may even be better if he is not. His own disbelief wi
free to direct his attention to the social and political theme
German romances develop.

The deliberate deceptions serve a number of thematic purposes. They
illustrate how easy it is for a shrewd and determined band to delude even
those men who do not believe in apparitions, and they serve as a particular warning to others whose faulty education or disposition of mind
may predispose them to accept the deceits of pretended sorcerers as
supernatural phenomena. Characters of all these types appear in the novels. In *The Necromancer,* for example, Hellfried and Herrman do not believe in apparitions, but they are utterly mystified by some strange experiences they have had. The Austrian recruiting officer, on the other
hand, though a stable, respected, and fully rational man, has come to accept apparitions because he has observed phenomena that he cannot
otherwise explain. Other characters are even more prone to error. The
Prince in Friedrich von Schiller's *The Ghost-Seer* (1795) has not been
properly educated, and he has in his character a fondness for the marvelous that makes him especially susceptible to the Armenian's deceptions.
And Miguel in Cajetan Tschink's *The Victim of Magical Delusion* (1795)
is deceived by an apparent apparition "because his philosophy and experience are not sufficient to explain it in a natural manner."[28]

All of these characters have apparently made the same mistake. If they
had followed reason, believed unconditionally in the order of nature,
and interpreted all strange events as either mental aberrations or misapprehended natural phenomena, they would have escaped the delusions
that cause their embarrassment or ruin.[29] What makes their task most
difficult is that all are opposed by shrewd and unscrupulous men who
plan their deceptions with such care that they are difficult to detect. The
pattern was set by Schiller in *The Ghost-Seer.*[30] The Armenian, an agent
of the Inquisition, captures the attention of the Prince by a series of
strange events and coincidences that precede the main deception. That
deception itself is carefully organized. A Sicilian promises to raise the
ghost of the Marquis de Lanoy, the Prince's departed comrade, but
when the apparition appears, it is interrupted by a second ghost that
claims to be the true one and shows the Sicilian's vision to be a fraud.
The Armenian thus hopes to use an unmasked deception to convince the

Prince of the reality of the second apparition, win him to Catholicism, and eventually convert his future subjects to the same belief. Though the Prince sees through the attempt in that part of *The Ghost-Seer* that appeared in English, the second part of the book, merely summarized at the end of the English version, reveals the success of the Armenian in recruiting the Prince to his cause.

The deceptions in these romances, therefore, are designed to achieve a political or social end. Just as the Prince is ensnared in a plot which eventually leads to his downfall, so too is Miguel in *The Victim of Magical Delusion* lured into a series of plots that finally destroy him. This novel has a firm historical basis. The action takes place in 1640, just at the time of the Portuguese revolt that freed the country from Spanish domination and put the Duke of Braganza on the Portuguese throne. Miguel is subjected to a series of wonderful occurrences instigated by a mysterious character known as both the Irishman and Hiermansor, who wants to manipulate him into taking part in the revolt. He first deceives Miguel with a number of strange phenomena; then, when Miguel discovers the truth, he explains away the deceptions as a test of him; and, having fully won his confidence by this apparent honesty, he deceives him further with a seemingly inexplicable apparition. When the revolution succeeds, however, Miguel falls under the influence of another political manipulator, called Alumbrado, who undoes the work of the Irishman and leads Miguel to destruction in an abortive attempt to restore the Spanish rule.

Stories of this kind were popular in the 1790s largely because of the current interest in secret societies, especially the Society of the Illuminati, a German association that was said to maintain a shadowy influence over political events. Thus, even though the story itself deals with the Inquisition, the translator of *The Ghost-Seer* appended a note at the end of his English version to connect the tale with the German society. The story, he writes, "appeared at a time when the sect of the *Illuminated,* as it is called, was beginning to extend itself very rapidly in Germany. These people, it is well known, were accustomed to seduce the ignorant and the superstitious, by extravagant and incredible tales of supernatural powers and appearances. This story being calculated in some measure to expose these miraculous accounts, would, of course, be received with avidity."[31] Material of this kind was, without question, ideal for the purposes of the romancer, and Karl Grosse's *Horrid Mysteries* (1797) was specifically designed to meet the interest of contemporary readers. Indeed, the preface to the English edition of the book contains a long discussion of such societies, including the Secret Tribunal, which figures in Christiane Naubert's *Herman of Unna* (1794), and "the secret order of the Illuminators,"[32] who seem to have attracted the greatest attention, and whose machinations are the subject of Grosse's romance.

Horrid Mysteries is an especially interesting book in that it is much more successful than the others in creating a sense of mystery and terror. Some of the false apparitions are extremely well done. They flash upon the mind of Don Carlos like dazzling visions and are sometimes so utterly disconnected from normal time and space that they ring with conviction. In form, too, the romance is rather effective. Don Carlos begins his tale with a number of disjointed episodes in which he is first lured into the secret society and then, once he feels he is being unduly manipulated, attempts to escape from it. Mystery follows mystery as characters appear and disappear, and Don Carlos is never sure of his relationship to them or theirs to him. Nor does he understand who, or what, the ghostly Genius is who sometimes appears. The reader is often as much in the dark about what is happening as the narrator himself, and the book therefore communicates at times something of the anxiety and terror that the protagonist feels. Even the conclusion brings no final revelation. Though the secret society has reportedly been dissolved, a series of incidents suggests that it may still exist, and Don Carlos—and the reader—are left with a sense of uncertainty about the future.

Although *Horrid Mysteries* is probably the most successful of the German romances, one other tale, *The Necromancer,* is also worthy of note both for the subject matter it contains and the manner in which it is told. Because it treats a far-ranging band of robbers instead of secret societies or groups of politicial conspirators, this tale of the Black Forest stands somewhat apart from the other German romances in having relatively little social purpose.[33] It exploits, rather, a sense of mystery derived primarily from its skillful use of a multiple point of view. A number of strange adventures are described by at least four different narrators in widely separated times and places, adventures that seem at first glance to be totally unrelated. Only toward the end of the book are all of them brought together and revealed as the work of Volkert, a master of disguise who early won the reputation of being a sorcerer and who eventually used his talents for deception to help the band of robbers who terrorize the countryside. Like the Armenian, the Irishman, Alumbrado, and the secret powers of *Horrid Mysteries,* Volkert is adept at creating skillful magical delusions. He differs from them only in his lack of a strong political purpose.

It was through such characters as these and their skillful manipulation of others that the German romancers of the late eighteenth century made their main contribution to the developing Gothic mode. Though they surely sought to create some sense, at least, of terror in their works, their primary concern was clearly with rationalistic themes. The kind of supernatural event one finds in the tales of Walpole, Reeve, or even Lewis becomes in their hands merely an elaborate trick designed to dupe the unwary. Yet unlike such British rationalists as Radcliffe and Smith, who also explain away their most terrible effects, the Germans seem little concerned with depicting the psychological reactions of their characters to the phenomena they experience. They focus their attention, rather, on externals: on exposing supernatural phenomena as mere delusion, on revealing the dangers inherent in secret societies whose members work behind the scene and are not accountable for their acts, and on showing the important social and political consequences that might ensue if men should surrender to superstition and allow themselves to be influenced by deliberate deceptions. In focusing on these themes, they write what are, without question, the most rationalistic of Gothic romances.

To analyze in this way the Gothic fiction in English available to Americans in the closing years of the eighteenth century is to present a more orderly picture than the contemporary reader is likely to have perceived. A large number of romances were competing for his attention, and examples of all four types of the Gothic mode were simultaneously available in the bookstores and lending libraries, all arranged in the catalogues, with other novels and romances, alphabetically by title. Despite the apparent confusion, however, certain patterns do emerge, and even in that day an intelligent young man like Charles Brockden Brown, eager to launch his own career as a novelist, must surely have perceived them. An avid reader himself, he was undoubtedly well aware of the literary taste of his contemporaries—as, indeed, his use of the Gothic mode in most of his major romances so clearly indicates. Within that mode, however, he sought his models, not among the supernatural tales of a Walpole or Lewis, but among the rationalistic ones of the German romancers and of the Radcliffe school—a decision made necessary perhaps by the intellectual climate of the times, and one of considerable consequence to the subsequent development of American fiction.

THREE

Charles Brockden Brown

To discuss the novels of Charles Brockden Brown only in terms of contemporary Gothic fiction is to view them from an admittedly limited point of view. A man of strong intellectual curiosity, Brown read widely in both traditional and contemporary literature. Echoes of Shakespeare and Milton are heard throughout his works, and the influence on his books of both the fiction and nonfiction of his own age was great. Biographers have stressed the importance of William Godwin, Mary Wollstonecraft, and Robert Bage in the development of Brown's ideas, and no single book was perhaps more important than Godwin's *Caleb Williams* (1794) in teaching the young man about the form and purpose of fiction. To emphasize these influences, however, is to create a bias in favor of the liberal ideas that are introduced, discussed, and tested throughout his works—a bias that warps our view of Brown away from his real importance as the father of American fiction.[1] For however important those liberal books and ideas may have been to the aspiring young writer of the 1790s, it was the side of his fiction derived from the British and German Gothic writers that gave him his characteristic mode of expression and established a kind of fiction that was to become peculiarly American.

In developing the Gothic strain, however, Brown confronted a problem that would trouble many of his successors in nineteenth-century America: how to adapt a European mode of fiction to the very different conditions of American life. The Gothic novel had begun in England as a tale of Gothic times, set in the distant past and pretending to imitate the manners of the medieval age. Even those novels detailing more recent events were either set, like *The Italian,* on the continent of Europe, or, if laid in Great Britain, like *The Old Manor House* or *The Children of the Abbey,* used an old and usually decaying castle or similar ancient building as a source of Gothic terror. Neither of these alternatives was suitable for an American writer of the late eighteenth century who wished to develop a distinctively American literature, and in his preface to *Edgar*

Huntly (1799), Brown announced to his public that he had eschewed the "puerile superstition and exploded manners, Gothic castles and chimeras" (4: 4) usually employed to engage the interest of the reader. But although Brown turns in that book to scenes of the wilderness and the incidents of border warfare to embody his theme, the fact that he makes the statement at all indicates that he was without question thinking of his book in terms of the contemporary Gothic mode.

How much Brown learned from contemporary Gothic fiction remains an open question, for his sources in this genre have never been properly explored. Some critics have mentioned both Schiller's *The Ghost-Seer* and Tschink's *The Victim of Magical Delusion* as possible sources for *Wieland* (1798), while others have suggested the romances of Ann Radcliffe as a possible influence on him.[2] The problem, of course, is that Gothic devices soon became the property of all the practitioners of the mode, and one can never be sure whether a specific device is a source or an analogue for another's use of it. Thus, although Carwin in *Wieland* may resemble in some respects both the Armenian and Hiermansor in Schiller's and Tschink's romances, he is also much like Volkert, the pretended sorcerer in Kahlert's *The Necromancer*. And if both Clara Wieland and Constantia Dudley face terrifying situations alone in their rooms at night, so too do the heroines of not only Ann Radcliffe's romances but also those of practically every other book by her numerous imitators. To seek a specific source from among so many possible contenders is difficult at best and may in the final analysis be simply futile.

One can point out, nonetheless, some interesting parallels. Eliza Parsons's *The Mysterious Warning* (1796), for example, stands in a close relationship to Brown's *Wieland* in the important use they both make of apparently supernatural voices. Ferdinand, in the former book, believing himself to be disinherited, hears a voice in the chamber of his dead father promise him pardon and peace. Though he has always discredited "supernatural interpositions," he is convinced that the voice is "not the illusion of his senses" (p. 12), and his certainty is reinforced when it warns him against his corrupt brother and later tells him to avoid his unfaithful wife. Since both he and his wife hear the third message, he believes he must accept it as a warning from the dead. Though all three messages are the work of Ernest, an old steward who is loyal to Ferdinand, his corrupt brother, Rhodophil, begins to hear voices too. Since those that Rhodophil hears have no objective source in the real world, they must be the product of his guilt or of a diseased fancy. The parallel with *Wieland,* where Carwin's biloquial tricks are interpreted by Clara and Theodore Wieland as supernatural messages, and where Wieland himself begins to hear other voices not made by Carwin, is perfectly obvious.

An equally interesting analogue to *Wieland* may be found in Kahlert's *The Necromancer* (1794), a story told through the use of a multiple point of view. Each of three characters recounts the striking experiences he has had independent of the others, and it is not until the end of the book, when the culprit confesses, that each experience in turn is revealed to have been the deception of a man named Volkert. He early learned how easy it is to play on the credulity of others for his own purposes and soon acquired the reputation of being a sorcerer. Besides the fact that Volkert bears some resemblance to Carwin, in form *The Necromancer* may have provided Brown with a model for *Wieland,* where a series of strange events also occurs, only to be explained finally in the confession of Carwin. One can, of course, make too much of such parallels. The voices of *The Mysterious Warning* and the technique of *The Necromancer* may—or may not—have influenced Brown when he was composing *Wieland.* But the question of sources is not really the point. What the parallels certainly indicate is the close relation of Brown's fiction to the kind of thing being done by his British and German contemporaries.

We should seek the sources of Brown's inspiration, therefore, not so much in specific works as in general types of fiction. Though a writer may sometimes borrow a particular episode or event from another, he is usually more profoundly affected by the broader aspects of the fiction he has read. Brown's probable use of the German romance is a case in point. What he got from the fiction of Schiller and Tschink, and perhaps also of Grosse, was the use of a mysterious band of political adventurers who seek to manipulate others for their own advantage. Since each of their books deals with a different kind of political intrigue, Brown could only have derived from them the general idea. He had to select for himself the kind of society he wished to use. He found what he wanted in the Society of the Illuminati, a real group that was much discussed in those days. Both the end-note to the English edition of *The Ghost-Seer* and the long introduction by Peter Will to his translation of

Horrid Mysteries contain information about it, and John Robison's *Proofs of a Conspiracy* includes a long discussion of it.[3]

When William Dunlap read the manuscript of "Memoirs of Carwin, the Biloquist" in 1798, he immediately saw what Brown was about, for he wrote in his diary on September 14: "read C B Browns beginning for the life of Carwin—as far as he has gone he has done well: he has taken up the schemes of the Illuminati."[4] Though Brown does not mention the society by name in any of his fiction, it figures prominently in at least two of his important works, and suggestions of it appear as well in *Wieland.* In both "Memoirs of Carwin" and *Ormond* (1799), he includes a mysterious character who belongs to a utopian society and who, like the secret leader in *Horrid Mysteries,* recruits promising young men to the cause. Ludloe, in the former work, seeks to enlist Carwin when he learns of his talent as a ventriloquist, but the fragment ends before we discover the use that is to be made of him. Ormond, in the latter book, has at his command "numerous agents and dependants" (6: 170-71), such as the surgeon who cures Stephen Dudley's blindness, all of whom are used for the furtherance of his political goals.

This political purpose is so veiled in secrecy that only the vaguest hints and most oblique allusions suggest to the other characters what is really afoot. Even Sophia Westwyn Courtland, the narrator of *Ormond,* tells us twice that she does not have complete knowledge of Ormond's actions and that it would not be prudent for her to reveal the means by which she acquired the information which she does have. Carwin's fragment breaks off long before he learns much of Ludloe's plans, but both he and Sophia reveal enough to suggest that the secret societies aim, in her words, at nothing less than "the new-modelling of the world, and the subversion of all that has hitherto been conceived elementary and fundamental in the constitution of man and of government" (6: 245). Though subversion seems to be part of their schemes, both Ludloe and Ormond are also concerned with constructing new societies in unexplored parts of the world. Carwin discovers a map among Ludloe's things which places his colony on some islands in the South Pacific,[5] and though Ormond conceals the location of his society, Sophia believes that it must be in some out-of-the-way place: "on the shore of an *austral* continent, or in the heart of desert America" (6: 245).

For the furtherance of their schemes, these utopian projectors use powers that are so mysterious as to border on the incredible. Like Hiermansor in *The Victim of Magical Delusion* or Don Carlos's servant, Alfonso, in *Horrid Mysteries,* Ormond is the master of disguise. Having once been the dupe of misleading appearances, he has used his talent to penetrate the duplicity of others and has been so successful in each attempt that he uses this means repeatedly to attain his ends. Both he and Ludloe, moreover, are extremely adept at penetrating the secrets of others. Carwin is amazed to learn that Ludloe knows all about an event in his life which he has taken great pains to conceal, and he even produces a paper that Carwin thought he had burned. In a similar fashion, Ormond reveals to the astonished Constantia Dudley his total knowledge of conversations she had had with Sophia Courtland—conversations that had taken place under such conditions that it would appear impossible for anyone to have overheard them. Thus, like their German counterparts, both Ludloe and Ormond seem to possess a number of powers that border upon the miraculous.

But Brown does not exploit the marvelous aspects of this material. Unlike the German romancers, whose pretended sorcerers use spectacular displays to play upon the credulity of their victims, Brown avoids any suggestion of deliberate magical delusion. Even Carwin employs his voices in *Wieland* not to dupe the superstitious but first to extricate himself from tight situations and later to test the fortitude and rationality of Clara Wieland and Henry Pleyel. In no instance does he attempt to delude them for a political or social end. In a similar fashion, the powers of Ludloe and Ormond are not manifested through the magical tricks of their German counterparts, nor do they attempt to create a feeling of superstitious fear in their victims. They never pretend that their powers are anything but natural, and Ormond even admits to Constantia toward the end of the book that he has merely used secret passages and canvas walls in acquiring his knowledge of her private affairs. A sense of mystery is, of course, present in all these incidents, and *Wieland,* in particular, has about it an aura of the supernatural, but Brown has avoided even the suggestion that his projectors employ either real or supposed supernatural means to attain their ends.

In other matters, too, Brown's use of this material differs sharply from that of the German romancers. For Schiller, Tschink, and Grosse, the political theme is the center of focus, and for the former two, the story exists merely to show how clever men may play upon the superstition of others for their own ends. In Brown's completed works, however, the mysterious projectors play only a subordinate role. Although Carwin's use of ventriloquism in *Wieland* may remind one of the magical deceptions of the Germans, the main emphasis of the book is on Clara and Theodore Wieland and the intellectual problems posed to them by the seemingly inexplicable phenomena they perceive. In *Ormond,* the main point of the book is not the secret machinations of the projector but the strength and fortitude of Constantia Dudley, who, because of her rational education, is able to act with intelligence and resolution when confronted with all kinds of challenging situations.[6] Only in "Memoirs of Carwin" did Brown attempt an entire book focused upon the material he found in the German romances, but he did not bring the work to completion. His primary interest apparently lay in other directions.

Brown was concerned, not with political themes or attacks upon superstition, but with the serious moral and intellectual issues raised by the principles and actions of his utopian projectors, questions like the relation of means to ends and the value of unrestrained intellectualism as a guide to life. He gives his projectors a fair hearing for their ideas, but the actions of his books make clear the appalling consequences that can result from the application of those principles. Though "Memoirs of Carwin" is only a fragment, the fate of Carwin in *Wieland,* accused of robbery and murder by his erstwhile benefactor and pursued as a common criminal, clearly indicates the fate of one who, for whatever reason, incurs the wrath of the secret society. The arrogant intellectualism of Ormond leads him into hideous excesses: the murder of Constantia's father and the attempted rape of the girl herself. And the biloquial tricks of Carwin in *Wieland* illustrate clearly the danger of setting in motion, even in an innocent manner, a chain of events the end of which no one can predict. In developing his books in this way, Brown greatly improved on his sources. He turned a limited kind of fiction—at once both sensational and aridly rationalistic—into an interesting vehicle for testing significant ideas.

Brown's handling of other Gothic materials—the Gothic horror, for example, that was just coming into prominence at that time—illustrates further his ability to adapt a convention to his own artistic ends. In *A Si-*

cilian Romance, Ann Radcliffe had included a brief episode in which two characters are trapped in a vault with the decaying bodies of some bandits' victims, and Karl Grosse, in *Horrid Mysteries,* includes a series of episodes in which a character named Elmira seems to die and reappear, undergoes premature burial, and even reappears once after her husband has retained her dead body until there can be no doubt that it must be buried. In Matthew Gregory Lewis's *The Monk,* moreover, such materials are given an unusually prominent place for British Gothic fiction. The story of the Bleeding Nun and the description of putrescence and physical decay in the charnal house of the convent are among the most striking and sensational elements in the book. One would expect, perhaps, that a young intellectual like Brown, so deeply concerned with moral and philosophical questions, would have had little interest in such material. Yet in *Ormond* and *Arthur Mervyn* (1799–1800),[7] Brown includes a number of elements that are closely related to it.

The yellow fever epidemic in Philadelphia in 1793 provided Brown with the means for creating a sense of Gothic horror without resorting to the kind of device he dismisses in the preface to *Edgar Huntly.* In *Ormond,* for example, a character named Whiston flees in terror when he learns that his sister is infected, only to die alone in a barn, his body left to decay because everyone fears to approach it. Another, named Baxter, is watching the house of a Frenchman one night when he sees the man's daughter drag a body from the house to bury it in a shallow grave. When she pauses a moment in her work, she looks up, catches sight of Baxter's face, and shrieks. He, in turn, flees in such panic that the disease, which he otherwise might have resisted, takes hold of him and kills him. A feeling of intense fear pervades these scenes in *Ormond.* The characters face the horror of the plague with enervating terror and perceive the gruesome effects of sickness and death. The stench of the disease fills the atmosphere, and the horror of physical dissolution is constantly held before the eyes of the onlooker.

Brown develops an even greater sense of horror in the first part of *Arthur Mervyn.* Though he certainly had no use for tales like that of the Bleeding Nun, he does allow Arthur Mervyn to experience the psychological equivalent of perceiving such an apparition. In plague-ridden Philadelphia, Mervyn has learned that a man he has been searching for is dead, and looking through his house to recover what property he has left, he hears footsteps approach him.

The door opened, and a figure glided in. The portmanteau
dropped from my arms, and my heart's-blood was chilled. If an
apparition of the dead were possible, and that possibility I could
not deny, this was such an apparition. A hue, yellowish and livid;
bones, uncovered with flesh; eyes, ghastly, hollow, woe-begone,
and fixed in an agony of wonder upon me; and locks, matted and
negligent, constituted the image which I now beheld. My belief of
somewhat preternatural in this appearance, was confirmed by recollection of resemblances between these features and those of one
who was dead. In this shape and visage, shadowy and death-like as
they were, the lineaments of Wallace, . . . whose death I had conceived to be incontestably ascertained, were forcibly recognized.
[3: 166-67]

Though Wallace turns out to be alive, Mervyn has for the moment perceived him as a specter.

Nor is this all. The men who collect the dead sometimes thrust living
persons into the coffins, and Mervyn himself almost undergoes premature burial. While searching a house in the hope of finding Wallace,
Mervyn looks into a mirror and thinks he sees an apparition approaching
him. When he turns to confront it, a blow to his forehead renders him
senseless. He dreams that two gigantic figures are trying to cast him
into a pit, and he awakes to find two men who, thinking him dead, are
about to place him in a coffin and nail down the lid. Other men in the
city collect the sick and carry them to the hospital, the equivalent, in
Brown's universe, of the charnal house of the conventional Gothic romance. Here Wallace had been sent when he contracted the fever, and
he was placed on a mattress "whose condition proved that an half-decayed corpse had recently been dragged from it" (3: 173). The horrors
of the sick and the dying are made worse by the carousals of those who
are supposed to care for them, and a dying victim is sometimes forced by
his position to look at "the ghastly writhings or deathful *smile* of his
neighbour" (3: 173).

Passages like these are closely allied to the kind of Gothic horror that
Lewis includes in *The Monk* and that was to become a staple of one type
of Gothic fiction down to the works of Edgar Allan Poe, Ambrose
Bierce, and even William Faulkner. What makes Brown's use of the
material so interesting is his ability to create the effect of Gothic horror

without resorting to the more conventional literary devices. His use of
the yellow fever may, in fact, have intensified that effect. The threat of
death and the horror of dissolution are especially frightening during an
epidemic, the fear of premature burial becomes a very real as well as a
deeply psychological terror, and the sights and smells of the hospital create a sense of horror not to be matched by those of a charnal house in the
vaults of an ancient convent. By describing a real situation, moreover,
Brown was able to use these Gothic materials for a serious social purpose. The hospital scenes, in particular, serve an important function in
revealing what were, after all, the true conditions of the time, and some
of the incidents clearly show the strength and weakness of human nature in the face of such actual terrors.

Brown was equally adept at turning the Gothic strain of Ann Radcliffe and her successors to his own artistic ends. The influence of this
school is especially strong in *Wieland,* where many of the devices of British Gothic fiction appear. Clara Wieland, who narrates the book, resembles in some ways the Gothic heroines of the Radcliffe school. She flees
in terror once from apparently inexplicable phenomena, she is threatened with rape, and she is separated from her lover for a time before
their ultimate reunion and marriage. The setting, too, sometimes takes
on a Radcliffean atmosphere, and it affects the mind of the heroine in
the expected way. Alone in her room at night and frightened by a mysterious voice, Clara observes: "Solitude imposes least restraint upon the
fancy. Dark is less fertile of images than the feeble lustre of the moon. I
was alone, and the walls were chequered by shadowy forms. As the
moon passed behind a cloud and emerged, these shadows seemed to be
endowed with life, and to move. The apartment was open to the breeze,
and the curtain was occasionally blown from its ordinary position. This
motion was not unaccompanied with sound. I failed not to snatch a
look, and to listen when this motion and this sound occurred" (1: 86).
Though the style is his own, Brown is attempting to create the kind of
effect made popular by the British romancers.

Yet numerous though such Gothic devices may be, they receive in
Wieland a markedly different emphasis, derived in part from the serious
treatment given the whole question of supernaturalism. Instead of the
somewhat trivial purposes it sometimes serves in even Radcliffe's romances, it provides the intellectual center for the entire book. The tenor
is firmly established in the opening chapters when the elder Wieland

dies under extraordinary circumstances, his arm hurt, his body burned, and a strange light pervading the atmosphere. Though his death may be explained as the result of spontaneous combustion, his own report, before he expires, of what had happened to him in his temple of worship—a report which suggests that he has not told all that occurred—leaves open the question of whether or not some nonmaterial influence may have been present.[8] A degree of uncertainty is thus introduced in the minds of his children, which leaves them prone to believe that direct supernatural intervention may have been instrumental in bringing about their father's death. When Carwin later projects his voice, therefore, both Theodore and Clara Wieland are prepared to believe that messages may be received from supernatural powers.

Wieland is thus inclined from the beginning to accept the voices produced by Carwin as supernatural phenomena, and his view of the world is such that he sees his decision as a perfectly rational one. In the course of the novel, however, Wieland goes insane and believes he hears a voice that has no basis in reality. When it tells him to murder his family, he assumes he has received a divine command and proceeds at once to obey it. Clara, on her part, is much more likely to weigh the evidence and balance one interpretation of strange phenomena against another. But she is soon subjected to a series of frightening experiences, all directly caused by Carwin, in which a voice seems to preserve her from harm and warn her away from danger. Clara is not superstitious. She scorns the tales of ghosts and apparitions that so often unnerve the unwary, and she considers herself "a stranger even to that terror which is pleasing" (1: 45). So real and so inexplicable are the events that happen to her, however, that she begins to believe an invisible protector is shielding her from evil.

Because it lays such stress on the question of supernatural intervention, *Wieland* stands somewhat apart from the novels it most resembles. Though the use of Carwin's ventriloquism to suggest supernatural events may remind one of the romances of Schiller, Tschink, and Kahlert, Brown does not dismiss the phenomena as merely political trickery or magical delusion, and in the mania of Wieland he adds a dimension to the problem of interpreting strange phenomena untouched by the German romancers. In a similar fashion, though Clara Wieland bears an obvious resemblance to the heroines of Ann Radcliffe and her imitators, her encounters with mysterious occurrences are more ex-

tended and more terrifying than those of her British counterparts, and
her ultimate descent into madness, after Wieland murders his family,
sets her further apart from them. Clara is depicted, too, as more intelligent and better educated than the usual Gothic heroines, she ponders
more deeply on the strange events she experiences, and in the course of
her adventures she exhibits psychological depths not to be found in
them. To reveal her psychic state Brown employs two stock Gothic devices that he had undoubtedly picked up in his reading, but which, char-
acteristically, he turns to his own purposes: the presentiment and the
prophetic dream.

Early in the book, Clara experiences a strange but accurate presentiment of what is to come. When she first sees Carwin, she is much disturbed by the strange inconsistency she perceives between his melodious
voice and his unattractive countenance. She quickly sketches his visage,
and during the stormy day that follows, she spends her time in deep
contemplation of both the image and the tempest. When night returns,
her mind is "absorbed in thoughts ominous and dreary" (1: 54). She sees
in the tempest a possible sign of impending ruin, the portraits of her
brother and his children increase her mournfulness, and although their
images are as serene as ever, she thinks of them "with anguish. Something whispered that the happiness we at present enjoyed was set on
mutable foundations" (1: 54). As yet she is unaware of any connection
between Carwin and her family, and though the stormy day may have
had a depressing effect on her, there is no reason for Clara to expect an
early end to their happiness. Yet her foreboding is accurate: Wieland in
his madness will soon destroy his wife and children, and Clara herself
will eventually be driven to insanity.

A presentiment of this kind is a far cry from those to be found in *The
Mysteries of Udolpho* or *The Italian,* for it seems to rise from a source
deeply imbedded in the character's psyche. So too does an odd series of
experiences that Clara undergoes in which a prophetic dream and presentiments of the future are strangely intermixed. Having fallen asleep
in the summerhouse one evening, Clara dreams that she is near her
brother's house and walking toward a pit of which she is unaware. Her
brother stands on the other side, beckoning to her and bidding her make
haste. But just as she is about to plunge into the abyss, a voice cries out
"Hold! hold!" and she starts awake (1: 62). In the waking world the
voice is Carwin's, but as so often happens in sleep, it also functions in

her dream. Clara is of course disturbed by this occurrence, but she is more deeply affected by the voice she subsequently hears than by the dream itself. Indeed, it does not recur to her memory until one night when she is alone in her room and she has another presentiment of evil.

On this occasion Clara is about to go to her closet to get her father's manuscript, which she intends to read. Because she has previously heard voices there threatening her life, she is understandably nervous, but as she approaches the door, she feels "unconquerable apprehensions. A sort of belief darted into my mind," she writes, "that some being was concealed within, whose purposes were evil" (1: 84). Though Clara does not know it, Carwin is concealed in the closet, and when she puts her hand on the lock, she hears the same command she heard in the dream. This cry makes her remember who it was in the dream that beckoned her to destruction, and she leaps at once to the conclusion that Wieland lurks within and is waiting to kill her. From one point of view, of course, her presentiment is wrong. There is no one there with any intent to harm her, for Carwin has simply been led to her room by a desire to see her father's manuscript. From another, however, the presentiment is deadly accurate. It is Wieland she must fear, and before the book is finished, he will come to kill her in that very room.

In the ensuing action Clara undergoes a series of experiences that confirm at last the prophecy of her dream. The death of Wieland's wife and children drives her temporarily insane before she can learn who the murderer is, and when she recovers her sanity, she assumes it is Carwin. It is only then that her uncle reveals to her that Wieland has confessed his crimes, and he places in her hands her brother's testimony before the court. Shocked though she is, she requests to see him, only to be told that Wieland considers his task as yet incomplete, and should she enter his dungeon, he would try to kill her. Indeed, he had already twice escaped in an attempt to complete the murders that he thinks are commanded by God. At this point Clara recalls her dream in the summerhouse. "I recollected the omens of this destiny; I remembered the gulf to which my brother's invitation had conducted me; I remembered that, when on the brink of danger, the author of my peril was depicted by my fears in his form: Thus realized, were the creatures of prophetic sleep, and of wakeful terror!" (1: 189-90). From a deep recess in Clara's mind there has arisen a fanciful image of her true danger.

Other aspects of Gothic fiction also receive an emphasis in *Wieland* not usually found in the genre. Like most of its British and German predecessors, the book is concerned with the problem of perception: the characters are mystified by the phenomena they perceive and, in some cases, interpret them as supernatural. In most of the British romances, however, the uncertain vision is only a subordinate element usually employed to project the fears of the isolated heroine, and in the German books it is always presented as a deliberately induced delusion. In *Wieland,* however, the problem of perceiving reality is of the utmost importance in the book, the interest in it is sustained throughout, and the source of the delusion is as much internal as it is externally induced. In addition, Brown lays heavy stress on the sense of hearing rather than that of sight. This in itself was an important shift in emphasis from the typical Gothic romance, where most apparitions are visual. An aural delusion cannot be dismissed by a simple change of light or shift from night to day, and since sight is the primary sense on which the characters must rely for knowledge, they are likely to believe that the voices they hear have no physical source when none is visible.

In their reactions to the problem, moreover, the characters in *Wieland* differ from those most often found in Gothic fiction. Both Clara and Theodore Wieland are intelligent and educated persons whose qualities of mind should prevent their succumbing to the kind of belief in supernatural agencies usually reserved for the ignorant lower classes, but their strange family history and personal psychology render them incapable of penetrating the appearances they perceive to the truth that lies behind them. Even their rationalist friend, Henry Pleyel, whom Clara loves, is markedly different in his behavior from the character he most resembles in the British Gothic. Both he and Lord Mortimer in Roche's *The Children of the Abbey* fall prey to mistaken perceptions deliberately caused by others. They believe the evidence of their senses that the heroines of the books, Clara Wieland and Amanda Fitzalan, have become the mistresses of unsavory characters, Carwin and Colonel Belgrave. Each confronts the girl with his accusations, but whereas Lord Mortimer, in true sentimental fashion, is immediately convinced of Amanda's innocence when she explains what has happened, Pleyel insists in his passion that his senses have reported the truth, and he leaves Clara protesting, but unable to prove, her innocence.

Because the delusions of the characters in *Wieland* are so strong and deepseated, the cure is by no means as easy to effect as it usually is in the romances of the Radcliffe school. There the sources of error are always clearly presented as superstition, emotion, or an ardent imagination, and the cure is brought about by a return to the rule of reason, which enables one to distinguish fact from fancy. In Brown no such unqualified solution appears. Though he, like his predecessors, clearly recognizes the deceptive power of the imagination and the influence of the emotions in leading men astray, he makes it abundantly clear that the cause of error is not simple nor the cure easy. Wieland, after all, insists that he put the passion of love aside and acted reasonably in following the evidence of his senses—the divine command he imagines he heard—in destroying his family, and both Clara and Pleyel are equally sure that they have acted on sensory evidence and arrived at rational conclusions, even when the one believes that she is under supernatural protection and the other is certain that he has perceived her dishonor.

Reason, of course, does enter the book in the character of Clara's uncle, a rationalist physician who nurses her back to sanity after her ordeal and who arranges for Carwin to disabuse Pleyel of his mistaken opinion of her. But so thoroughgoing is Brown's treatment of the unconscious sources of human error that reason cannot be seen as ever in full control, not even at the end of the book. Throughout, the characters are lost in the maze of their own perceptions, and even after her uncle's explanation, Clara's final analysis of the characters' "errors" does not really establish a basis on which sound knowledge could have been derived from their perceptions. Despite all the evidence to the contrary, she still perceives Carwin as a "double-tongued deceiver" and the author of the evils they have experienced (1: 244), whereas the action of the book clearly reveals to the reader that the sources of error lie within and cannot be so glibly assigned an external cause. Brown permits no easy solution to the problems he raises, and unlike the Gothic novelists from whom he derived so much, he retains an aura of ambiguity and uncertainty right to the end.

What Brown did in *Wieland,* therefore, was to take the problem of perception that he found in the British and German Gothic romances and examine it in terms of its deepest philosophic meanings. In his hands, the device of mistaken perception is used not merely to suggest that people frighten themselves with chimeras, but to examine the very basis of human knowledge and to probe, as he writes in the preface to *Wieland,* "the moral constitution of man" (1: 3). He looks deeply into the springs of human motivation, touches the unconscious sources of terror, and suggests that the causes of madness—the ultimate misapprehension of reality—may lie in one's childhood experience or in the traits inherited from one's forebears. Though the book must surely be seen as derived primarily from one branch of the late eighteenth-century Gothic mode, it goes far beyond its predecessors in adapting that form to a serious psychological purpose. *Wieland* marks a real advance over the Gothic tales of Ann Radcliffe and her successors, and it establishes once and for all in America a type of Gothic fiction that was to undergo a great deal of additional development.

The most original use that Brown made of this material was undoubtedly in *Edgar Huntly,* a book which, true to its preface, employs no major Gothic devices, but which represents nonetheless the culmination of Brown's Gothicism. Many of its most striking effects derive, of course, as do those of the usual Gothic romance, from the characters' misapprehension of the reality that impinges upon them and their inclination to interpret the strange phenomena they experience as supernatural. But there are significant differences, too. The characters in *Edgar Huntly* do not confront bizarre external phenomena. There are no spectacular deaths like that of the elder Wieland to suggest supernatural interference in the affairs of men, no voices like those projected by Carwin to baffle interpretation, indeed, no accurate presentiments of evil, no truly prophetic dreams. The world that the characters face is by and large the natural one, and the sense of mystery and terror derive not so much from the external world itself as from the inner workings of their individual minds. What they perceive, therefore, is an index to the world that lies within, and the book, perhaps even more than *Wieland,* is deeply psychological.

Consider the reactions of three of the characters to the strange experiences they have in the actual world. All three suggest supernatural explanations for what has occurred, and each interpretation reveals the mental state of the character. The skeptical Sarsefield, for example, is undismayed by a series of seemingly miraculous events he has observed. While searching for Huntly during the Indian incursion, he twice witnesses his apparent death and return to life, he becomes aware of the incredible distance Huntly has covered in a short period of time, and he sees the Indians Huntly had killed while presumably unarmed. Thus, when he finally meets Huntly in a farmhouse where he least expects to find him, he declares himself ready to abandon his lifelong spirit of skepticism. Though he has never placed "credit or trust in miraculous agency" (4: 232), were he called upon to testify, he would have to swear that Huntly has been dead and restored to life, and has exhibited preternatural powers. Sarsefield, of course, is not really serious in this statement. To rely on his senses alone would indeed enforce this conclusion, but as a rational man he believes there must be a natural explanation, and he actively seeks it.

Edgar Huntly, on the other hand, draws a quite different conclusion when he discovers that some papers he had hidden in a secret cabinet are missing. Utterly unable to account for the phenomenon, he experiences a feeling of ominous terror—"a whispering intimation that a relic which [he] valued more than life was torn forever away by some malignant and inscrutable destiny" (4: 128). This sense of helplessness before a mysterious force stays with him. After he awakes in the cave totally at a loss to explain how he got there, he fancies, in a kind of wakeful dream, that he has been imposed upon by "some tyrant who had thrust [him] into a dungeon of his fortress" (4:154), and even when he escapes from the cave, he wonders if "some mysterious power [had] snatched [him] from the earth, and cast [him], in a moment, into the heart of the wilderness" (4: 164). Finally, when he rediscovers his papers in the farmhouse where he meets his mentor, Sarsefield, he can only conclude that the power who has afflicted him is beyond conjecture. Though Huntly's experience has, of course, been much more disturbing than Sarsefield's, his mind is more apt to leap to a belief in a supernatural agency.

A related but much more ominous conclusion is drawn by Clithero Edny, who undergoes an even stranger experience. While he was still in Europe serving a Mrs. Lorimer, he became involved in a series of events that led him to kill Arthur Wiatte, her evil twin brother. Clithero is innocent of any intent to murder. He fired in self-defense at an assailant whom he did not recognize. His mind, however, goes through a strange and irrational series of thoughts which eventually leads him to conclude that because of this deed he must kill Mrs. Lorimer as an act of benevolence, and he immediately sets out to do so. When he fails in his attempt to murder her, Mrs. Lorimer faints, and Clithero leaves the scene convinced that she has died because of her strange belief that her life must end with that of her twin. In telling his story to Edgar Huntly in America, however, Clithero insists that some evil power had ordained this fate for him. He believes that his mind had "been perverted by diabolical instigations" (4: 65) and that the act of attempted murder was not actually his but that of the daemon who possessed him.

Though Clithero draws by far the darkest interpretation of events, both he and Huntly are alike in seeing themselves as pawns in the hands of some inscrutable power. The influences they feel are, to be sure, entirely subjective and derive from aberrations of mind, but they seem to them as real as any demonstrable influence in the physical world. Of the two, Clithero is, as his interpretation suggests, the more seriously disturbed. His behavior is obviously bizarre. When Huntly first sees him, he is burying a box beneath an elm tree while asleep; on the second occasion he wanders through the wilderness of Norwalk at night and darts into a cave; and after telling his story to Huntly, he flees to an isolated peak in the wilderness where he intends to starve himself to death. From their first encounter Huntly realizes that Clithero is a sleepwalker, and he knows that the inability to sleep soundly is the sign of a "sorely wounded" mind (4: 13), but he also believes that a sympathetic and understanding friend may restore him to sanity. For this reason Huntly makes several trips to the wilderness retreat to seek him out, fells a tree across a chasm in order to reach him, and brings him food so that he will not perish.

What Huntly fails to perceive is that he himself is so mentally disturbed that his judgments are not to be trusted. He is aware, of course, of some of his own aberrations. He knows that his friend Inglefield has had to correct "the wanderings of [his] reason and [his] freaks of passion" (4: 24), and he recognizes the folly of repeatedly searching the spot where another friend, Waldegrave, was killed in the hope of finding some clues to his murder. When he decides to help Clithero, however, he thinks he is acting rationally, even though his pursuit of him becomes increasingly strange. He begins, indeed, to resemble the man he is trying to help, for, completely unknown to himself, he has become a sleepwalker. While in the somnambulent state, he, like Clithero, hides papers from himself, goes wandering into the wilderness, and enters a cave. Unlike his double, he falls into a pit in the cave and later awakes with no recollection of how he has come there, but on his return to the settlements he discovers a bloodthirsty side of himself that he did not know he possessed, and he feels, in killing some Indians, as if "a spirit vengeful, unrelenting, and ferocious" has taken possession of him (4: 184).

The aberrations of mind from which Huntly suffers create a world that is intensely Gothic in its effects. Because of his compulsive search for clues to Waldegrave's murder and his obsessive pursuit of Clithero through the wilderness, Huntly both perceives and describes for the reader a number of strange and mysterious scenes: Clithero digging under the elm tree late at night, and the tangled labyrinth of Norwalk through which they move in darkness. Huntly's gradual return to consciousness when he awakes in the cave, moreover, provides a series of adventures filled with mystery, and his journey back to Solesbury during the Indian incursion, his encounter with the warriors, his flight from apparent pursuers by diving into the river at night, and his strange adventures in the houses he enters provide the kind of suspense and terror that other Gothic novelists had created through the use of more conventional devices. What is especially significant in *Edgar Huntly*, however, is that the universe of the book is a reflection of Huntly's mind. It must be dark and mysterious so long as Huntly remains a man unknown to himself.[9] Should he acquire self-knowledge, he would presumably see a world approximating that of Sarsefield.

Such enlightenment seems to come when Huntly meets Sarsefield in the farmhouse and, in the course of their long conversation, the mystery of what has happened to him is at last unraveled. Once he learns from his mentor that he, like Clithero, has been a sleepwalker, the disappearance of his papers and his presence in the cave are easily explained, and as he and Sarsefield recount their adventures to each other, what had seemed strange and inexplicable becomes perfectly clear. Huntly's return to rationality, therefore, would seem to have been easily effected by the interposition of Sarsefield's mind, which, viewing the phenomena dispassionately and observing their true meaning and significance, can help him to reestablish in his mind the rational order of things. Huntly believes that something like this has indeed happened, for after the experience is over and he begins to write the narrative of his adventures, he exclaims: "What light has burst upon my ignorance of myself and of mankind! How sudden and enormous the transition from uncertainty to knowledge!" (4: 6). Huntly retains this view throughout the book, concluding his account of what has happened in the assurance that all mysteries have been solved and his return to rationality is complete.

The book does not end with Huntly's narrative, however, but goes on to a final episode that brings this conclusion into serious doubt. Huntly's career has so closely paralleled Clithero's that a question remains of whether Clithero too can be saved. Sarsefield does not think so. He believes that Clithero is probably an incurable maniac, and he tries to persuade Huntly to this opinion. Huntly, on his part, should have learned by now that he ought to distrust his own judgment, but he still believes that Clithero can be cured. Three letters appended at the conclusion of Huntly's narrative show the results of his acting upon that assumption. As he did in the early part of the narrative, Huntly seeks out Clithero in the wilderness in an attempt to cure him of his madness by revealing that Mrs. Lorimer is alive and in America. But much to Huntly's dismay, the insane Clithero sets out at once to murder her. Despite his vaunted self-knowledge and enlightenment, Huntly has acted rashly, and only a hasty letter to Sarsefield prevents a total disaster. Mrs. Lorimer is not killed, but she loses the child she is carrying, and Clithero ends a suicide.

As he did in *Wieland,* therefore, Brown ends his book not with the triumph of reason but with the major character still deeply disturbed and inclined to fall into the same error he has succumbed to through the book. Though the voices of Clara's uncle and of Sarsefield reaffirm an ideal of reason, the action of both books seems to indicate the fallibility of the human mind, the powerful influence of its unconscious forces, and the inability of men to predict the outcome of their actions. The dark world of Gothic terror would seem therefore to be more real than the bright and ordered world of the rationalists, even though that Gothic world derives from the consciousness of the characters who perceive it. If this interpretation is correct, the Gothic novels of Charles Brockden Brown are significantly different from their English and German counterparts. The external world of Gothic terror in *Wieland* and *Edgar Huntly* is no chimera that can be easily dismissed by the influx of light, either physical or mental. It is, rather, an accurate indication of the reality that lies within the tortured minds of the protagonists—a reality that is not to be changed by any simple means.

The Gothic devices that Brown uses are for this reason more highly charged with symbolic significance than are those of his predecessors.

The best of the British Gothic romancers had, of course, always sought to make their settings more than mere sources of terror. The castles and abbeys, darkened rooms, moonlit galleries, and subterranean labyrinths that abound in their books not only provide an appropriate atmosphere but sometimes suggest as well the physical and mental condition of the characters who move through them. An abbey set deep in the woods in Ann Radcliffe's *The Romance of the Forest* appropriately suggests not only the physical isolation of the central characters but also to some extent their psychological insecurity, while the intricate paths through which Ferdinand wanders when his mind is distraught in Eliza Parsons's *The Mysterious Warning* are an effective physical representation of his psychological state. But few, if any, of the British Gothic writers develop the material so fully as Brown does in *Wieland* and *Edgar Huntly.* In his hands some of the objects of the external world take on a symbolic meaning, which, closely related to the mental condition of his characters, is consistently maintained throughout the book.

Like all Gothic romances, Brown's two books are full of enclosures—the temple, the summerhouse, and Clara's bedroom and closet in *Wieland*, and the cave in *Edgar Huntly*—all of which reflect the various characters' minds.[10] The temple in *Wieland,* for example, isolated on the top of a steep hill and used for different purposes by its successive owners, is clearly the counterpart of the minds of those who possess it. As the bare and forbidding site of the elder Wieland's solitary worship, it appropriately reflects the mental state of a man whose religious obsessions separate him from his family and eventually consume him. As a place of social and intellectual pleasure for his children and their friends, on the other hand, it comes to represent, with its harpsichord and bust of Cicero, the supposed enlightenment of minds that have been educated according to just principles. But because the temple, however changed, remains the one in which their father perished, it serves as the constant reminder of a mysterious past from which their minds can never be entirely free. The temple is thus much more than merely a physical object. It embodies as well a large amount of thematic meaning of the utmost importance to the development of the story.

In a similar fashion the many isolated enclosures in which Clara finds herself become symbolic of her mind. Both the summerhouse, where she has her prophetic dream, and the bedroom of her residence, where it is almost fulfilled, are isolated places. The summerhouse can be reached only by a difficult path, her house is far removed from that of her brother, and her upstairs bedroom with its adjoining closet is her most intimate retreat. All of these places are violated by the voice of Carwin, which, operating by chance with the material of her dream, sets her mind working in a way that reveals her unconscious fears of her brother. What happens in these enclosures is happening in Clara's mind, so that in a sense the two become one. It is therefore highly significant that, once she faces the murderous Wieland and survives, she retires to her house and refuses to leave—an obvious retreat into her own inner consciousness—and it is not until her house is destroyed by purging flames and her uncle takes her away to Europe that Clara is able to recover the degree of sanity that she reaches at the end of the book.

A related enclosure, the cave, appears in *Edgar Huntly,* though here it achieves its fullest significance only if seen in relation to another device of equal import, the journey through an intricate maze or labyrinth. Both Clithero and Huntly thread their way through the tangled wilderness of Norwalk, only to plunge into a cave or penetrate to another wilderness retreat. Because the most important of these journeys take place while they are asleep, the maze through which they go may be seen as a mental one, and the place where they arrive as the inner self to which they withdraw when reality is more than they can face. Though Clithero leaves his innermost retreat, he never really emerges from the labyrinth of his mind. He takes up his permanent abode in Norwalk, and there he would have remained had Huntly not provoked him to seek out Mrs. Lorimer. Huntly, on his part, emerges from the labyrinth only with the greatest difficulty. After awaking in the cave and gradually reorienting himself to reality, he manages to work his way back to the external order of the settlements. But his recovery is not complete. Huntly still faces the danger of repeated relapse, as his final trip to the wilderness and its disastrous results so clearly show.

Because he lays such stress on the psychological state of his characters, the major Gothic romances of Charles Brockden Brown make a new and significant contribution to the developing Gothic mode. The works that he found on the shelves of the bookstores and lending libraries of New York or Philadelphia had no doubt taught him much about the craft and purposes of fiction, and one can certainly trace the influence of some of these books on his own romances. But Brown was not the slavish imitator of any school of fiction, and although he might derive what he could from a Schiller or Tschink or Radcliffe or Parsons, he developed the material in a highly individual way. He apparently saw at once the possibilities of the Gothic mode as a vehicle for psychological themes, and he quickly found a way to relate the mental states of his characters to the objects of external reality. In both *Wieland* and *Edgar Huntly* he established at once his own version of Gothic, creating thereby an American branch of the mode that was to reach its fullest development a generation later in the works of Edgar Allan Poe and Nathaniel Hawthorne.

FOUR

New European Developments

While Charles Brockden Brown was creating his version of Gothic, writers in England and Germany were turning the mode to their individual purposes. In England the influence of Ann Radcliffe, Matthew Gregory Lewis, and the German romancers continued strong, of course, and practically all the Gothic novels that followed showed the effect of their works. Some were hardly more than popular imitations, some attacked them satirically, and some made important advances on them in both form and theme. Short Gothic stories were also becoming popular. In England sensational tales that played upon the predicament of a protagonist in some frightening situation began to appear in the journals, and the genre was brought to its fullest development in *Blackwood's Edinburgh Magazine,* which soon became identified with it. From Germany, on the other hand, there came a popular kind of tale, based on folklore and legend, that made no attempt to explain away the strange or fantastic but presented a whole range of supernatural creatures as actual beings living and interacting with human characters in the objective world. As the century wore on, moreover, the various strains of Gothic became so intermixed that all of them might sometimes be found in the works of a single author.

Satiric attacks on the Gothic mode began when its vogue was highest. As early perhaps as the late-1790s, when Ann Radcliffe's novels were winning wide acceptance, Jane Austen wrote *Northanger Abbey* as a corrective to the absurdities she perceived in the form, and although the book was not published until 1818, it was completed and sold to a bookseller in 1803.[1] Austen's primary target is *The Mysteries of Udolpho,* and she shows in the course of the novel how Catherine Morland makes herself the victim of "a voluntary, self-created delusion" by reading that and other Gothic romances. Because she has developed "an imagination resolved on alarm,"[2] Catherine transforms the commonplace objects and occurrences of the abbey into sources of Gothic fear. She tries to live the experience of Emily St. Aubert, to recreate the fictive world of *Udolpho* in the commonplace reality of late eighteenth-century England, and she becomes acutely embarrassed when she at last perceives that her imaginative flights have no basis in reality.

A different kind of satire appears in Thomas Love Peacock's *Nightmare Abbey* (1818). In his attacks on the morbidities of modern literature, Peacock includes both the German romance, typified by Karl Grosse's *Horrid Mysteries* with its band of Illuminati, and the ghostly tale of apparitions who stalk through haunted abbeys in their winding sheets. Following his usual practice, Peacock fills his novel with characters of various opinions and persuasions who present a variety of points of view on the subjects discussed, but he pokes particular fun at Scythrop Glowry (Shelley) who, in his passion for reforming the world, becomes enamored of the Illuminati, sleeps with *Horrid Mysteries* under his pillow, and even builds a secret chamber into the walls of his apartment. Another target is Mr. Flosky (Coleridge) who, while discoursing on his belief in ghosts, is put to headlong flight when "a ghastly figure, shrouded in white drapery, with the semblance of a bloody turban on its head" (actually a servant walking in his sleep) enters the apartment.[3] Flosky and the after-dinner companions he is addressing have, as one might expect, prepared themselves for the consternation they all experience by telling ghostly anecdotes to one another.

Yet clever as these two novels most certainly are, they had little if any influence on the development of the Gothic mode, especially in America. Much more important were the works of two writers of some substance whose books were imported into America as soon as they were published and reprinted in this country within a year or two of their appearance. William Godwin and Charles Robert Maturin took the Gothic romance as it came to their hands and used it for purposes much more serious than had Radcliffe or Lewis. Neither was much concerned with adopting exclusively either a rationalistic or a supernatural stance in the mode, but assumed each in their novels as it best fit their themes. Maturin's *Fatal Revenge* (1807) and Godwin's *Mandeville* (1817) contain natural explanations of the Gothic effects they include, but Godwin's *St. Leon* (1799) and Maturin's *Melmoth the Wanderer* (1820) are unabashedly supernatural.[4] All four of these books avoid the mere titillation so common in much Gothic fiction to develop instead a group of themes of considerable significance.

Fatal Revenge is the most conventional of these books. Two brothers,

Ippolito and Annibal Montorio, undergo the usual experiences of terror, the former perceiving bizarre spectacles that seem to foretell that he is to kill his father, the latter receiving less obvious suggestions that he is divinely commissioned to perform the same deed. Though the brothers are fundamentally superstitious, both, insofar as they are able, resist the suggestions of the supernatural manifestations they perceive, but over a period of time their resistance is broken and "under the influence of visionary terror,"[5] they perpetrate the deed. Up to this point the reader is led to believe that they are indeed under the influence of supernatural powers, but at the end of the long romance a confession by the monk Raffaello Schemoli—supposedly the boys' uncle, but actually their real father—reveals that all the supernatural paraphernalia have a natural explanation and have been created by the monk to wreak revenge on his brother, who has wronged him grievously.

Described thus baldly, *Fatal Revenge* would appear to be a romance of the Radcliffe school. Schemoli bears an obvious resemblance to Schedoni in *The Italian,* and the explanation of the supposedly supernatural events bears the imprint of the Radcliffe formula. In addition, the influence of *The Monk* and perhaps of the German romances may be detected in some of the more bizarre incidents of the romance. *Fatal Revenge* should not be dismissed, however, as a mere imitation of such books. Creaking though its Gothic machinery may be, Maturin employs it for an important thematic purpose. In pursuing his revenge, Schemoli adapts his devices to the psychological make-up of his presumed nephews. Ippolito, the "volatile and impetuous," is subdued "by the force of spectacle and sensible representations," the "dark and deliberate" Annibal by "the influence of solitary terror, and the supposed incumbency of a task assigned him by a spiritual agent" (2: 286-87). Since Maturin believed that no one escapes from "*the fear arising from objects of invisible terror*" (1: 3)—even in mature manhood—the book suggests that different means may be used to influence almost any personality type to experience such fear.

This focus on character motivation and analysis sets *Fatal Revenge* apart from its predecessors in the Gothic mode.[6] So too does the change that occurs in Schemoli, who plots his revenge in the belief that Ippolito and Annibal are his nephews, but learns just before the murder that they are really his sons, long thought dead, and that he has done his work so well that he is powerless to stop them. To turn the horror of the plot back upon its instigator in this way marks a significant departure from the conventional Gothic formula. It humanizes Schemoli and makes plausible his confession at the end of the romance. He must confess that his sons were acting under his overpowering influence if he is to save them from execution for the murder of their uncle, though in doing so he of course seals his own doom. *Fatal Revenge* is at times a clumsy and confusing book, but in its emphasis on the psychological motivation of its major characters, it marks a real advance in the evolution of the Gothic romance.

Much more important in the development of Gothic fiction, however, is William Godwin's use of the mode, which, despite his liberal philosophy, seems to have had a real attraction for him. There are so many Gothic touches in his most famous novel, *Caleb Williams* (1794), that the book is often seen as on the periphery, at least, of the genre. The mystery of Falkland's trunk, the robbers who live amid supposedly haunted ruins, and the mad delusions of Miss Melville, whose disturbed imagination conjures up visions of violence and horror, are unquestionably well within the Gothic tradition, and critics are certainly justified in pointing out the novel's relation to the Gothic mode. Yet despite these effective touches, *Caleb Williams* is not really a Gothic novel. These incidents are minor and play no vital role in the total action of the book. *St. Leon* and *Mandeville,* on the other hand, may truly be classed in the genre, for the sources of Gothic terror in each lie at the heart of the book and are intimately related to both the form and the theme that Godwin wished to develop.

In *Mandeville* most of the Gothic devices are firmly based in reality. Charles Mandeville is reared by a recluse uncle in a decaying mansion, part of which is closed off and deserted. The early experiences of his life, combined with some later disappointments, cause him to have frightening dream visions, both waking and sleeping, wherein the death of his parents, which as a child he had witnessed during a Catholic uprising in Ireland, is mixed with other images that have no recognizable source. These visions or dreams are clearly the result of his traumatic experience and can be rationally explained. Only once in the book does Godwin include what could be interpreted as a truly supernatural occurrence. After the Catholic insurrection the ghosts of the slaughtered Protestants are seen for many days half rising from the river, but even here Godwin includes a footnote attesting to his historical accuracy and including a reference that, he says, attributes the phenomenon to a natural cause.[7] *Mandeville* thus falls into that class of Gothic novels (it was inspired by Godwin's reading of Charles Brockden Brown's *Wieland*[8]) in which all the unusual phenomena can be rationally explained, or, most particularly, derive from the mind of the character who has the bizarre experience.

Like Theodore and Clara Wieland—as Godwin apparently interpreted them—Charles Mandeville is led to a mad misperception of reality by the untoward events that influenced his childhood and youth. The death of his parents, his isolated boyhood in a decaying house under the influence of a bigoted Presbyterian tutor, his early infatuation with honor and chivalry in his support of Charles Stuart, the misinterpretation of his actions by society in general, and the success of a rival, Lionel Clifford, whom Mandeville blames for his failures—all contribute to his misanthropic madness. Like Edgar Huntly, too, he even becomes so distraught on one occasion that he runs madly through a wild forest and falls insensible into a pit. Though he is nursed back to health by his sister Henrietta, his view of reality becomes increasingly distorted as the story progresses. He perceives the innocent Clifford and Henrietta as hating him; he misinterprets his sister's reactions while he raves at her; he violently curses her impending marriage to Clifford, who has become a Catholic; and he even attempts to kill Clifford, who in defending himself blinds one of Mandeville's eyes and leaves a hideous scar on his cheek that distorts his face into a grisly smile. Mandeville has become the victim of his own misapprehensions of reality.

The Gothic effects in *St. Leon*, on the other hand, are quite a different matter. In this book Godwin follows the alternate stream of British Gothic fiction to present a tale in which the supernatural events are accepted as real. Because he has lost his wealth at gambling and is forced to live a simple life in Switzerland, Reginald de St. Leon, a French count, is offered the secrets of the philosopher's stone and the elixir of life by an old Venetian who must surrender them to another before he can be permitted to die. After some hesitation, St. Leon accepts and pledges himself to absolute secrecy. In the ensuing story he undergoes a number of Gothic experiences. He is three times imprisoned in dungeons, and he is haunted by ghosts of the mind when he thinks of those whose deaths he has caused. Both St. Leon and Bethlem Gabor, with whom St. Leon allies himself, have forebodings that prove to be true, and St. Leon has a recurring prophetic dream of rescue from a dungeon by a youth who, when the event occurs, turns out to be his son. All these incidents, however, are relatively minor. The important elements of the story are the two great secrets that St. Leon acquires.

With the wealth and extended life he has come to possess, St. Leon believes he can play a godlike role in the world, but he leaves behind him instead a trail of misery and death. He arouses the suspicions of many—including governmental authorities—because he cannot account for his newly acquired wealth, and little by little he brings his family to ruin. Though he tries to do good with his wealth and power, he achieves only partial success. Potential rivals hate him, and even those he helps turn against him when things do not go well. Worst of all, he is alone. He cannot reveal his secret to anyone—not even his wife—and he goes through the world after her death without friend or companion. He becomes, in effect, a kind of Wanderer, cut off from human sympathies and in utter isolation. St. Leon failed to value sufficiently the idyllic life he could have lived in Switzerland after he lost his fortune, and in grasping for wealth, power, and longevity, he condemned himself to loneliness. His son estranged from him and his daughters, resettled in France, thinking him dead, St. Leon at the end of the book possesses his secrets in miserable isolation.

Godwin deliberately used such "incredible situations" mixed with "human feelings and passions"[9] in order to win his readers to an understanding of his theme. In other words, he turned the Gothic mode into a vehicle for the exposition of his social and philosophic concepts, and wrote, in both *St. Leon* and *Mandeville,* truly Gothic tales that, different as they are in their handling of the mode, are alike in the themes they develop. Both protagonists are men with chivalric pretensions, both are strongly affected by the social milieu, both miss the saving influence of human intercourse and sympathy, and both end in miserable isolation. Both, in Godwin's view, are victims of their educations and of the societies in which they live. But one need not accept this Godwinian philosophy to appreciate what Godwin accomplished in these two books. Even more than Maturin's *Fatal Revenge,* which appeared between them, *St. Leon* and *Mandeville* turn well-worn Gothic devices to important thematic purposes and develop for the reader intellectual concepts far beyond any to be found in the works of Radcliffe and Lewis.

Even more successful than Godwin's two novels, however, is Charles

Robert Maturin's *Melmoth the Wanderer,* perhaps the finest of all Gothic fictions. This long and complex book is practically a compendium of all the devices Gothic writers had been using since *The Castle of Otranto* over half a century before, but they are handled in such a way as to support convincingly the great romantic themes that Maturin develops. Early in the romance we find the dusty, half-legible manuscript and the mysterious painting that by 1820 had long been the stock in trade of Gothic writers, but in *Melmoth the Wanderer* both perform important functions. The manuscript leads the younger Melmoth into the first of several stories in which the Wanderer figures, and the painting helps him both to identify his ancestor, who has already been alive over a hundred and fifty years, and to begin to appreciate the kind of person he has become. Moreover, when Alonzo de Monçada, who tells the remaining stories, appears, he carries a miniature of the same person, thus assuring both him and young Melmoth that they have encountered and are discussing the same man. Both devices thus possess an artistic validity that they had long ceased to have in the works of lesser practitioners of the genre.

Maturin is also careful to adjust the kind of Gothic effect to the character and situation. Though supernatural events occur throughout the romance, they are generally limited to the Wanderer himself. Others live in a world of natural cause and effect, and many of the frightening sights they see have rational explanations. The vision of demons clothed in fire that Monçada awakes one night to find in his monastic cell is a deliberate deception intended to terrify him. The demons are only "hideous figures scrawled in phosphorus" that fade away with the dawn.[10] Other objects of terror derive from the distraught minds of the characters. They are phantoms of the imagination or the illusions of madness. The final moments of a dying man are haunted by specters of conscience, and the judges of the Inquisition view Monçada with terror because they look at him "through a distorting atmosphere of mystery and suspicion" (p. 181). *Melmoth the Wanderer* thus resembles Matthew Gregory Lewis's *The Monk* in that both present supernatural phenomena as real but also recognize that many of the objects thought to be supernatural are nothing more than projections of the disturbed minds of the perceivers.

Like *The Monk,* too, *Melmoth the Wanderer* contains a number of episodes of grisly terror. When Monçada attempts to escape through the subterranean passages of the monastery, he conjures up terrors of seeing a feast of ghouls and demons feeding upon the corrupted flesh that lies in the vaults, and when Isidora is wed to the Wanderer, the scene is one to rival anything in Lewis's romance. Though the wedding takes place on a midsummer night, she feels an occasional blast of cold, and "pale, meteoric lightning" flashes in the sky (p. 295). She moves with her bridegroom at great velocity through the darkness until they reach a ruined monastery where a hermit-priest is said to live. Left alone for a moment by Melmoth, Isidora perceives a shadowy figure move through the graveyard, and sees the ghost of an old servant in one of the ruined windows. When Melmoth returns to lead her into the chapel, the moon sinks behind a cloud and the wedding takes place in perfect darkness. Isidora hears only mumbled words as she holds the Wanderer's hand, but when she feels that of the priest, it is as cold as death. Only later does Isidora learn that her wedding was performed by a specter.

Such incidents are not Maturin's major concern, however. More important are those elements which *Melmoth the Wanderer* shares with William Godwin's *St. Leon.* Both protagonists are men who, having acquired supernatural powers, are condemned to become Wanderers, forever separated from their fellow human beings. Yet if both are Faustlike in seeking such powers, Melmoth is a much more terrible figure because of the Mephistophelean qualities he also possesses. St. Leon acquires the philosopher's stone and the elixir of life because he imagines that he can do good for others, and by the end of the book he is pictured as victim, not villain. Melmoth, on the other hand, becomes a tempter who deliberately seeks out those whose lives are desperate—the sane man betrayed into a madhouse, the prisoner of the Inquisition, or the honest man whose children are starving—in order to offer them release in exchange for their immortal souls. Melmoth is thus a titanic figure—both Faust and Mephistopheles, Cain and the Wandering Jew[11]—whose burning eyes and mirthless laughter reveal his inner state. As such, he is a much more awesome protagonist for a Gothic romance than any who had gone before him, and the themes developed through him are commensurate with his stature.

Part of Maturin's theme, it has been suggested, lies in the common thread that runs through the tales, of men oppressed by institutions and corrupted by money or social arrogance;[12] and part, no doubt, is contained in Maturin's preface: the belief, expressed in one of his sermons, that no one in all the earth would exchange his hope of salvation for "all that man could bestow, or earth afford" (p. 3). Melmoth's experience clearly supports this idea, for the Wanderer utterly fails to persuade even one soul to consent to its own damnation. Beyond all this, however, there is yet another theme implicit in the romance: the fate of one who, in seeking forbidden knowledge and power, raises himself in many ways above his fellows, but who, in doing so, cuts himself off from their saving communion. This theme had a powerful appeal to the romantic mind, and Maturin's handling of Melmoth reveals the attraction-repulsion that many must have felt toward this type of character, Satanic in his treatment of the desperate, human in his love for Isidora, perhaps even tragic in his final awareness of the futility of his quest, the knowledge that his seeking has been for nought, that he has succeeded only in damning himself.

No other Gothic romance even approaches the success of *Melmoth the Wanderer* in its fusion of Gothic convention with significant theme. Mary Shelley's *Frankenstein* (1818) has a similarly serious purpose in its development of the Promethean theme, and presents in the character of the monster both Adamic and Satanic qualities as interesting as anything suggested by Melmoth's Wanderer. But *Frankenstein* cannot really be called a Gothic romance. Though in Victor Frankenstein and his creation the book contains an interesting variant on the device of the double,[13] the Gothic elements play, on the whole, a much less vital role than they do in *Melmoth*. The philosopher's stone and the elixir of life that had figured so largely in *St. Leon* are dismissed almost in passing, and the best of the Gothic touches—the appearance of the monster for the first time in his creator's bedroom, for example, or at the window of his laboratory in the Orkneys—are minor elements in a book that contains only a few such devices. Though *Frankenstein* is without question an important book in its own right, it cannot rival Maturin's romance as a work of Gothic fiction.

Much of Maturin's success derives from his use of traditional European lore, most notably the legend of the Wandering Jew and the Faust-Mephistopheles story. Except for *The Monk* and *St. Leon*, material of this type had played no major role in the British Gothic romance, and Maturin's brilliant handling of it in *Melmoth the Wanderer* sets him apart from most of his British predecessors and links him to the German romantic school that was just coming into prominence in England when

his book appeared. Though most of the German Gothic fiction translated into English during the 1790s had been strongly rationalistic, a second kind of German tale, frankly supernatural and drawn from folk
sources, had also been imported. *Popular Tales of the Germans,* a selection
from the stories of Johann August Musäus, had appeared in 1791, and
Matthew Gregory Lewis, as we have seen, borrowed directly from German horror literature for his romance. After the turn of the century,
however, the tide of German literature that had run so strong in England during the 1790s began to ebb, largely the result of the protracted
Napoleonic Wars. But with the return of peace in 1815, the tide began
again to flow.[14]

German romantic fiction came to the English reader in a number of
different ways. The British journals reviewed translations of German
books as they were published, and many British readers became acquainted with German fiction through these reviews and through individual stories that occasionally appeared in the magazines. A few important novels were also translated, among them the Baron de la Motte
Fouqué's *Undine* (1818), a tale of water sprites, and E.T.A. Hoffmann's
The Devil's Elixirs (1824),[15] a sensational story, obviously derived from
Lewis's *The Monk,* that develops the romantic theme of the double.
Most important, however, were collections of German tales. A translation of Grimms' Märchen was published in two series, in 1823 and
1826; and in the latter year four anthologies appeared: Richard Hol-
craft's *Tales from the German,* Thomas Roscoe's *The German Novelists,*
George Soane's *Specimens of German Romance,* and R.P. Gillies's *German
Stories.* The following year Thomas Carlyle's *German Romance* marked
the crest of the tide that had been flowing for at least a decade. Through
all these books the folk collections of Musäus, Grimm, and Otmar, and
many of the fine romantic tales of Fouqué, Hoffmann, and Ludwig
Tieck became known in Great Britain and, as a matter of course, in the
United States.[16]

The tales themselves are of many different types, some of which were
by no means new to the British reader. The episode of the specter barber
in Musäus's "Dumb Love," for example, resembles the kind of tale that
Lewis had brought to England during the 1790s, and the prophetic
dream through which the story is resolved had long been used by Gothic
romancers. But the Germans also included materials that had as yet
played no significant role in British Gothic fiction. By accepting folk be-

liefs as the basis for their stories, they created a fictional world in which goblins, elves, witches, and elemental spirits are no less real than the human beings who encounter them. The goblin Rübezahl in Fouqué's "The Field of Terror" is simply accepted as a creature from a different order of being. So too are the elves who live in a dark patch of fir trees in Tieck's "The Elves," or the wood, earth,and water spirits who haunt the forest through which the knight Huldbrand rides in *Undine*. In all these stories the supernatural order impinges on human reality, most often creating a problem or conflict that must be resolved in the course of the narrative.

In "Dumb Love" and "The Field of Terror" all ends happily for the human characters. After the specter barber has shaved the face and head of Franz, who spends the night in the haunted castle, the young man returns the service, and the specter, released by this means from his bondage, tells him in gratitude what he must do to solve his problems. And Rübezahl, a frolicsome rather than a malignant goblin, ends up helping the young farmer who, despite his taunts and tricks, is not afraid to till the field of terror or, for that matter, to chastise the goblin when, in an outburst of high spirits, he frightens the farmer's children. Rübezahl is so impressed with the young man's integrity that he leaves the haunted field to his peaceful cultivation forever. "The Elves," on the other hand, ends more darkly. When Mary, whom they have befriended, breaks her vow to keep their existence a secret, the elves are forced to leave the grove of firs. But because their presence there was indispensable to the prosperity of the nearby human community, their departure brings about its utter ruin.

Other of Tieck's stories come to equally dark conclusions. When Christian, the young hunter in "The Runenberg," falls under the influence of a mysterious figure he meets on the mountain, he becomes so obsessed with a desire for wealth that he turns his back on life and love to seek the treasures that he believes lie hidden underground. As a result, his family is brought to disaster, and all that Christian gains for his sacrifice is a sack of gravel and pebbles, which he, in his delusion, takes for precious jewels. An even more terrible fate befalls Emilius, a sober young man who becomes enchanted in "Love Magic Some Centuries Ago." In a scene of grotesque horror, bathed in the blood-red light of the setting sun, Emilius explodes into violence when released from a spell that has blacked out his memory and frozen his will. He kills his bride and the witch who cast the love charm for her in a bloody ritual that he himself witnessed. The world of Tieck's tales is a sinister one in which strange and mysterious powers can affect the life and happiness of the human beings who encounter them.[17]

The sinister side of these folk traditions appears as well in Fouqué's *Undine,* a story usually praised for the charming character of the heroine and her faithfulness to Huldbrand, her human lover. Undine is indeed a delightful character, and the tale contains perhaps more than its share of sentiment. But beneath the surface of the romantic narrative, there runs a current of terror, especially in the character of Kühleborn, Undine's uncle, and the power of the elemental forces he can release in the world. These forces become an ever-present threat to the human characters when Huldbrand neglects Undine for Bertalda, a human girl, and eventually drives the sprite away with angry words. Undine has heretofore protected them from Kühleborn's wrath, but when Huldbrand marries Bertalda, his fate is fixed. The law of the water sprites demands that Undine must kill her faithless human lover. As long as he stays away from her element, he is of course safe, but when Bertalda, seeking some water to beautify her face, removes the seal from a nearby fountain, Undine rises from the waters, seeks out Huldbrand, and drowns him in her tears. Once again, the supernatural world triumphs.

The people who are affected by these mysterious, powerful, and sometimes hostile forces are not always able to confront them openly. Goblins and witches can change their forms at will, so that men can never be quite sure of what they are facing; elves remain invisible unless some chance or accident reveals their presence; and elemental spirits sometimes appear in ambiguous forms. In *Undine,* for example, a character may think he sees a white old man nodding at him and perceive a moment later only a stream flowing through the forest. He reads the man as illusion, the stream as reality, yet in the universe of the book both perceptions are true. What has happened is simply that human vision has caught a glimpse of, but has failed to penetrate to, the supernatural realm that lies beyond. Misperception had, of course, always played an important role in the Gothic mode, but here the emphasis is different. It is not so much misperception that the characters experience as alternating perceptions of two valid actualities: the human world and the spirit world that, in *Undine,* meet in the flowing water.

The perception of co-terminous worlds received a rich and suggestive development in the works of E.T.A. Hoffmann, who stands somewhat apart from his compatriots in his handling of romantic material. No less fantastic than those of Fouqué and Tieck, Hoffmann's tales focus our attention on a world in which everyday objects and people can change before the eyes of the protagonist into strange and bizarre forms. A good example is "The Golden Pot," one of Hoffmann's best tales and well known to English readers through its inclusion in Carlyle's *German Romance*. It is the story of a clumsy student in Dresden who has a series of wonderful visions. Anselmus hears crystal bells and sees little green-gold snakes in an elder tree, he watches while a doorknob turns itself into the contorted face of a witch, and he sees an elderly man, the Archivarius Lindhorst, fly away from him in the form of a large bird. Most important of all, he sees his commonplace world transformed at times into beautiful things, and he grasps for the magical realm he perceives as the truer reality.

These wonderful transformations may of course be read realistically as merely the projection of the student's disordered mind, and we get occasional clues that the world considers him mad. But Hoffmann will not permit so simple an interpretation. Though Anselmus eventually disappears from the story and so may simply have withdrawn into his own fantasy world, Hoffmann holds out the possibility that he may indeed have perceived a better and truer world than that in which he eked out his meager existence. Hoffmann intervenes at the end of the tale to inform the reader in the final vision that he has himself seen Anselmus alive in Atlantis, a world that has existed since before the time when the spark of thought was kindled. Through the imagination, Anselmus has penetrated to a higher realm where poetry reveals "itself as the sacred Harmony of all Beings, as the deepest secret of Nature."[18] It is a place that can be reached only through the magic of art, but it is not for that reason any less real than the workaday world or, for that matter, the realm of goblins and spirits through which Hoffmann's German contemporaries had developed their themes.

Hoffmann's flights of fancy were generally condemned by British critics, who considered the extravagant incidents of his tales too far out of the ordinary for British taste. Even Carlyle, who recognized Hoffmann's genius, saw "too little meaning in [his] bright extravagance,"[19] and Sir Walter Scott, in an important review of three of Hoffmann's books, considered "his taste and temperament" as directing "him too strongly to the grotesque and fantastic."[20] Scott used his review, however, for a broader purpose than merely the criticism of Hoffmann's books. He considered the use an author might properly make of supernatural materials in fiction, and he included in his discussion examples drawn from English, French, and German literature, including the works of Musäus and Fouqué. He even treated two of Hoffmann's stories, "The Entail" and "The Sandman," at considerable length. Scott's opinions in this matter are important. Because he used a large number of Gothic devices in his own romances—books that were extraordinarily popular in both Europe and the United States—he inevitably played a significant role in forming the taste of a large number of readers and in creating a precedent for the romance writers who followed him.

Scott had read widely in the fiction of his age, had broad knowledge of the Gothic romance in all its forms, both British and German, and maintained throughout his life a deep interest in tales of the supernatural. In the series of essays he wrote for Ballantyne's Novelists Library in the early 1820s and later collected with some additions in *Miscellaneous Prose Works* (1827), he discusses at some length the novels of Horace Walpole, Clara Reeve, Ann Radcliffe, and Charlotte Smith; and he reviewed, in addition to Hoffmann's books, such current works as Maturin's *Fatal Revenge* (1810) and Mary Shelley's *Frankenstein* (1818).[21] Though written for the most part after he had become a successful writer of fiction, these essays provide the best evidence for his view of the Gothic as a literary genre. In general, Scott preferred Walpole to Radcliffe. He strongly approved the use in fiction of those supernatural elements that would have been accepted as real at the time the story takes place, and he criticized Radcliffe's technique of "referring her prodigies to an explanation founded on natural causes."[22]

Scott saw no reason why supernatural phenomena should be explained away in what is, after all, an admitted fiction, and he raised a number of objections to the practice. It disappoints the reader by providing a cause inadequate to the feelings of terror he has been induced to feel, and it asks him to accept at times explanations that are more incredible than the supposed apparitions themselves. Scott was especially critical of the German rationalists in this matter and preferred an honest ghost to their mechanical contrivances. He realized, of course, that in a rationalistic age the supernatural must be managed with great delicacy and that not all writers handle it equally well. Musäus, he believed, showed great skill in dressing up ancient tales to suit the modern taste, and Fouqué was highly successful in treating the water sprite in *Undine*. But other writers managed the material badly. Both Godwin, in *St. Leon*, and Maturin, in *Fatal Revenge*, are too unremitting in their use of the terrible to achieve the effects they aim for. The reader's emotions are soon exhausted by their excess.

Scott's own use of the Gothic began in the extravagantly supernatural vein. Strongly influenced by Lewis's *The Monk* and the German romantic writers, he translated Gottfried August Bürger's popular specter ballads, "Der Wilde Jäger" and "Lenore" (1796), published a version of Goethe's "Erlkönig" (1798), and contributed some pieces to Lewis's *Tales of Wonder* (1801). The influence carried over into his original work. Gothic materials derived from these sources appear in such poems as *The Lay of the Last Minstrel* (1805) and *Marmion* (1808),[23] and when Scott abandoned poetry for fiction in 1814, he continued to use Gothic elements in his historical romances. Despite his opinions and early practice, however, Scott did not limit himself to a single strain of the mode. Like Godwin and Maturin he saw no need to maintain a consistent point of view throughout his fiction, but uses the supernatural or the "explained" Gothic as it suits his immediate purpose. His romances therefore reflect just about every aspect of the Gothic mode that had appeared in both British and German fiction since the time of Walpole, including the German rationalist school that he attacked so severely in his critical essays.

Scott's attitude toward these Germans was at best ambivalent. At times he treats them with humor. In the opening chapter of *Waverley* (1814), he makes fun of their predilection for such secret and mysterious societies as the "Rosicrucians and Illuminati, with all their properties of black cowls, caverns, daggers, electrical machines, trap-doors, and dark lanterns,"[24] and he attacks them more specifically in *The Antiquary* (1816) through his treatment of Dousterswivel, a German adventurer who employs the techniques so often found in their books. Said to be an Illuminé and to use the tricks of the Rosicrucians, Dousterswivel bilks Sir Arthur Wardour of money by encouraging the hope that he will gain great wealth through the German's supposedly supernatural powers. Dousterswivel employs the usual hocus-pocus of occult signs and burning chemicals to create his effects, but the tables are turned on him at last by some down-to-earth Scots, who not only expose him as a common swindler but also frighten him with an apparition that they have themselves created. Though the novel itself develops a rationalistic theme, Dousterswivel is treated with none of the seriousness accorded his counterparts in German romance, but is instead held up to ridicule.

In two later novels, however—*Woodstock* (1826) and *Anne of Geierstein* (1829)—Scott uses techniques that closely resemble those of the Germans. The magical delusions employed by the Royalists for political ends in *Woodstock* remind one of the sort of thing to be found in Schiller or Tschink. To keep the Royal Lodge at Woodstock empty as a hiding place for Charles Stuart, they use mechanical deceptions to cause supposedly supernatural phenomena. Some are simply crude devices for overturning beds or dousing them with water, but others rival in ingenuity the kind of illusion found in the German romances. Markham Everard, a young Puritan, wakes one night to find the apparition of a long-dead man and veiled lady in his room, but when he fires a pistol at them, they laugh at him and vanish. Suspecting trickery, Everard thinks his pistols may have been unloaded while he slept, but he finds the bullet lodged in the wall and knows it must have passed through the figure of the man. The illusion is never explained, even when all the mechanical devices are revealed, but the whole tenor of the book is so completely rationalistic that the reader never believes that the apparitions are real.

Since *Woodstock* is laid in England during the Civil War, Scott could not include the secret society of conspirators that is sometimes associated with such political deceptions, but in *Anne of Geierstein,* set in Burgundy and Switzerland during the fifteenth century, he had the opportunity to introduce it. One source of terror here is the German Secret Tribunal, or Vehmic courts, which had appeared in fiction as early as Christiane Naubert's *Herman of Unna.* Scott knew the Vehme also from Goethe's drama *Götz von Berlichingen,* which he translated, and Veit Weber's *Die Heilige Vehme,* which he adapted,[25] and he uses it in *Anne of Geierstein* in much the same way as his German predecessors. An Englishman, the Earl of Oxford, traveling incognito in Europe, in 1474, is seeking help to restore the Lancastrians to the throne of England, and hoping to further his cause, he becomes politically involved with the Duke of Burgundy. But in the course of his adventures he runs afoul of the Vehme and is taken before the court, where the judges, hooded and robed, bring him to trial in a subterranean vault. Though Oxford is not convicted, he is deeply shaken by the terrifying experience.

The Vehme figures in other incidents, too, and helps explain a number of elements that seem at first to be supernatural. *Anne of Geierstein* herself appears so mysteriously in places where she is least expected and at times when she is believed to be elsewhere, that some of the characters think her a doppelgänger, with power to be in two places at once—a power thought to derive from her maternal grandmother, who is said to have been an elemental spirit of fire. A lurid story is told about that grandmother's death, and Anne's surprising appearances in unusual places lend credence to the belief that she has such close connections with elemental spirits that they can assume her form at will. Much of the mystery surrounding her ancestry, however, was caused by her grandfather's office as judge of the Vehme, and Anne's mysterious appearances are made at the direction of her father, the Count of Geierstein, who also turns out to be a judge of the Secret Tribunal. *Anne of Geierstein* ends, therefore, much like a German rationalistic tale: the apparently supernatural events are finally shown to derive from the machinations of a secret society.

Yet if Scott made *Anne of Geierstein* a rationalistic romance, he wrote a thoroughly supernatural one in *The Monastery* (1820). The White Lady of Avenel is presented throughout as a real naiad, an elemental spirit of water who dwells in a fountain in a sequestered glen and who is linked by mysterious ties to the House of Avenel. She rose from the fountain first when that House had its beginning, her life is coexistent with its duration, and she will be annihilated at its fall. As Scott himself admitted, he modeled the White Lady of Avenel on Fouqué's *Undine*, and he even used some of the same techniques in handling her. Like the white old man in the German tale, she is sometimes only half perceived by human eyes. Father Eustace, for example, riding along in a contemplative mood, thinks he sees "in his path the form of a female dressed in white," but when he tries to fix his vision on the spot, it always seems that he has "mistaken some natural object, a white crag, or the trunk of a decayed birch-tree with its silver bark, for the appearance in question" (p. 82).

Scott departs from his model, however, by making the White Lady a much less spritely character. So deeply attached is she to the House of Avenel that she helps the family in times of trouble and thwarts those who oppose them. But in doing so she loses much of the delicacy that had made her prototype so effective. She throws one monk in a stream and strikes another from his horse when they try to remove an English Bible from Lady Avenel's possession; she takes young Halbert Glendinning, who loves Mary Avenel, to an underground cave where he must draw a book with his bare arm from a strangely flaming fire; and she even engineers a duel between him and a pretended aristocrat—a duel which she manages in such a way as to make each man think he has killed the other. She thus interferes in the story in so direct and so physical a manner as to exhibit a kind of grossness inappropriate to her character. The White Lady was criticized from the moment the book appeared, and Scott went to some lengths in his 1830 introduction to defend the character and explain his reasons for including her in the book.

Another water sprite appears in *The Bride of Lammermoor* (1819), but although she plays an important role in establishing the curse that falls on the family of Ravenswood, she is kept well in the background and is treated with a delicacy that makes her more effective than the White Lady of Avenel. Her love for a mortal man, an ancestor of the present Master of Ravenswood, brings about her death when, moved by distrust and fear that she might be a demon, he breaks the rules by which alone he may meet her: he keeps her with him beyond the appointed time in the hope that she will then be forced to reveal herself in her true form. Instead, she disappears with a shriek in the fountain, leaving behind a trail of blood to betoken her end.[26] From that time forward, the legend goes, the fountain where she died is believed to be fatal to all Ravenswoods, and the course of the tale amply bears out the truth of that belief. The fountain is where important events occur which link the Master of Ravenswood to Lucy Ashton in so fatal a bond that both of them perish in the dark dénouement of this somber tragedy.

Most of these books also contain elements derived from both strains of the British Gothic tradition, though Scott is careful to maintain the integrity of his works by including in each only those devices that are appropriate to the general tenor of the romance. In *The Monastery* he introduces a ghost who resembles the ones in Clara Reeve's *The Old English Baron*. Because she was born on All Hallows Eve, Mary Avenel has the power to perceive apparitions, and she sees one night the ghost of her dead father, whose brother has seized the inheritance that should rightfully be hers. This ghost is never explained away in the book, but takes on a kind of objective reality when he is later seen by two other people entering Avenel Castle in triumph before his daughter Mary, who—much like the dispossessed Edmund in Reeve's romance—finally takes possession of it at the end of the tale. Another real ghost appears in *The Bride of Lammermoor* when the wraith of old Alice, a blind seer, briefly appears near the naiad's fountain to warn the Master of Ravenswood just at the moment she dies a considerable distance away in her hut.

In *Woodstock,* on the other hand, two ghosts appear that belong to the "explained" supernatural of the Radcliffean school. One, indeed, is no ghost at all but a living man thought dead by the one who perceives him.[27] The other turns out to be a dual deception: a person disguised as the apparition of a murdered man so works on the conscience of the one who killed him that the guilty one begins to imagine he sees the victim even when no one is there. The physical deception thus produces a mental one. In *The Antiquary,* too, apparently supernatural events turn out to have rational causes. Sleeping in a supposedly haunted chamber, Lovel, the young hero, seems to have a prophetic dream in which he is shown an inscription in a language he cannot read. When he later sees the words in one of the Antiquary's books, Lovel is ready to take them as a special message for himself, until Oldbuck, the Antiquary, explains to him that the evening before the dream, Lovel had been distracted when Oldbuck had shown the words in the book to another. They had thus unconsciously stuck in Lovel's mind, only to surface later in his sleep.

Not every Scott romance falls neatly into one of the two main types of Gothic fiction. Some of the books are deliberately ambiguous in their treatment of supernatural events, leaving the reader with two or more possible but irreconcilable interpretations. Scott adapted a number of techniques to achieve this effect. He had learned from the German romantics the value of folklore in Gothic writing, and he early recognized that his native Scotland was rich in such materials. He also shared the belief of many Gothic writers that fear of the supernatural appears most often not in the higher but in the less sophisticated lower classes. It was a simple matter, then, to construct his tales in such a way that the two types of Scottish characters could be brought into contrast. At times, of course, the more sophisticated character is shown to have the truer perception. Thus, when Hobbie Elliot, a farmer, and Earnscliff, the educated hero of *The Black Dwarf* (1816), first see a very real dwarf on the supposedly haunted Mucklestane-Moor, Hobbie, who believes the tales of spunkies, kelpies, bogles, and witches he has heard since childhood, holds back in terror from what he fears is an apparition, while Earnscliff simply advances to question the man.

But in other of Scott's romances, especially those in which the folk beliefs of the Highland Scots are placed in contrast to the rationalistic views of the Lowland and Saxon characters, the nature of the supposedly supernatural event is not so easily established. Fergus Mac-Ivor, a Highland chief in *Waverley,* twice sees the Bodach Glas, the spirit of a man killed by one of his ancestors, that always foretells impending doom to his race. The spirit appears to him first on the night before the skirmish in which he is captured, and a second time on the evening before his execution. In *A Legend of Montrose* (1819), moreover, Allan M'Aulay, a reputed seer, has a thrice-repeated vision in which a Highlander, whose face he cannot see, stabs the Earl of Mentieth. When Allan reverses his plaid, the wraith does the same, making it clear—as Ranald MacEagh, another seer, explains—that Allan has seen his double, or shadow self. The vision means, therefore, that Allan will eventually stab the earl, an act he does indeed commit in a fit of jealousy when Mentieth is about to marry Annot Lyle, whom Allan also loves.[28]

Both phenomena, of course, have rational explanations, as the English and the educated Scots are quick to point out. Waverley tries to dismiss the first appearance of the Bodach Glas as "the operation of an exhausted frame and depressed spirits working on the belief common to all Highlanders in such superstitions" (p. 527), and both he and the priest-confessor treat the second as a deception of the imagination. The Saxons consider Allan M'Aulay's visions as only "the delusions of an overheated fancy," and the Earl of Mentieth tries to explain them away as the result of neither enthusiasm nor imposture but of true "judgment and reflection" that Allan mistakes for "supernatural impressions on his mind" (pp. 268, 65). Fergus and Allan, however, remain convinced of the authenticity of their experiences, and the two views of the world are brought into irreconcilable conflict. Neither prevails. The Bodach Glas and shadow self are as real to the Highland Scots as material events are to the rationalists. The reader is left, therefore, with an ambiguous world where reality depends to a large extent on the nature of the mind that perceives it.

Scott achieved a similar effect in his use of interpolated tales of goblins and devils in some of his long romances. Taken by themselves, both

"The Fortunes of Martin Waldeck" in *The Antiquary* and "Wandering Willie's Tale" in *Redgauntlet* (1824) are stories of the German romantic kind in which human beings find themselves involved with supernatural creatures, but the context in which they are placed suggests that the stories need not be taken at face value. Both are excellent tales of the supernatural. In "The Fortunes of Martin Waldeck," the main character, a charcoal burner, obtains from a tutelary demon of the Harz mountains the gold he uses to rise in society, but he is later severely punished for his pride and presumption in assuming too high a status with his goblin gold. And in "Wandering Willie's Tale," a blind fiddle player recounts the adventures of his grandfather, Steenie Steenson, who journeys to hell to get a receipt for the rent he paid Sir Robert Redgauntlet, who died in agony before he could write it—the money, meanwhile, disappearing amidst the confusion. Each tale is a self-contained unit and could be printed apart from the romance in which it appears.

The conditions under which they are told, however, give ample opportunity for the rationalist to explain them away. Though both describe events that are supposed to have really happened, they are recounted long after the time of the stories by persons who are at one or more removes from the original narrators. "The Fortunes of Martin Waldeck" is brought from Germany by Dousterswivel, who swears to its truth as he is "an honest man" (p. 238), and it is written down by Miss Wardour, who turns it into a romance. "Wandering Willie's Tale" was long kept secret, known only to Steenie and his minister, but when the minister dies, Steenie's wife reveals the story, and Steenie, now an old man, must tell it or be accused of being a warlock—though by this time, it is intimated, his judgment and memory may not be the sharpest. There is even the suggestion that the Covenanters may have told the story because of their hatred of Sir Robert, who was a persecuting prelatist. Both tales are highly effective pieces that treat supernatural events with perfect seriousness, but the circumstances of their telling leave room for the rationalistic interpretation that is hinted at but never finally established.[29]

The ambiguity that Scott built into some of his tales and romances is probably his most significant contribution to the Gothic mode, but his use of other Gothic devices has an importance that is difficult to overestimate. It is true, of course, that he did not use his fiction for philosophic purposes, as did Godwin and Maturin, nor did he develop the psychological aspects of the mode, as did Godwin and Brown. Scott is not, after all, primarily a Gothic artist but an historical romancer, and he used the devices—both British and German, supernatural and "explained"—as subordinate elements in fundamentally historical fiction. But his work was so extensive, so popular, and so filled with various kinds of Gothic devices that he undoubtedly helped keep alive an interest in literary Gothicism in all its many aspects. His influence was especially important in the United States, where his books were republished as soon as they appeared in England, and where a whole generation of romancers profited by his example. Writers as diverse as Washington Irving, James Fenimore Cooper, and Nathaniel Hawthorne learned at least part of their craft from the practice of the great Scottish romancer.

FIVE

Washington Irving

The American writers who followed Charles Brockden Brown in the early years of the nineteenth century did not pursue the line of development that he had opened with his Gothic romances. Although George Watterston, in *Glencarn; or, The Disappointments of Youth* (1810), and the pseudonymous Adelio, in *A Journey to Philadelphia: or Memoirs of Charles Coleman Saunders* (1804), include plot elements reminiscent of Brown's novels,[1] most of the Gothic devices in these and other books by American writers derive from European sources. Both the anonymous *Adventures in a Castle* (1806) and Sarah Wood's *Julia, and the Illuminated Baron* (1800) reveal their ancestry in their very titles, and Isaac Mitchell's *The Asylum; or, Alonzo and Melissa* (1811) even goes to the extreme of placing a castle in Connecticut during the American Revolution! Mitchell greatly admired Ann Radcliffe, and the most extended Gothic episode in his novel, in which smugglers frighten Melissa while she is imprisoned in the castle,[2] obviously derives from similar incidents in *The Mysteries of Udolpho* and Charlotte Smith's *The Old Manor House*. None of these American writers perceived what Brown had accomplished, and all of their books imitate British models.

The next major advance in American literary Gothicism came from a group of writers who were not much affected by the rage for such fiction that had characterized the closing decade of the preceding century. Although they undoubtedly knew Brown's works and those of the British Gothicists, the Knickerbocker wits drew upon a different tradition of eighteenth-century literature and wrote their first works in the satiric mode. One need only turn to *Salmagundi* (1807–1808), the series of papers written by William and Washington Irving and James Kirke Paulding, to see that their interests lay in a completely different direction. Not that the Irvings and Paulding were totally uninfluenced by the Gothic. Touches of it appear even in *Salmagundi,* and as the century wore on both Washington Irving and, to a lesser extent, Paulding included the Gothic in their works. But the strong intellectual bias of the satiric mode and its primary purpose of social amendment set their minds in a way that prevented their ever becoming practitioners of the Gothic in the style of Charles Brockden Brown. They developed instead a second strain of the American Gothic, one that can best be understood through a close look at the works of Washington Irving.

Although Irving grew up in New York just at the time when the flood of Gothic romances was reaching its crest and Brown was publishing his own remarkable books, there is little in Irving's earliest work to suggest that he was at all influenced by any of them. His first published works—newspaper pieces that he did not gather into his collected edition—are attempts at social and political satire that show no trace of Gothicism. *The Letters of Jonathan Oldstyle, Gent.,* published in his brother Peter's *Morning Chronicle* (1802–1803), is most noteworthy for its satire on the contemporary theater, and Irving's contributions to *The Corrector* (1804), insofar as they can be identified, are ephemeral political pieces.[3] That Irving met Brown is certain, for the novelist is reported to have called on him in 1803, after the appearance of the Jonathan Oldstyle papers, to request a contribution to his own Philadelphia *Literary Magazine, and American Register,* and the men may have met later since both were inducted into the New York Historical Society in 1809.[4] But if Irving could not have failed to know about Brown and his works, we have no indication of which if any of them he read at that time.[5]

We can be reasonably sure, however, that by the end of 1804 Irving had read at least two of the romances of Ann Radcliffe. In a journal entry of August 8, 1804, he describes a castle he had seen on the banks of the Garonne while traveling from Bordeaux to Toulouse. Day is just breaking as he views it, and the dramatic lighting of the scene, the first gleams of morning falling upon the decaying towers, reminds him immediately of Radcliffe's descriptions. Since in *The Mysteries of Udolpho* the chateau of Monsieur St. Aubert stands on the banks of that river and significant parts of the novel take place in Gascony, Irving must surely have had that romance in mind as he wrote his journal. In the following month, moreover, Irving bought a French translation of *The Italian,* and he recorded in his travel notes for October 9 that he had lent the book to a French physician who was traveling with him.[6] Though Irving was later to write that Mrs. Radcliffe stood "at the head of her line,"[7] her influence on him at this time seems to have been minimal. On the evidence of his writing after his return to America in 1806, we can only

conclude that he merely followed the lead of most of the Gothic writers
in ascribing reports of supernatural events to the superstitious fear of the
ignorant.

In both *Salmagundi,* in which Irving did a major part of the writing,
and the first edition of *A History of New York* (1809), supernatural tales
of ghosts, goblins, and witches are universally attributed to such people,
who, like some of the characters in British Gothic romances, frequently
terrify themselves and others with them. Caesar, an old black in *Salmagundi* who peoples the neighborhood with imaginary beings and scares
the boys at Cockloft Hall with tales of them,[8] has his counterpart in the
first edition of Knickerbocker's *History* in "some old crone of a negro,
. . . who, perched like a raven in a corner of the chimney, would croak
forth for a long winter afternoon, a string of incredible stories about
New England witches—grisly ghosts—horses without heads—and hair-
breadth scapes and bloody encounters among the Indians."[9] Both books,
moreover, make fun of the simple old women and ignorant country folk
who put themselves into a panic with tales of strange and marvelous occurrences, and they satirize those who not only are prone to believe reports of witches and witchcraft, but quickly find proofs to support them
whenever the alarm is raised.

The comic potential of such material is readily seen, in Knickerbocker's *History,* in the death of Antony van Corlear, who, sent by Peter
Stuyvesant to rouse the Dutch to the defense of New Amsterdam, first
eats a hearty dinner, drinks some Hollands, and drowns in an attempt to
swim across the Harlem River at night. His end is witnessed by "an old
Dutch burgher, famed for his veracity," who claims that he saw the
devil himself seize Antony by the leg and drag him under. Because he
had sworn to swim the river *"en spijt den Duyvel,"* Antony becomes a
kind of Flying Dutchman whose "restless ghost . . . still haunts the surrounding solitudes" and whose trumpet, for which he was famous, "has
often been heard by the neighbours, of a stormy night, mingling with
the howling of the blast."[10] Written in the spirit of good fun that ani-
mates the entire book, the passage bears little relation to the works of
earlier Gothic writers. It serves instead to satirize the ineptitude of the
Dutch, to poke fun at folk superstition, and to provide a comic source
for the name of Spuyten Duyvil Creek. For Irving in 1809, the Gothic
mode was hardly more than a means for projecting Diedrich Knickerbocker's humor.

Irving's attitude changed in 1810 when he became acquainted with the theory of perception as presented in contemporary Scottish Common Sense philosophy and began to consider seriously the sources of superstition and its effect upon the mind. How much philosophy Irving read that year remains an open question, but the Notebook of 1810 contains a number of entries copied from some unidentified philosophic work and includes the brief but important statement: "Perception / We percieve external objects thro the medium of impressions and sensations"[11]—very much the Common Sense view of the subject. Acceptance of such a concept entailed, of course, some important consequences. In their insistence upon the objectivity of the physical world and the ability of men to perceive it through their sensations and impressions, the Common Sense philosophers not only confirmed Irving in his fundamentally realistic attitude but opened the way for him to develop the Gothic mode in a new and fruitful direction. Because they distrusted the imagination, which could substitute isolated concepts for realities, Common Sense philosophers sought a rational explanation for supernatural phenomena, such as ghosts and goblins, which people think they see but which have no basis in material reality.

The Common Sense position was ably stated by James Beattie in *Dissertations Moral and Political* (1783). Aware of the popular belief in apparitions and prophetic dreams, Beattie argues that both derive most frequently from natural causes. He does not deny that some prophetic dreams and supernatural manifestations have occurred in the past, nor does he believe that their occurrence in the present is impossible. But he argues strongly that most dreams derive from memory or from impressions made on the organs of sense while one is asleep, and he maintains that what most people take for apparitions are natural phenomena misinterpreted by the senses or misconstrued by the imagination. He even gives examples of such errors drawn from his own experience: an apparition seated by his bedside one night that turned out to be only some clothes laid over a chair, or the appearance of a coffin in his room that was only an illusion made by a stream of yellow light. The cure for each delusion was simply to get up and investigate the cause of the apparition, but he admits that in the latter case the appearance continued to impose upon his sight until the light of morning dispelled it.[12]

Irving need not have read Beattie to have arrived at a similar understanding. The belief that apparitions must derive from faulty perception, a diseased imagination, or out-and-out madness was widely held, and he could have found it expressed in a number of different places. It appears in the works of Dugald Stewart, whom Irving mentions three times in the Notebook of 1810,[13] and it had played an important role in British Gothic fiction, where apparitions were often presented as psychological phenomena. If Irving perceived this aspect of Mrs. Radcliffe's writings, however, he made no use of it in the works he wrote immediately after he read her romances, for he did not attempt to depict the psychological source of apparitions in either *Salmagundi* or the first edition of *A History of New York*. He dismissed them, rather, as merely the follies of superstition. But with his new interest in philosophy as revealed in the Notebook of 1810, Irving began to consider the role of the imagination in the perception of supernatural phenomena, and, though he did not know it at the time, he initiated a process of thought that was to have a far-reaching effect on his art.

His intellectual position, then and later, was a thoroughly realistic one that insisted upon the chimerical nature of all supposedly supernatural phenomena. In the Notebook of 1810 he attributed popular superstition to the imaginations of the ignorant: "The reason being too weak to pierce the mystery that envelopes every natural phenomenon, the imagination takes it up—and dresses it out in forms & colours of its own[.] Hence the singular fables of Fairies, sylphs & enchanters by which ignorant nations attempted to explain the prodigies of nature—." Though such beliefs, he writes, are "charming & fanciful," they are merely illusions of the mind which, as knowledge advances, "the clear light of philosophy" soon dispels.[14] Irving was firm in this belief, and, while serving as editor of the *Analectic Magazine* (1812–1814), he selected for inclusion in that journal at least three items which explain away apparitions, banshees, and familiar spirits as the result of ocular deception, malfunctioning bodily organs, or predisposed imaginations.[15] Although not all items in the magazine can be taken as examples of Irving's opinions, the views expressed in these three articles are completely consistent with those that Irving avowed, and they clearly reveal his interest during these years in the philosophical position they maintain.

The thoroughgoing realism of this intellectual position could have influenced Irving in a number of different ways. He might simply have eschewed any use of supernatural phenomena to develop further his fine talents for social and political satire. Or he might have followed the lead of so many Gothic romancers, both British and German, in building up Gothic terror only to explain it away at the end of his works. In fact, he did neither. By turning his attention instead to the function of the imagination in causing faulty perception and retaining at the same time his penchant for humor, he opened for himself some excellent new possibilities for Gothic fiction. Heretofore he had merely poked fun at the credulity of the ignorant, who scare themselves with tales of ghosts and goblins. Now that he understood the ultimate cause of terror in the misapprehension of reality, he could extend the humor to more situations and tie it in more closely with the specific nature of the character who suffers the delusion. Irving introduces this practice in the story of Oloffe the Dreamer, an episode he inserted in the second edition of Knickerbocker's *History of New York* (1812).[16]

The episode satirizes in part the Gothic device of the prophetic dream, for whenever an event of consequence happens at Communipaw, the site of the earliest settlement, Oloffe declares that "he had previously dreamt it; being one of those infallible prophets, that always predict a thing, after it has come to pass." More important, however, Oloffe is "a great seer of ghosts and goblins, and a firm believer in omens." His mind is thus predisposed to perceive supernatural phenomena when he and a small band of Dutchmen set off in canoes and a round Dutch boat to seek a new site for the settlement. He fears to land on Governor's Island, suspecting it to "be the abode of demons and spirits"; he believes they are "in the hands of some supernatural power" as the tide hurries them up the East River; and when they arrive at Hell Gate and the vessels are swept about in the turbulent water, he perceives all kinds of strange phenomena: specters fly through the air, hobgoblins yell, the water feels scalding hot, and several strange beings, perched on a rock, appear to skim it with ladles. Oloffe accepts these perceptions as real, but others who hear his tale interpret them "as mere phantasies of [his] imagination."[17]

In the story of Oloffe the Dreamer, Irving created for the first time the kind of sportive Gothic tale, based on the credulity of the superstitious, that was to appear again in such well known stories as "The Legend of Sleepy Hollow" and "The Spectre Bridegroom." Tales of this type resemble, of course, the sort of thing he had done in both *Salmagundi* and the 1809 edition of *A History of New York,* but they represent, nonetheless, a real advance in his Gothic art. Instead of merely commenting upon the superstitious fear of his credulous characters, he reveals the mental state that makes them act as they do. Once he had accomplished this, the way was open for further artistic development. Irving was well aware that others besides the ignorant and naive were affected by supposed apparitions, and he knew that there was a kind of pleasure to be derived, even by the sophisticated, from tales of the supernatural. His Notebook of 1810 makes this attitude clear. The strongest mind, he observes, will sometimes dwell with fondness "on the superstitions of the nursery," and "we often endeavour . . . to conjure up past scenes and dream ourselves for a moment into the pleasing feeling of superstition we once felt."[18]

This perception led to a major development in Irving's handling of the Gothic mode, for, in permitting the use of other than merely ignorant and credulous characters, it enabled him to achieve a range of sophisticated effects far beyond anything in his earlier work. The results are apparent in his first books written in Europe—*The Sketch Book* (1819–1820), *Bracebridge Hall* (1822), and *Tales of a Traveller* (1824)— where a major advance in technique, combined with a new kind of subject matter, enabled him to produce his most interesting Gothic tales. From Sir Walter Scott, whom he visited in Abbotsford in 1817, Irving acquired an awareness of the riches of German romantic literature, and he found in the folk collections of Musäus, Otmar, and Johann G. Büsching materials that he turned to his own purposes in "Rip Van Winkle" and "The Legend of Sleepy Hollow."[19] Irving set out to learn German, and during his residence in Dresden in 1822–1823, he became increasingly familiar with German legends, some of which, like that of Die Weisse Frau—the ghost of a woman dressed in white who returns to haunt the place where she once lived[20]—turn up in a few of his tales.

Yet Irving's enthusiasm for German romantic literature, though unquestionably real, had no profound effect on his literary practice. Because of the "common sense" view he had acquired from his reading in 1810, he could not accept the German tales at face value, and he made no attempt in the books of the 1820s to create a dual world in which human beings can interact with goblins, ghosts, and specters. This rationalistic attitude was no doubt supported by two German books with which he became familiar before he completed *The Sketch Book*. The first he bought in Liverpool: Christoph Martin Wieland's *Die Abentheuer des*

Don Sylvio von Rosalva (1772), which satirizes the current interest in the supernatural. The second he merely recorded by title in his Notebook of 1818: Samuel Christoph Wagener's *Die Gespenster* (1797), which attributes supposed apparitions to natural causes.[21] Works like these could only have confirmed Irving in his mode of writing and may perhaps have influenced him to use the German romantic tales he collected over the next few years in ways consistent with the treatment of supernatural material in his earlier books.

The Gothic tales that Irving wrote for *The Sketch Book, Bracebridge Hall,* and *Tales of a Traveller* derive, therefore, from the many influences Irving had felt over the preceding decade and more, and they reveal the great skill he had developed as an original Gothic artist. Whatever their sources may have been—and much too much has sometimes been made of them—the primary value of the tales lies in Irving's adroit handling of his material. The stories are varied in both content and tone. They include not only the boisterously comic and grimly macabre, but also the mildly ironic and pensively sentimental. Several of them make excellent use of chilling Gothic effects, but all are treated in such a way as to do no violence to Irving's "common sense" belief that ghosts, goblins, and apparitions are nothing more than mental deceptions. The key to Irving's success is his careful manipulation of point of view. All three books are presented as the work of Geoffrey Crayon, a persona with the kind of mental attitude which permits the use of Gothic materials in a rationalistic context.

Crayon assumes an intellectual position that firmly controls both the Gothic material he presents and the manner of its handling. In *The Sketch Book* and *Bracebridge Hall* he takes a thoroughly rationalistic view of supernatural phenomena, an attitude which prevents him from treating the Gothic mode completely seriously. A man of imagination and sensibility, Crayon is attracted to the stories of fairies, ghosts, and goblins that he has picked up during his travels, and, reflecting a view Irving expressed in the Notebook of 1810,[22] he half regrets that the time is past when men could take pleasure in the fanciful creations of the mind. But however much he may lament the changes in popular belief that have banished such fancies from the minds of men, he knows very well that they were "creations of ignorance and credulity," and he is "convinced that the true interests and solid happiness of man are promoted by the advancement of truth." Crayon is thus a realist. He accepts the "true philosophy," in whose light, he believes, the creations of superstitious belief must vanish (9: 233). Hence, he reports supernatural phenomena as either deceptive appearance or the creation of a superstitious mind.

In *Bracebridge Hall*, for example, he explains how such apparitions can result from faulty perception. They are sometimes no more than optical illusions or the effect of deceptive light. Even a rational man like himself can be deceived. On entering a dusky passage in the Hall, he has thought that a full-length portrait of a knight in armor, "thrown into strong relief by the dark panelling against which it hangs," was actually advancing toward him. To a superstitious mind, moreover, "predisposed by the strange and melancholy stories that are connected with family paintings," the light of the moon or a flickering candle may "set the old pictures on the walls in motion, sweeping in their robes and trains about the galleries." The mind perceives an uncertain image, and, having been led to expect a supernatural occurrence, readily perceives it. Old houses, moreover, with their dusky corners, faded pictures, and strange noises are particularly liable to "produce a state of mind favourable to superstitious fancies" (9: 227). In Crayon's view, the apparitions reported to have been seen in them have no objective reality but result from the imaginative creation of minds predisposed to perceive them.

Such minds exist, he believes, largely among the common folk in isolated rural areas, for "the general diffusion of knowledge" in England "and the bustling intercourse kept up throughout the country" have spread such enlightened views that only in "a retired neighbourhood" like Bracebridge Hall can belief in popular superstitions still be found. Even here they are fading away, and the people themselves are reluctant to reveal their beliefs to strangers—or, for that matter, to the gentry— lest they be laughed at. Yet the beliefs persist. The parson at Bracebridge Hall assures Crayon that some of his parishioners still remember the bar-ghost, which was said "to predict any impending misfortune by midnight shrieks and wailings" (9: 228), and he tells a group assembled around the supper table that he knows a number of common folk who have maintained a lonely vigil on St. Mark's Eve for three successive years in the belief that on the third night they would see enter the church a ghostly procession of those to die in the coming year. Some claim to have actually seen it, much to the perturbation of others in the village who fear such persons may have advance knowledge of their deaths (9:81).

The favorite ghost of the neighborhood, Crayon learns in *The Sketch Book,* appears to be that of a crusader whose effigy is carved on his tomb by the church altar. The good wives of the village have always viewed it with superstition, and the usual stories are told about him. Some say he walks at night because of a wrong left unredressed at his death or because of a hidden treasure "which kept the spirit in a state of trouble and restlessness." His picture in Bracebridge Hall is viewed with awe by the servants, who believe its eyes follow them as they walk about, and the porter's wife avers that in her youth she heard it said "that on midsummer eve, when it is well known all kinds of ghosts, goblins, and fairies, become visible and walk abroad, the crusader used to mount his horse, come down from his picture, ride about the house, down the avenue, and so to the church to visit the tomb." Some of the rustics often laugh at these tales, but when night comes on, many of the strongest disbelievers in ghosts will not venture alone on the path across the churchyard (8: 188).

Yet Crayon knows that the common folk are not the only ones affected by such tales. Even the more educated act at times in similar ways and for the same reasons. The parson himself, Crayon believes, is "somewhat tinctured with superstition, as men are very apt to be, who live a recluse and studious life in a sequestered part of the country, and pore over black letter tracts, so often filled with the marvellous and supernatural" (8: 188). A "naturally credulous" man, the parson spends so much of his time in searching out the supernatural tales he tells "that his mind has probably become infected by them," and though he "never openly professes his belief in ghosts," he cites "the opinions of the ancient philosophers" and "quotes from the fathers of the church" in defense of the supernatural (9: 82-83). The mind of the parson has been predisposed to belief in ghosts by the antiquarian habits he has developed, and the more he studies the popular lore of his and other nations, the more he is likely to lend credence to the stories he uncovers—a mental process not unlike that of the common people who feed their superstition with the tales they constantly retell.

Master Simon, too, a relative of Squire Bracebridge, can become as unnerved as the common folk by what appears to be a strange occurrence. He has heard of the ghost of a hard riding earlier squire who is said to gallop "with hound and horn, over a wild moor a few miles distant from the Hall." Crayon is inclined to believe that this story has been set abroad by the present squire, who, though himself a disbeliever, does not want to see the popular superstitions die, but Master Simon hints that there may be truth in the tale. He has "heard odd sounds at night, very like a pack of hounds in cry," and once, when returning home rather late from a dinner, he saw a galloping figure on that very moor. But, he goes on to say, "as he was riding rather fast at the time, and in a hurry to get home, he did not stop to ascertain what it was" (9: 228). Though Master Simon is not depicted as a superstitious man, his actions on this occasion are little different from those of the rustics who fear to cross the churchyard, or the dairy maid who will not venture after dark near a wood where an old owl is hooting (9: 194).

Crayon's irony is light in these passages, for he wants to poke only mild fun at the parson and Master Simon. They are not so different, after all, from other educated people who find themselves at least partially affected by tales of the supernatural. Whenever such stories are introduced into social gatherings, they are frequently met with smiles, but no matter how gay or enlightened the audience may be, if the tales are continued long, they will soon absorb the interest of the listeners. "There is," Crayon believes, "a degree of superstition lurking in every mind; and I doubt if any one can thoroughly examine all his secret notions and impulses without detecting it, hidden, perhaps, even from himself. It seems, in fact, to be a part of our nature, like instinct in animals, acting independently of our reason" (9: 82). Crayon, indeed, detects it in himself, for after an evening of such stories, he finds he cannot sleep, so strong a hold do they take on his imagination. The room he sits in, hung with tapestries whose faded figures "look like unsubstantial shapes melting away from sight," fosters a state of mind which turns naturally to supernatural things (9: 83).

As he gazes out of the window on the "quiet groves and shadowy lawns, silvered over, and imperfectly lighted by streaks of dewy moonshine," his mind is filled with fancies concerning spiritual beings, and he wonders if they do indeed exist. Though he knows that belief in the return of departed spirits "has been debased by the absurd superstitions of the vulgar," he sees it "in itself [as] awfully solemn and sublime," and because it is so prevalent in all times and places, it seems to him "to be one of those mysterious, and almost instinctive beliefs, to which, if left to ourselves, we should naturally incline." He wonders, then, if such belief can ever be eradicated, whatever "pride of reason and philosophy" may say, and he entertains, at least for the moment, the possibility of reunion with the dead he has loved (9: 84-85). Crayon is, of course, under a kind of spell at this point, one generated by the stories he has heard, the room in which he sits, and the silvery landscape over which he gazes. In the full light of day he will turn again to the disbelief in ghosts that more usually characterizes his thought.

The Gothic tales that Crayon includes in his books, moreover, are markedly influenced by his philosophic view. In accordance with his usual practice, Crayon tells none of the stories in his own voice but merely reports what he has heard from others, sometimes as much as twice removed from himself.[23] Thus the actual narrator of "The Spectre Bridegroom" is a corpulent Swiss with "a pleasant twinkling eye" (8: 120) who tells the story in a Flemish inn. "The Legend of Sleepy Hollow," "Dolph Heyliger," and "Wolfert Webber" all come from the posthumous papers of Diedrich Knickerbocker, but the first is told by an old gentleman "with a sadly humourous face" at a meeting of the Corporation of the city of Manhattoes (8: 296), the latter two by "John Josse Vandermoere, a pleasant gossiping man, whose whole life was spent in hearing and telling the news of the province" of New York (9: 250), and who is generally considered to be "one of the most authentic narrators in the province" (7: 392). Finally, "Strange Stories by a Nervous Gentleman," the first section of *Tales of a Traveller,* is told by the same person who recounts "The Stout Gentleman" in *Bracebridge Hall,* but each story told at the hunting dinner has its own narrator.

Because Crayon himself assumes no responsibility for any of these tales, he is able to achieve through his narrators a wide variety of effects. Both "The Spectre Bridegroom" and "The Legend of Sleepy Hollow" in *The Sketch Book* are told by somewhat roguish men whose purpose is to make their audiences laugh. In their hands, therefore, the Gothic mode becomes a vehicle for humor, the Gothic terrors turned against the credulous characters and converted into material for comedy. "Dolph Heyliger" in *Bracebridge Hall* and "Wolfert Webber" in *Tales of a Traveller,* on the other hand, are told by a man deeply interested in the past. Though he too has his humorous side, he creates in both the tales a Gothic tone that is not completely destroyed by their comic conclusions. In "Strange Stories by a Nervous Gentleman," moreover, the use of different narrators for each tale permits a considerable range of tone, from the rollicking mood of "The Bold Dragoon" to the somber horror of "The Adventure of the German Student." But whatever the effect achieved, each of the stories is firmly based in the realistic philosophy that Crayon professes, and illustrates well the function of the mind in the perception of Gothic terrors.

In "The Spectre Bridegroom" and "The Legend of Sleepy Hollow," for example, the Gothic terrors experienced by the Landshort household and Ichabod Crane are shown to derive ultimately from their superstitious natures. In each case, however, the imagination is stimulated by external events that create the proper conditions for the credulous mind to mistake what it perceives. When Herman Von Starkenfaust arrives at the Landshort castle, the Baron Von Landshort, a man who delights in supernatural tales, gives him no opportunity to announce the death of the expected bridegroom, the Count Von Altenburg. Instead, the Baron mistakes him for his murdered friend and entertains him handsomely. Because of the awkwardness of his situation—made more difficult by the feud between their families—Herman becomes increasingly dejected and melancholy as the evening progresses. His "unaccountable gloom" chills the gaiety of the feast, the singing and laughter are stilled, and the company soon falls into its favorite pastime of telling "wild tales, and supernatural legends" (8: 128). The story of the fair Leonora who was carried off by the goblin horseman[24] gives Herman an idea of how to extricate himself. Announcing his own death and imminent burial in Wurtzburg Cathedral, he thoroughly frightens his superstitious hosts and leaves them fully convinced for a time that they have been entertaining a specter.

A similar mental process occurs in "The Legend of Sleepy Hollow." Much like the Landshort household, Ichabod Crane is a credulous man who frightens himself with the tales he reads in Cotton Mather, who listens with "fearful pleasure" to the stories of ghosts and goblins told by the old Dutch wives, and who tells in return the tales of witchcraft, omens, and portents that he has brought from his native Connecticut. But the pleasure he gains from such tales when he sits in the chimney corner is dearly bought on his homeward walks when his path is beset by frightening "phantoms of the mind" (8: 277-78). Ichabod Crane is already ripe for the scare of his life well before Brom Bones drives him from Sleepy Hollow. On the night of the party at the Van Tassel farm, the usual stories of ghosts and goblins are told, but most especially that of the Headless Horseman of Sleepy Hollow. By the time Ichabod leaves, therefore, his mind is so deeply affected that he begins to see specters and hear ghostly groans even before he arrives at the spot where Brom Bones awaits him. Small wonder, then, that when he sees the horse with its apparently headless rider, he immediately believes it is the well known specter and flees in terror.

In both of these stories the usual Gothic devices are converted by knowing characters into the kind of practical joke that reveals the credulity and superstitious fears of those taken in by them. They are thus completely consistent with the realistic views expressed by Crayon, who attributes to the minds of the ignorant and superstitious the perceptions they report of supernatural beings and occurrences. Other of Irving's stories, however, handle the Gothic mode in a somewhat different way. "Wolfert Webber" and "Dolph Heyliger," the tales told by John Josse Vandermoere, have about them an aura of the legendary that permits a more truly Gothic tone. Already an old man when Diedrich Knickerbocker hears the stories from him (and Knickerbocker himself writes them down many years later) Vandermoere is far removed from the present age, and he tells his tales of times more distant still. Indeed, imbedded in both "Dolph Heyliger" and "Wolfert Webber"—stories of the early eighteenth century—are tales that are set in an even earlier period: "The Storm-Ship," a supernatural tale of the days of Dutch rule in New York, and "The Adventure of the Black Fisherman," a story laid in a time many years before it is heard by Wolfert Webber.

Twice removed from Crayon himself and set in the distant past, Vandermoere's stories may contain strong Gothic elements without doing violence to Crayon's avowed disbelief in ghosts and goblins. Yet at the same time, "Wolfert Webber" and "Dolph Heyliger" cannot be considered purely Gothic tales. Both have their humorous aspects, and both contain obvious references to the realistic philosophy that consistently appears in Crayon's treatment of the supernatural. Where these stories differ from "The Spectre Bridegroom" and "The Legend of Sleepy Hollow" is in the narrator's willingness to allow a Gothic mood to form before it is undercut by the usual humor. Of the two stories told by Vandermoere, "Wolfert Webber" is the more closely related to "The Spectre Bridegroom" and "The Legend of Sleepy Hollow," for the hero is rather credulous and his main Gothic adventure is turned at last into a hilarious rout. The story as a whole, however, is not so broadly humorous as the other two, and it contains some truly threatening elements, most especially the supposed pirate who for a time dominates the village inn, and the group of smugglers who provide a real element of danger in the story.

The Gothic elements are common ones. Wolfert Webber dreams a prophetic dream that a fabulous treasure lies concealed in his cabbage garden, a dream that unexpectedly comes true when the city runs a street through his land and Wolfert becomes rich by parceling it out in building lots. Moreover, when he looks for pirate gold, Wolfert's adventures involve him in a number of Gothic episodes: he blunders into a tomb where a human skull lies exposed; he later sees what appears to be the red-capped ghost of a drowned seaman enter the vault; and at the moment he thinks he has found the gold he seeks, he confronts the grinning visage of the red-capped sailor. What all these events actually mean is never fully explained in the story, the narrator merely providing a number of alternative interpretations. What is strongly suggested, however, is that Wolfert's path has crossed that of a group of smugglers, and the fears and terrors he undergoes are the result of a mind so filled with tales of ghosts and pirate gold that on the night of his great adventure he converts the red-capped smugglers into a legion of ghosts and goblins. This explanation, however, is not allowed to dominate the story, which, despite its humor, still manages to maintain something of a Gothic tone.

"Dolph Heyliger," on the other hand, is for most of its length a more serious Gothic tale. The hero sees a real ghost in a haunted house; he dreams a prophetic dream that leads him to believe he is under a supernatural influence; he journeys from New York to Albany, where he sees a picture resembling the ghost in a house he is visiting; and the ghost eventually reveals to him in a dream the well in New York where a wonderful treasure lies hidden.[25] Dolph himself is not a credulous character. He tries to persuade himself that the ghost is "a mere freak of the imagination, conjured up by the stories he had heard" (9: 265), and he later attempts to explain it away as merely a dream (9: 266). Indeed, he begins to doubt at one point "whether his mind was not affected, and whether all that was passing in his thoughts might not be mere feverish fantasy" (9: 269). "Dolph Heyliger" thus appears to be a most unusual story in that the character who has the series of strange experiences is just the kind who, well aware of the deceptive quality of the imagination, ought to be able to see through the supernatural phenomena to a realistic explanation.

Yet for all its supernatural events, "Dolph Heyliger" is not inconsistent with the realistic psychology that underlies Irving's other Gothic tales. Unlike Ichabod Crane and Wolfert Webber, Dolph is a shrewd man who does not permit his imagination to run away with him. He takes things as they come and, despite his real fears, maintains his equanimity even under the most unusual circumstances. Far from being frightened by imaginary terrors, he refuses to permit even a real ghost to intimidate him. The ghost, on the other hand, may not be real at all. Dolph Heyliger is the sole authority for the strange events that occur, and he tells the story to a few old cronies at his private table only after many years have passed. By this time Dolph is rich, the result apparently of the treasure he found in the well. No one ever contests the supernatural parts of his story, but that should not be surprising. Dolph, the narrator informs us, "was noted for being the ablest drawer of the longbow in the whole province" (9: 300). The story may thus be merely a tall tale told by the shrewd Dolph Heyliger to conceal the source of his wealth.

"Dolph Heyliger" is not unique among Irving's Gothic tales. "Strange Stories by a Nervous Gentleman" contains three similar ones, but because they are integrated into a larger whole, they must be seen in relation to the overall meaning of the entire sequence. The stories are told by a group of men, marooned by a winter storm, after a hunting dinner. Four are told the first evening, after which the Nervous Gentleman, who presents the entire series, undergoes a disturbing experience with a mysterious portrait in his chamber. The following day their host tells a long story to account for the strange picture, after which the guests are given the opportunity to test their own reactions to it. The sequence of stories thus has a purpose that goes beyond the individual tales the guests tell. The point of the series concerns the reactions of the guests both to the stories themselves and to the suggestion that the portrait they see may have a disquieting effect upon them. Their response, it is clear, results from the growing influence of the various stories on their imaginations.

The first three tales are comic and are partly designed by the narrators to take in their audience. All resemble "Dolph Heyliger" in the way the

main characters react to the supernatural. In "The Adventure of My
Uncle" the protagonist is a shrewd old traveler not easily frightened by
strange occurrences, and although he is chilled to the marrow by the
eyes of a ghost that appears in his room, he refuses to be disturbed. He
simply pulls the covers over his head and goes to sleep. Though he attempts to learn the reason for the ghost's appearance and the narrator
leads the audience on to expect some disclosure, the story is finally left
up in the air with no explanation given. "The Adventure of My Aunt"
is quite the opposite. Alone in her room when she hears a suspicious
noise and sees the eyes of the portrait of her dead husband move, she
takes matters firmly in hand, refuses to panic, and, leading a band of her
servants, drives out an intruder who is hiding behind the picture. In
"The Bold Dragoon," finally, an Irish soldier tells an improbable tale of
goblins and dancing furniture in his room to conceal a midnight adventure with the landlord's daughter. And much like Dolph Heyliger, he
makes his story stick because of his obvious skill "with sword or shille-
lah" (7: 53).

All of these stories are snares to catch the unwary, to lead the credulous on with a promise of Gothic terror that is left unfulfilled. As the
narrator of the first tale remarks, all three had "a burlesque tendency"
(7: 54). He proposes, therefore, to tell a fourth which is a different thing
entirely. "The Adventure of the German Student" recounts the experience of a young man in Paris during the French Revolution. With a
melancholy temperament, a mind filled with German philosophy, and
fear that some evil hangs over him, he is alone and unhappy. Haunted
by a recurring dream of a beautiful young woman, he finally meets her
one stormy night near the guillotine. Highly striking in appearance but
simply dressed, she wears around her neck "a broad black band . . .
clasped by diamonds" (7: 59). The student takes her home and spends
the night with her. Believing he has formed a permanent union, he
leaves next morning to seek a better apartment. On returning to his
room, however, he finds her dead and learns from the police that she
had been guillotined the previous day. When the officer unclasps the
band around her neck, her head rolls on the floor.

Starkly horrible in its suggestion of necrophilia, "The Adventure of
the German Student" adds a new note to the sequence of stories and
turns it in a new direction. Not that the story departs completely from
the sportive tone of the tales that precede it. However much it may seem

to be a truly Gothic tale, its tone is undercut by a humorous conclusion that dissolves the Gothic effect. In providing authentication for the tale he has just completed, the narrator informs his listeners that he has the story on the best authority: he heard it from the German student himself—in a madhouse in Paris! Yet if this revelation makes the reader smile, the explanation has a significance beyond the humor. If superstition or a diseased imagination can affect one's perception of reality, how much more powerful is out-and-out madness in distorting a person's vision.[26] Seen in these terms, the tale can be accepted as the mental projection of a mad protagonist. Even this tale of horror, then, is perfectly consistent with the "common sense" philosophy to which Irving always subscribed.

"The Adventure of the German Student" has yet another significance that cannot be overlooked. Though added to the group as almost an afterthought on Irving's part,[27] the tale is actually the keystone of the series. Related to the earlier stories through the humorous undercutting at its conclusion, it helps to stimulate the Gothic adventures that are to follow. Throughout most of its length, this tale, like "Dolph Heyliger," closely resembles conventional stories of ghosts and goblins. Though the narrator's final words may deny the relation, the effect it has had on the listeners cannot be wholly erased. Thus, by the time the story is finished, the assembled company has become engrossed in the subject of ghosts. No matter how sportively the evening may have begun, the characters would have gone on telling such tales if the spell had not been broken by the "loud and long-drawn yawn" of one of their number who had fallen asleep (7: 63). The company decides instead to disperse for the night. At this point, the host informs his guests that one of them will sleep in a haunted chamber, but none shall know in advance who it will be. The assignment of rooms will be left "to chance and the allotment of the housekeeper" (7: 64).

Thus the stage is set for the events of the evening to begin to have an effect on the company. When the Nervous Gentleman goes to his room, he smiles "at its resemblance in style to those eventful apartments described in the tales of the supper-table." He draws a chair to the hearth, stirs up the fire, and sits "looking into it, and musing upon the odd stories [he] had heard" (7: 64). Overcome by fatigue and the wine he has drunk, he soon falls asleep. Restless, as he believes, because of the heavy dinner he has eaten, he has a frightening dream in which he feels oppressed by something evil. Struggling in his dream to throw it off, he starts awake. The light of a flaring candle falls on a hitherto unnoticed portrait which gives him a growing sense of unease. The eyes of the picture seem to charm him, and although he instinctively tries "to brush away the illusion," it is in vain (7: 65). Only one picture of all those in the room has this effect upon him, and he notes: "it was some horror of the mind, some inscrutable antipathy awakened by this picture, which harrowed up my feelings" (7: 66).

Despite his nervous condition, the narrator is a rational man who knows full well how events can influence the mind. "I tried to persuade myself that this was chimerical, that my brain was confused by the fumes of mine host's good cheer, and in some measure by the odd stories about paintings which had been told at supper." But although he determines "to shake off these vapors of the mind," he finds he cannot do it (7: 66). When he goes to the window, he sees the picture reflected in a pane of glass; when he turns his back, he feels it looking over his shoulder; when he goes to bed, he finds he has a full view of the portrait. Even when he puts out the light he has no peace. The fire on the hearth gives an uncertain light to the room, but the picture is left in darkness, and the chamber itself, to his "infected imagination," begins "to assume strange appearances." He cannot convince himself that he is tormented only by his "diseased imagination" (7: 67), and realizing that a nervous agitation can only increase the longer it continues, he quits the room to sleep on a drawing room sofa.

When on the following morning his companions discover that he has not slept in his assigned room, the Nervous Gentleman becomes the butt of their laughter. Though protesting that he is not superstitious and asserting his lack of faith in "silly stories" of haunted rooms, he maintains nonetheless that he has "met with something . . . strange and inexplicable" in his chamber: a picture that has had a "most singular and incomprehensible" effect upon him (7: 71). The merriment of his companions merely makes him affirm more insistently that he has indeed experienced an unusual phenomenon, and the host soon has to come to his rescue. He tells his guests that he does indeed possess a picture which has an unsettling effect on all who view it. In fact, he would have had it covered the preceding night "had not the nature of our conversation, and the whimsical talk about a haunted chamber, tempted me to let it remain, by way of experiment, to see whether a stranger totally unacquainted with its story, would be affected by it" (7: 72). This announcement instantly stills the banter of his guests, all of whom become anxious to hear the story behind the mysterious portrait.

The host tells a long tale of a young Italian he met and befriended in Venice. This young man, who had studied to be a painter, suffered grievously at the hands of the world. Rejected by his wealthy father, he endured a long series of misfortunes culminating in his betrayal by a man he had trusted. In love with a girl named Bianca, the young Italian was forced to leave her to attend his ailing father, with whom he had become reconciled. In his absence, however, the friend married Bianca after first convincing her that her lover was dead. Infuriated by his friend's treachery, the young Italian killed him, only to be haunted by a pursuing figure. This might have been either "an illusion of the mind" resulting from his early education at the hands of some monks, or "a phantom really sent by Heaven to punish" him (7: 113), but in either case it pursued him relentlessly. The young Italian was finally influenced by a deep religious experience to give himself up, and he left with his English friend a manuscript detailing the story of his life and the horrible portrait he had painted of the phantom that had pursued him.[28]

At the end of this tale, of course, the whole company wants to see the mysterious picture, and the host agrees to let them, on one condition. The guests must go into the chamber one at a time. He gives the appropriate instructions to his housekeeper, and when the guests return, they all have felt the influence of the portrait: "Some affected in one way, some in another; some more, some less; but all agreeing that there was a certain something about the painting that had a very odd effect upon the feelings." The Nervous Gentleman is deeply impressed and quickly concludes that there must indeed be "certain mysteries in our nature, certain inscrutable impulses and influences, which warrant one in being superstitious. Who can account for so many persons of different characters being thus strangely affected by a mere painting?" The host, however, reveals to his nervous friend that none of his companions have seen the mysterious portrait. Because he saw that some of them were in a bantering mood, and not wishing the Italian's painting to be made fun of, he had instructed his housekeeper "to show them all to a different chamber!" (7: 115).

Because "Strange Stories by a Nervous Gentleman" ends in this way, it can be read as simply an extended joke, the final revelation designed to subvert the Gothic mood that has gradually been developed. The immediate effect is, of course, comic, but the ultimate purpose is serious. Sportive though most of them may be, Irving's Gothic tales are fundamentally concerned with a problem of human perception, the reasons why people sometimes fail to perceive the world as it is but see instead a world of Gothic terror. Most of those who fall prey to these self-engendered delusions are men whose minds are filled with superstition, much like the common folk whom Geoffrey Crayon describes in *The Sketch Book* and *Bracebridge Hall.* Others, however, are hardly men of this type. The guests at the hunting dinner in *Tales of a Traveller* are by no means credulous men like Ichabod Crane or Wolfert Webber. Rather, the very stories they tell clearly reveal their disbelief in ghosts and goblins, and their initial response to the Nervous Gentleman's experience with the mysterious picture is to laugh uproariously at his discomfort.

As Crayon observes in *Bracebridge Hall,* however, men like these are not immune from feeling Gothic effects, especially if they submit themselves, however lightheartedly, to the influence of supernatural tales. This is, of course, the point of the Nervous Gentleman's stories. All the guests eventually feel the effect of even the sportive stories that have been told, and the comic conclusion makes it especially plain that what happens to them when they view what they think is the mysterious picture bears no relation to reality. They have simply projected into the real world a mental state that derives from a chain of circumstances which began with the sportive tales and ended with the host's story of the young Italian. Their imaginations have led them to perceive what their reason would deny. But the comic conclusion serves yet another purpose. In revealing the purely mental basis of the Gothic experience, it returns the series of stories to the world of actuality from which it began. In effect, it affirms the reality of the world perceived through reason—the world of common sense and prosaic daylight in which the Gothic tales of these three books are always firmly anchored.

Although Irving continued to use the Gothic mode for the next quarter of a century, he did not reach again the success he achieved with it in *The Sketch Book, Bracebridge Hall,* and *Tales of a Traveller.* Legends of ghosts, goblins, and Moorish enchantments abound, of course, in *The Alhambra* (1832); the popular superstitions of Newstead Abbey are described in *The Crayon Miscellany* (1835); an occasional tale of the supernatural appears in the papers he wrote for *The Knickerbocker* (1839–1841) and later collected in *Wolfert's Roost* (1855); and an additional tale of enchantment and brief Gothic sequence appear in the revision of *The Alhambra* that Irving made in 1850. But in none of these works does his use of the Gothic mode undergo any further development. At his weakest, Irving tends to repeat the devices of his earlier fiction and to publish faded reflections of his better work. But even at his best—in the many legends of Morisco Spain with which he filled *The Alhambra*—he failed to provide the firm philosophical foundation and the nice adjustment of narrator, context, character, and circumstance that had characterized the Gothic tales in his first European books.

Such a judgment, however, should not be allowed to obscure his real success with the Gothic mode in the works of the 1820s. Like Radcliffe and Brown before him, Irving drew on the strong rationalistic strain that influenced most Gothic writers at the close of the eighteenth century, and developed a kind of psychological Gothic that is similar to but not the same as theirs. Though as thoroughgoing a rationalist as Mrs. Radcliffe, he did not, like her, simply explain away the Gothic effects that his characters experience, nor did he, like Brown, become completely immersed in the workings of their minds. He maintained, rather, a kind of intellectual balance, firmly committed to an objectively real and knowable external world, but admitting at the same time the power of the imagination to create a world of appearances that has a psychological reality for the mind that perceives it. Irving constructed a Gothic world that does justice to both of these principles, makes telling comments upon human foibles and failings, and yet allows room for the sometimes pointed but always good-natured humor that, in the last analysis, is his unmistakable trademark.

SIX

Further American Developments

By the early 1820s, when Washington Irving's most Gothic works were appearing, the mode had become so popular in America that many books which are not in themselves Gothic frequently contain an episode or incident that unquestionably is. For thirty years and more, literary Gothicism had flourished on both sides of the Atlantic, and American readers had grown fond of Gothic fiction. They might treat "with sovereign contempt," as James Kirke Paulding put it in 1819, tales of "magic, and supernatural agency" laid in their native land, but they viewed "with great respect" stories "of second sight, or witchcraft . . . laid in the Highlands of Scotland, or some one of the western isles," and tales of "poisons, assassinations, adulteries, monkish villany, and sheeted spectres" set "in the Appenines, in an old ruined castle."[1] Few American writers, of course, would directly imitate Radcliffe, Lewis, or Scott, but Gothic works were so widely read and admired that even those American authors who were more strongly attracted to the quite different fiction of Henry Fielding and Laurence Sterne felt the need to include some kind of Gothic material in their works.[2]

They had many models to choose from. All were influenced, to some extent at least, by the strong European strain that had been developing since the 1790s. Ann Radcliffe remained a major influence on American writing well into the nineteenth century, Matthew Gregory Lewis continued to be read, William Godwin and Charles Maturin were both well known, and Sir Walter Scott, of course, took America by storm. Though most American writers of the 1820s and 1830s strove to maintain independence from Europe and sought to develop a native American literature, many borrowed material from these writers and used it for their own purposes. Some remained close to their sources, some transmuted them into new and different forms, but none fully escaped their influence. A number of American writers, however, drew on sources closer to home. Some followed the lead of Irving in using Gothic devices for humor in fundamentally realistic fiction, and others drew on Charles Brockden Brown to develop further the psychological themes he had initiated. For twenty years or so, the American Gothic seemed to move in many directions at once as writers sought an appropriate way to integrate the popular material into their fiction.

Most clearly related to the European Gothic are works containing the familiar trappings that had long been associated with the mode: Italian or German settings, forbidding castles and dark caves, spectral or diabolical characters, old manuscripts that recount mysterious tales, and the like. American writers sometimes resorted to these with varied success. In *Monaldi,* written in 1822 but not published until 1841,[3] Washington Allston sets the scene in Italy and uses some of the devices that one might expect to find in romances of the Radcliffe type; while in "The Spirit Bridegroom" (1837), a serious tale set in Germany, William Gilmore Simms obviously draws on "Lenore," the specter ballad of Gottfried August Bürger that had provided Washington Irving with material for comedy. The tale also shows the influence, acknowledged by Simms in a footnote,[4] of Goethe's *Faust,* and even borrows a detail from Maturin's *Melmoth the Wanderer.* The appearance of Albert, the title character, like that of Melmoth, is announced by the sound of ethereal music. Though Allston and Simms make significant changes, especially in terms of theme, in the sources they use, they remain rather close to them in subject matter and setting.[5]

In some other American works the familiar Gothic techniques are merely transposed to the New World. The strange lights and antic figures that terrify the settlers in the seventeenth-century Maryland of John Pendleton Kennedy's *Rob of the Bowl* (1838) have their source in the British and German romances of a generation before, and the settlers' reactions differ in no essential way from those of the British and German characters. The strange phenomena are caused by smugglers, much the same explanation as those provided for the frightening events in *The Old Manor House* and *The Mysteries of Udolpho,* and the freebooters use devices—"visors, masks, and strange disguises," and the burning of "chemical fires"[6]—that had appeared in the German romances of the 1790s. The trickery may have come to Kennedy by way of Sir Walter Scott—through *The Antiquary* or *Woodstock,* for example—but whatever the immediate source the American was drawing on a well established Gothic tradition for his explanation. The same sources provided, too, the human motivation for the settlers' fears: superstition among the ignorant and disturbed imagination among the more educated of the colonists, one of whom, lost in the wilderness at night, quails "before the conjurations of" his "excited fancy" (p. 294).

These and other causes of Gothic terror were widely used by American writers to suggest the same aberrations that had been depicted in British and German romance. In James Fenimore Cooper's *The Spy* (1821), for example, as in most Gothic tales, the superstitious fears of the ignorant cause them to perceive phantoms where none exist. The band of Skinners, a group of American irregulars who attack the house of Harvey Birch and rob him of his gold, are frightened into headlong retreat at the appearance of what they take to be the ghost of Harvey's father. Black Caesar, the Whartons' servant, and Katy Haynes, the Birches' housekeeper, also flee from the supposed apparition, and though Katy is later disabused of her error, Caesar remains forever convinced that he has seen a spook. Black characters, assuming the role of the European peasant, are often depicted in this manner, and Caesar, true to form, is afraid to approach a graveyard at night. Indeed, when sent on a mission to Sergeant Hollister, he so infects the soldier with superstitious fear that the sergeant, himself afraid of ghosts, is reluctant to lead his troops through the windy darkness.

A distempered imagination, on the other hand, is the cause of apparitions among those whose intelligence and education free them from the superstitious fears of the ignorant. Such a one is Philip Lindsay in John Pendleton Kennedy's *Horse-Shoe Robinson* (1835), a grave, thoughtful, retiring man and "ardent lover of books." His interest in speculative philosophy and "unhealthy appetite for the marvellous and the mystical" have led him to studies which, though "pursued with an acknowledgment of their false and dangerous tendency," seriously affect his imagination.[7] Few men, Kennedy writes, are ever wholly free from some degree of superstition, and a nervous temperament like Lindsay's is especially liable to its influence. Deeply upset by his daughter's love for Arthur Butler, of whom he does not approve, Philip Lindsay so works up his imagination that one moonlit night he sees the ghost of his dead wife in the garden, come to warn him against the marriage. Like Emily St. Aubert in *The Mysteries of Udolpho,* he has been impelled by his overwrought mind, his active imagination, and the lights and shadows of an illusory setting to conjure up an image that has no objective reality.

For a third group of characters, guilt is the cause of the terrible specters of conscience that they sometimes perceive. Like Sister Agnes in *The
Mysteries of Udolpho* and Spalatro in *The Italian,* the title character in
William Gilmore Simms's *Guy Rivers* (1834) is haunted by ghosts of
men he has murdered, and although he can put them down by shouting
"at them fiercely," their appearance "on the roadside, glaring at [him]
from bush or tree," does at times unman him.[8] Some villains perceive
the apparitions of men they only think they have harmed. Ben Pickett
sees the ghost of Richard Hurdis, in Simms's *Richard Hurdis* (1838), because he believes mistakenly that he has killed him, and he takes the
image of William Carrington, whom he actually killed in his place, for a
living man. In a similar fashion, the adventurer Sterling, in Robert
Montgomery Bird's *The Hawks of Hawk Hollow* (1835), sees in his
prison cell both the phantom of Henry Falconer, the man he killed, and
the specter of Hyland Gilbert, who he believes has been executed for the
crime on the basis of his false testimony. Like many a Gothic villain before them, these men are all tortured by phantoms of their own guilt.

With some Gothic devices, however, Americans made important
changes, adapting them to the very different conditions of American fiction. When Frances Wharton in *The Spy* ventures alone and at night to
the cabin of Harvey Birch to save her brother Henry, she is treading in
the steps of many British heroines who wander at midnight through the
dark hallways of haunted castles and abbeys. Although Frances encounters no sights or sounds that her mind can convert into specters, she does
experience a moment of real terror when, in the pale light of the moon,
she finds herself beneath the gallows on which her brother is sentenced
to hang and sees the rope swinging in the night air. Like many Gothic
writers before him, Cooper places his heroine in a situation of terror—
but he does it with a difference. Frances Wharton's adventure takes
place in the American countryside where her courage is tested in a situation that can have grave consequences for her brother. The journey is ar-
duous and the source of terror she encounters has a firm basis in reality.
Cooper has created an American version of the Gothic convention, and
without the sometimes absurd titillation of the British romances.[9]

Other Gothic devices underwent similar change as Cooper and his
contemporaries sought to retain a sense of Gothic mystery without
doing violence to the realities of American life. The prophetic dream,
long a staple of Gothic fiction, provides a good example of their prac-

tice. American writers of the early nineteenth century were deeply interested in dreams, presenting them as the unconscious blending of deep
memories, recent mental disturbances, and at times sensory stimuli from
the sleeper's immediate environment. Thus when Lionel Lincoln dreams
just as the Battle of Bunker Hill is about to begin, in Cooper's *Liönel
Lincoln* (1825), memories of the father he has not seen in years mingle
with the disturbing impressions he received on Copp's Hill the previous
evening and the sounds of the British bombardment of the American en-
trenchments, to raise visions of frightening specters in his mind. Lionel
dreams while he sleeps the deep sleep of morning, but the experience can
also occur while the person lies in the state halfway between sleeping
and waking, when, as Simms puts it in *Katharine Walton* (1851), the
mind "mingles the *real,* which assails the external consciousness, with
the dreaming method which employs it."[10]

American writers found this theory useful in providing a rational
basis for an Américan version of the prophetic dream or other mysterious warning. Ralph Colleton in Simms's *Guy Rivers* is in a state between waking and sleeping when warned by Lucy Munro that his life is
in danger. When Colleton hears her warning, he raises himself on his
couch and passes "his hand repeatedly over his eyes," as, "half doubting
his senses," he tries to identify the voice and understand the message
(pp. 238-39). Though he finally wakes completely to find the girl in his
room, he perceives her warning first as something strange and mysterious. Arthur Butler in Kennedy's *Horse-Shoe Robinson,* on the other
hand, remains at least half asleep when Mary Musgrove, herself the victim of a frightening dream, tells him to avoid a certain route the following day; and Roland Forrester in Robert Montgomery Bird's *Nick of the
Woods* (1837) is briefly roused into wakefulness when given a similar
warning by Telie Doe. Recalling the message the next day, Butler cannot decide whether the voice he heard was dream or reality, but Forrester concludes that he has indeed had a prophetic dream.[11]

Interesting though these incidents may be, however, they do not
function very well as Gothic devices. Bird is less explicit than Simms or
Kennedy in providing the rational cause for the supposedly prophetic
dreams, but none of them really creates for the reader the sense of mystery which alone can justify the use of the technique.[12] James Fenimore
Cooper did much better in the dreamlike warning that Peyton Dunwoodie, an American major, receives in *The Spy.* Deeply concerned that

Henry Wharton, his fiancée's brother, has been arrested as a spy, Dunwoodie rises early after a restless night and, in a "disturbed state of mind," wanders into the mist-filled orchard just as the moonlight is giving way to the first rays of morning. There he encounters Harvey Birch, the suspected royal spy, who, standing above him on some rocks, warns him of danger and vanishes. Since the major thinks that Birch is locked away in prison, he can hardly "persuade himself that the form he" perceives is "not a creature of the imagination"; and though roused by his approaching troops "from the stupor, which had been created by this strange scene," he is "unable to believe that all he had seen was not a dream" (pp. 223-26).

In his handling of this episode Cooper has gone much further than Simms, Kennedy, or Bird in adapting the Gothic device of the mysterious warning to the American landscape. He has also written a much more effective Gothic scene. He retains not a vestige of the prophetic dream itself, but creates, rather, just those conditions of mind and matter that allow reality to impress itself on the half-wakened consciousness of the major as if it were, in fact, a dream. As a result Cooper constructs a scene that does no violence to the rational predilections of his audience, yet still suggests that aura of the mysterious which they had come to relish in fiction. Part of his success derives, of course, from the setting in which the incident is embedded. The Neutral Ground, where most of the action occurs, evokes a sense of danger, uncertainty, and mystery much like that found in the conventional Gothic environment. And part derives from the character of Harvey Birch himself—a "mysterious being," as Dunwoodie calls him (p. 224)—whose background, appearance, and behavior reveal his relation to a whole range of traditional Gothic characters.

An elusive figure whose movements are hidden under cover of darkness, Harvey Birch comes from a family on which the judgment of God has fallen, and he moves through the world as a pariah who has no home among men. He is often associated, at least in the minds of the credulous, with the demonic; he appears and disappears, in Captain Lawton's words, "like a spectre" (p. 278); and he cannot find peace in his wanderings. But if certain aspects of Birch suggest, as one critic has argued,[13] the legend of the Wandering Jew, others seem to relate him to figures in German rationalist fiction. His great skill at disguise and deception links him to Charles Brockden Brown's Ormond, and through him to a whole group of German deceivers of the 1790s who, completely rational and political in their actions, make easy dupes of those who cannot penetrate their disguises—or their motives. In a sense Harvey Birch is both types of Gothic character, and he is neither. Cooper associates him with Gothic figures not to create an American version of the Wandering Jew or Schiller's Armenian but to suggest his function as the physical embodiment of those qualities that pervade his mysterious environment.

Seen in these terms, *The Spy* marks an important step in the domestication of literary Gothicism in America. Cooper found in the mode a useful means for evoking one aspect of the American landscape and for transforming so native a character as Birch, a New England peddler, into a creature of mystery. When he turned to the border romance, therefore, in *The Last of the Mohicans* (1826) and *The Prairie* (1827), it was natural for him to use those techniques in the new genre. The wilderness, after all, resembles the Neutral Ground as a place of danger, darkness, insecurity, and mystery, and the characters are placed in even more frightening situations than those in *The Spy*. The caves at Glens Falls and the Indian burial ground in *Mohicans* are clearly American versions of the Gothic environment, and the Indians serve as the counterparts of demons and specters in Gothic romance. Even Chingachgook, the friendly chief, frightens Alice and Cora Munro when he stalks, "a spectral-looking figure" (p. 56), out of the darkness of the cave, and both Magua in *Mohicans* and Mahtoree in *The Prairie* are depicted as Satanic figures, while their followers are seen as demons ranging the dark woods or galloping over the desolate prairies.

In both books, moreover, Cooper exploits the sense of Gothic terror. The wild cry, "neither human nor earthly," that rises in the night and rings through the cavern in *Mohicans* (p. 62) strikes fear into the hearts of all who hear it, and even the firmness of Hawkeye starts to give way before a danger he does not understand and cannot prepare to meet. Though the screams turn out to be those of a horse in mortal fear—a sound that Duncan Heyward at last identifies—Cooper develops the incident like a Gothic master to suggest the great insecurity of the whites in the forest wilderness. Similar incidents recur throughout the book. Alice and Cora cannot escape a feeling of horror when they take refuge in the Mohawk burial ground, and Duncan Heyward must suppress the fear that ghosts are walking among the dead who lie about Fort William Henry after the massacre. Indeed, near the end of the action the cave at the Huron camp, through which the whites and the Delawares pursue the fleeing Magua, appears "like the shades of the infernal regions, across which unhappy ghosts and savage demons were flitting in multitudes" (p. 405).

In *The Prairie,* too, "a band of wild horsemen" whirl silently across the plains as one might imagine "a troop of spectres would pass," and the group of warriors who scale the rock where Ishmael Bush makes camp appear "like naked demons flitting among the clouds" (pp. 36, 270). But by far the most Gothic scene in either book occurs when Ishmael Bush hangs his brother-in-law, Abiram White, for the murder of his son. Bush leaves him alone on a thin ledge with a noose around his neck, then waits at a distance for him to fall and die. The scene is one of appalling horror which Cooper underscores with Gothic effects. As Bush watches and listens, the rising wind sounds "like the whisperings of the dead," and he thinks he hears unearthly shrieks surging around him, now in the upper air and now "at the very portals of his ears." Unable to stand it longer, he starts toward the place where he left Abiram White, and there comes at last "a cry in which there could be no delusion [and] to which the imagination could lend no horror." Ishmael Bush is galvanized by the sound. It is followed by "a profound silence" (pp. 432-33).

The death of Abiram White is without question a most effective Gothic scene and comes as a kind of climax both to the novel itself and to the developing Leatherstocking series that had now grown to three tales. *The Pioneers* (1823), the first of the books, contains no Gothic incidents, for it is primarily a social novel that describes a secure if changing village set in a natural environment that white men are shaping to their will. In *The Last of the Mohicans* and *The Prairie,* on the other hand, Cooper focuses sharply on the darker aspects of the American landscape—the terrible insecurity felt by the whites who find themselves alone in the threatening wilderness, the terror inspired in them by the hostile Indians, and, in the latter book, the horror suggested by the lawless whites who have moved beyond the control of society and represent a world in many ways more frightening than that of the Indians. To represent these fears and insecurities through Gothic devices was a happy invention, for by their use Cooper was able to project the very real terrors of the wilderness in terms that would satisfy the Gothic taste of his readers.

Cooper turned away from the Gothic mode when he wrote the last two books in the series: *The Pathfinder* (1840) and *The Deerslayer* (1841). Though danger still lurks in the wilderness and hostile Indians threaten, Cooper chooses to emphasize not the dark but the bright expansive side of the American landscape—the harmony, "solemn grandeur," and "holy calm" of untouched nature[14]—qualities that are the very antithesis of Gothic darkness, enclosure, and fear. Thus, although Cooper does include a few Gothic touches—the superstition of the Scottish soldiers, an echo perhaps of Sir Walter Scott, in the former book, and the appearance of Hetty Hutter, specterlike, in the Huron camp, in the latter—the dominant tone of both is anything but Gothic. To follow the line of development that Cooper had opened in *The Last of the Mohicans* and *The Prairie*, therefore, we must turn to another writer, Robert Montgomery Bird, whose *Nick of the Woods* surpasses even *The Last of the Mohicans* in the darkness of its wilderness landscape, the demonic strain that runs through its violent action, and above all the evocation of Gothic terror in the mysterious being that gives the book its name.

To the Indians he is the Jibbenainosay, the Spirit-that-walks, "neither man nor beast, but a great ghost or devil that knife cannot harm nor bullet touch." The scourge of the Indian tribes, he brains, scalps, and carves a cross in the flesh of any warrior unfortunate enough to encounter him. Though all the tribes fear him, the Shawnee hold him in particular dread because of the havoc he has wrought among their warriors. To the settlers in Kentucky, on the other hand, Nick of the Woods, as they call him, is no less a devil, but he seems to be their guardian or protector because his bloody deeds have so frightened the redmen that they no longer dare to skulk around the settlements. Some of the white men claim to have seen him, "a great tall fellow with horns and a hairy head like a buffalo-bull," led by a bear that points the way through the deepest forest, and many more have seen the sign of his presence, the deep gashes in the bodies of his fallen foes that seem to indicate a "wantonness of . . . malice and lust of blood which even death could not satisfy" (pp. 65, 66, 123).

That Nick of the Woods turns out to be only a man does not detract in any way from the horror of the book, for the truth is more terrible than the superstitious delusions of both whites and Indians. He is actually Nathan Slaughter, a mild-mannered Quaker turned Indian hater by his treatment at the hands of Wenonga, the Shawnee chief. To show his good will and desire for peace, Nathan once handed his weapons to the chief, only to see them used to kill his wife and children. Wenonga then struck him in the head, scalped him, and left him to die. Though Nathan recovered from his wounds and still retains his reputation as a man of peace, the damage to his skull affected his brain, and Nathan is subject to epileptic fits from which he emerges transformed into Nick of the Woods. Indeed, in the final battle at the Shawnee camp, Nathan appears at his most terrible, the scalps of his wife and children, retrieved from the lodge of Wenonga, in his left hand, while in his right he brandishes an axe red to the helve with Wenonga's blood, and grasps the reeking scalp of the chief.

In a sense Nathan Slaughter is both madman and devil. Though he has been grievously wronged, he pursues his revenge with a single-minded purpose that is surely demonic. He proves himself to be at least as brutal as the most cold-hearted Shawnee warrior and even more hardened than the most callous Kentuckians, who treat the redmen like vermin. Nathan becomes, in effect, the very embodiment of frontier cruelty and violence, the most terrible figure in a brutal world where barbaric warfare is waged in the spirit of hatred and revenge. Bird depicts a fallen world in *Nick of the Woods*,[15] peopled by men whose actions seem to suggest that something demonic lurks in human nature, "as if, indeed, the earth of which man is framed had been gathered only after it had been trodden by the foot of the Prince of Darkness" (p. 327). So bleak a vision of reality demanded the dark landscape, lurid descriptions, and violent action that Bird provides, qualities that make the book not only the most Gothic of border romances but also the culmination of a line of development—the naturalization of Gothic techniques and devices—that Cooper had begun in *The Spy*.

Other American writers of the 1820s and 1830s viewed the Gothic mode in quite a different way—not, like Cooper and Bird, as a means for projecting some very real terrors of the American wilderness, but, like Washington Irving, as a source for humor. By the mid-1820s, especially in *Bracebridge Hall* and *Tales of a Traveller*, Irving had established the comic as an important aspect of American Gothicism. Success breeds imitation, and before the decade was over others had followed his lead.

Both William Cullen Bryant and James Kirke Paulding so admired "The Legend of Sleepy Hollow," perhaps the classic tale of the sportive Gothic, that they both wrote comic stories that closely resemble it. In Bryant's "A Border Tradition" (1826) and Paulding's "Cobus Yerkes" (1827), a superstitious man, made fearful by tales of ghosts and specters, is thoroughly terrified on his way home one night by a perfectly natural phenomenon: a girl dressed in a sheet who wants to scare him, in Bryant's tale, and his own dog, that Cobus takes for an incarnate devil, in Paulding's.[16] Both stories suffer, of course, from being such close imitations, but they indisputably show the strong influence of Irving on some, at least, of his contemporaries.

A much more original but nonetheless Irvingesque tale is "The Legend of the Devil's Pulpit" (1827). Written mostly by Bryant, in collaboration with Robert C. Sands and perhaps Gulian C. Verplanck,[17] it presents the experience of one William Vince, a cockney tailor in eighteenth-century New York, who takes a pair of black men for goblins, is transported by accident to New Jersey, and returns to New York with a tale of devil worship on the other side of the Hudson. The reader perceives at once that Vince, like Irving's Wolfert Webber in *Tales of a Traveller* (1824), has chanced upon a band of smugglers, and the treatment of his predicament is comic. In the latter half of the story, moreover, when the rationalist Dr. Magraw leads a party of frightened men to arrest the smugglers, the authors present the legend, tongue in cheek, as popular superstition has recorded it. In the intervening years, the tale has become a real devil story in which Dr. Magraw had to collar and chastise an actual demon! The comic tone is well maintained throughout to establish the tale as a good example of the sportive Gothic.

Yet another Irvingesque story appears in John Pendleton Kennedy's *Swallow Barn* (1832), a book written partly in imitation of, and partly in reaction against, *Bracebridge Hall* (1822). Although Kennedy burlesques incidents in Irving's book (most notably his treatment of falconry)[18] these loosely connected volumes of sketches are much alike in both content and form, and Kennedy's handling of the supernatural owes a great deal to Irving. The story of Mike Brown, the only Gothic element in the book, is a tale told in the Irving manner, twice removed from the original source. Hafen Blok, an ex-Hessian soldier, tinker, and purveyor of old ballads and legends, has told the tale of Mike's encounters with the devil to a group of educated listeners who encourage the telling but who do not really believe that they ever occurred. Mark Littleton, the narrator of the book, then recounts the tale for the reader with "some rhetorical embellishments" and places it in a context that clearly reveals his disbelief. He includes a comic paragraph burlesquing the usual Gothic setting; and, arguing that the devil and his progeny have long departed from the Atlantic states, he introduces the story as the "Chronicle of the Last of the Virginia Devils" (pp. 263-64).

The story itself has something of Irving's tone. Mike Brown, a black-smith and ex-Revolutionary cavalryman, is part Rip Van Winkle, part Bold Dragoon, with perhaps a touch of Dolph Heyliger. "A free and easy, swaggering, sociable chap" who loves his liquor and fears "neither ghost nor devil" (pp. 268, 273), Mike first encounters a specter horse and demon rider as he makes his way home one winter night after a long carouse. Mike is not intimidated. He shows the devil so little respect that the offended demon threatens to teach him some manners, and later that night Mike even refuses to shoe the hoof of a devil he sees dancing around his room. Some years later, however, the devil takes his revenge. He lures Mike into a neighboring swamp to rake the bottom of a pond for gold, and when Mike, who has been drinking heavily, comes to his senses, he is tired, wet, and none the richer for his efforts. Finally, after a long night at the tavern, Mike challenges the devil to a duel, but he is again tricked by the demon and ends up in the swamp, covered with mud and with green slime clinging to his shoulders.

Kennedy makes no attempt to create a sense of Gothic terror in his story, nor does he even pretend that the devils may be real. Mike sees them only when he has been drinking, and, except perhaps for the first appearance of the spectral horse and rider, all the encounters are comic. The method of presentation also contributes to the Irvingesque effect. Though the tale is supposed to be based on a first-hand account, the reli-ability of the source is undercut at all levels. Hafen Blok admits that Mike Brown, from whom he claims to have heard the tale, was "a mon-strous liar, and an uncommon hard drinker," and Mark Littleton, who has reshaped Blok's version for the reader, adds his own caution: since "Mike was a little prone to exaggerate when his personal prowess was in question, the judicious reader will make some grains of allowance on that score" (pp. 293-94). Of all who hear the tale from Hafen Blok, only the black slaves, who gather around the porch when he tells the story, accept the events in perfect faith as real occurrences in the actual world. The educated whites dismiss them with a quip.

Although stories like these clearly reveal the unmistakable mark of Irving's well known practice, they tell us little or nothing about the sportive Gothic as a literary mode outside his special forte, the short tale. Since Irving never produced an extended work of fiction, it remained for another to introduce the comic Gothic to the novel: James Kirke Paulding, his friend and collaborator in the first series of *Salmagundi*. Paulding and Irving were much alike in attitude and taste. Both were thoroughgoing realists with a strong penchant for satire and a keen sense of humor, but Paulding was more averse than Irving to the use of Gothic trappings, and he did not even toy with them, as Irving did in *Bracebridge Hall* and *Tales of a Traveller*. In his essay on "National Literature" (1820), he simply asserted: "The aid of superstition, the agency of ghosts, fairies, goblins, and all that antiquated machinery which till lately was confined to the nursery, is not necessary to excite our wonder or interest our feelings," and he based his own novels on realistic characters, natural events, and rational causes. [19]

Paulding's realistic principles had important consequences for his use of the Gothic mode. In his first two novels, *Koningsmarke* (1823) and *The Dutchman's Fireside* (1831), he portrayed the American past, including border warfare, in a realistic fashion, and although in the former book he does include an unusual clap of thunder that frightens the Indians and keeps them from burning their prisoners, it is presented as a natural—if providential—occurrence. But Paulding's fictional principles did allow room for the Gothic. Since some men in the real world do believe in ghosts, specters, and witches, they must be shown as they are, frightened at noises and shadows which their fears make them interpret as supernatural manifestations. The author, however, is free to reveal his own attitude toward them in any way he pleases. He may simply present his characters as sharing the common beliefs of a particular historical period, or he may turn to satire and comedy to ridicule their credulity. As historical novelist and satirist, Paulding found both means useful in treating the Gothic material he saw fit to include in his books.

In *Koningsmarke*, for example, Paulding develops a strong Gothic strain throughout a major part of the book, embodied in the person and actions of a black slave, Bombie of the Frizzled Head, the property of

Peter Piper, governor of Elsingburgh in New Sweden. Bombie behaves in so strange a manner and makes such oracular pronouncements that she is rumored to be a witch. Her "peculiar appearance and habits," coupled with reports of witchcraft in New England as recorded in Cotton Mather's *Magnalia,* strengthen these suspicions, for this is the seventeenth century, and such beliefs are general among the people. The reader, of course, soon learns that she is nothing of the kind. Bombie simply prowls at night and learns those "secrets of darkness" that seem to others to be "the result of some supernatural insight into the ways of men,"[20] but she plays her part extremely well, couching her speeches in figurative language and implying much more than she actually says. When pressed to explain, she merely repeats, "I have seen what I have seen—I know what I know" (1: 48 and passim). Small wonder, then, that the superstitious Swedes, including her master, are afraid of her.

Bombie is a serious character, and she is used for a serious purpose. She devotedly serves Christina, the governor's daughter, because of the kindness that Christina's mother has shown her, but she is hostile to Koningsmarke and opposes his marriage to the girl because she believes—mistakenly—that he was responsible for the mother's death years before in Finland. She is also devoted to her own son, Cupid, who brings her to grief by helping the Indians in their attack on Elsingburgh. Cupid is eventually apprehended by Lob Dotterel, the constable, and is tried and condemned for his treachery. The distraught Bombie pleads for her son's life, but the governor is obdurate, and she rails against the whole white race for what they have done to her people. Bombie assumes considerable stature in this episode and elicits a great deal of sympathy from the reader, especially when her son is hanged and she dies of grief, cursing the race that has enslaved her. Up to this point Paulding has well maintained the sense of mystery that surrounds her, and he even presents in a rather straightforward fashion the popular belief that Bombie's and Cupid's ghosts haunt the village and appear at night to Lob Dotterel.

But in one brief passage, Paulding undercuts whatever sense of the Gothic the book may have for the reader. When the men of the village, gathered one stormy night at the inn, discuss the recent events, Lob Dotterel is called upon to verify the visitations he is said to have received. He tells a tale of Bombie's appearing to him one night and of feeling her heavy hands press upon his shoulders until he falls into a faint. This tale leads to another. Wolfgang Langfanger recounts an experience he had twenty years before in his native Sweden. He took refuge during a stormy night in a ruined church and soon fell asleep. Awakened by the hooting of an owl, he confronted a terrible female figure with "lank face, hollow cheeks, and glaring eyes" who kissed him "with lips that semed covered with the damps and mildews of the sepulchre" (2: 167-68). Then, just as the fortress fired the signal gun for dawn, she kissed him again and disappeared in the darkness. Though he learned in the village next day that she was only a crazy woman who never harmed a soul, he was horrified to hear that she kissed only those who were very soon to die!

That twenty years have passed and Wolfgang Langfanger yet lives makes the reader smile. So too does the recognition that Wolfgang's tale is really a parody of Matthew Gregory Lewis's story of the Bleeding Nun, who plants repeated kisses on the lips of Don Raymond in *The Monk.* The reader is thus prepared for what follows. Master Lowright, a jolly peddler from New York, whets his listeners' appetite for horrors by telling a tale of his confrontation with a beggar who seems intent on killing him. When he ends the tale with the outrageous statement that the beggar in fact did so, his listeners start up and stare at him in horror, half afraid that they have been entertaining a ghost. At this point, a loud clap of thunder rolls, a terrible thumping noise and loud shrieks are heard in the garret, and the panic-stricken men fall over one another in terror—only to learn that the commotion was caused by a pair of fighting cats! The whole Gothic episode thus dissolves into laughter, as it so often does in the works of Washington Irving, creating a comic effect that undercuts as well the sense of mystery that Paulding has been developing, if only half seriously, throughout the book.

Two Gothic episodes in *The Dutchman's Fireside* serve the similar purpose of poking fun at the superstitious fears of the unsophisticated, in this case the black slaves and the Dutch. Paulding uses the device of a live man appearing as a ghost to those who think him dead when Sybrandt Westbrook, the hero of the novel, returns unexpectedly from the wilderness, where he was reported to have been killed, and terrifies the blacks, who think they have seen a spook. A second comic episode involves a Dutch captain, Baltus Van Slingerland, the skipper of a Hudson River sloop. He attributes "a wild shrill shriek or howl" heard from shore to the ghost of an old woman who is said to haunt the region, but each time he starts to tell the story to his passengers, the cries are repeated until they seem at last to come from the mast of the ship. As he begins for the fourth time, the supposed apparition, with "a tremendous scream," strikes him a blow in the face that sends him sprawling, and a great commotion is heard at the chicken coop. The spook turns out to be only a large owl.[21]

These two episodes are so brief and undeveloped, however, that by themselves they contribute little to the meaning or tone of the book. Much more important is the sportive Gothic imagery that Paulding uses to characterize his hero. Although Sybrandt Westbrook is an educated and accomplished young man, he has one flaw that seriously detracts from his character. He is ruled by a vivid and self-centered imagination which prevents him from functioning well in society. Paulding projects this aspect of his personality, in the first half of the book, through the use of Gothic imagery. Let someone only make a remark that Sybrandt can take as disparagement and the young man immediately applies it to himself. "His apprehensive pride [conjures] up specter after specter, grinning and pointing their fingers at him in bitter or playful scorn" (p. 54). His acute embarrassment turns the sufferer into himself, creates a false impression of his talents and abilities, and makes it impossible for him to join naturally in the social gathering. Sybrandt is thus bedeviled through much of the book, his emotional state revealed through a recurring image of phantoms and demons that seem to haunt him whenever he feels insecure in society.

This device was a particularly happy one, for it took a well established Gothic technique and reduced it to comedy. Gothic writers had often used such phantoms of the imagination to reveal a disordered mind or guilty conscience, and the specters raised by them are frequently objects of terror. To use the device, therefore, as Paulding does, to reveal the self-conscious embarrassment of an awkward and tongue-tied young man is to turn it to a comic purpose. However Sybrandt himself may suffer at such moments, he cuts a ludicrous figure in society, and the reader can only smile at his predicament. In Paulding's view, moreover, the cure is obvious. The demons will disappear when the young man comes out of himself, considers the needs of others, and joins with them in rational social intercourse. In other words, Paulding has used the sportive device of the demons to affirm his belief in fundamentally social values. He posits a world where outgoing men may act together in reason and common sense. Such a world, he believes, can provide no place for the Gothic terrors which he, like Irving, so often treats with humor.

Because the comic Gothic so strongly affirms a rational intellectual order, its use in American romance was short lived. Acting under the influence of new romantic ideas, many American writers preferred to turn their attention to the aberrations themselves, and following the lead of Charles Brockden Brown, began to examine the more serious aspect of mental delusion. Even those who accepted the rationalistic view contributed to this development, and the psychological Gothic eventually came to dominate the mode in America. Brown had not been especially influential during his lifetime, and only a few readers kept his memory alive after his death in 1810. But the appearance of William Dunlap's biography of him in 1815, the review of that book by E.T. Channing in the *North American Review* (1819), Paulding's praise of him in the second series of *Salmagundi* (1820), John Neal's treatment of him in *Randolph* (1823) and in *Blackwood's Edinburgh Magazine* (1824), and Richard Henry Dana's review of the first collected edition of his works in the *United States Review and Literary Gazette* (1827)[22]—all helped to revive his reputation. Moreover, three of these writers, including Paulding, wrote in the Gothic vein that Brown had introduced.

Charles Brockden Brown's appeal to American writers in the early nineteenth century is easy to understand. He had written the first—and, until the appearance of *The Spy* in 1821, the only—American novels of originality, substance, and power, novels in which the sense of immediacy is strong and the characters and incidents are memorable. In the period of strong nationalistic feeling following the War of 1812, Brown's novels could only be admired by men like Neal and Paulding, who, however they might differ from each other in their literary theory and practice, encouraged the development of a native American literature, free from the imitation of foreign models. Brown had shown that the popular Gothic romance could be written in the United States without recourse to the outworn trappings of its European form. He had also shown that the mode, as he had altered it, could be used for serious thematic purposes. By throwing the focus of interest into the mind of a disturbed protagonist, he had given the Gothic romance a strong psychological cast and opened the way for its vigorous development among American writers of quite different temperaments and literary persuasions.

The most radically romantic of them was John Neal, who distrusted intellectual patterning in fiction and developed his novels through the ongoing experience of his characters.[23] The material he includes is simply what they perceive. Some is directly borrowed from Brown's novels. The mysterious voices that Oscar hears in *Logan* (1822), first telling him to kill his sister and then ordering him to forbear, are clearly drawn from *Wieland,* and the overwrought Archibald Oadley's somnambulism in *Seventy-Six* (1823) reminds one unmistakably of *Edgar Huntly.* More interesting, however, are the many hallucinations and dreamlike visions that appear in *Logan,* especially the incident on shipboard in which Harold, smitten by conscience for the sin of incest, first transforms the ship's ropes on which he fitfully sleeps into crawling serpents, and then suffers intensely as he feels his flesh rotting away from the poison they spread on his body. *Seventy-Six* is more restrained in its Gothicism, but even in this tale of the Revolution the distraught characters sometimes perceive frightening images which have no reality except in their own disturbed minds, and they even hear mysterious rappings that warn of approaching death.

Neal's main contribution to the American Gothic, however, was his use of New England witchcraft in *Rachel Dyer* (1828), probably his best book. Because of his theory of fiction, Neal could not simply dismiss the belief in witchcraft among seventeenth-century New Englanders as mere mental delusion. He had to accept the sights and sounds they perceived as the accurate record of their experience. The book is filled, therefore, with passages that detail the signs and portents, shapes and apparitions which the common belief of the time accepted as objectively real: "stars" that fall "in a shower," "heavy cannon" that roar "in the deep of the wilderness," "apparitions" that walk "in the high way," and "evil spirits" that go "abroad on the sabbath day."[24] As the story unfolds, moreover, women are tried for witchcraft, a curse is laid on the town, and even the children are caught up in the excitement. At last, toward the end of the book, George Burroughs, a minister who has defended the witches, is himself accused and brought to trial, and a witness testifies that he has killed his two wives, both of whom will rise against him if he denies the murders.

Neal develops the episode very effectively, mixing the wild stories of the accusers with the more valid perceptions of those in the courtroom who see in Burroughs's "extraordinary voice," "bold haughty carriage," and "wonderful power of words" (p. 222) evidence of an ability well above the ordinary—but, in their view, an ability that may come from a demonic source. A violent storm arises as the trial progresses, the light grows progressively darker, and thunder and lightning seem to shake the earth. So wrought up do the people become and so conditioned are they to believe in the imminent appearance of supernatural beings, that when Burroughs denies that he killed his wives, the nearly hysterical onlookers, in a remarkable mass delusion, actually see the dead women come to confound him. In the midst of so great an uproar, even Burroughs himself begins "to fear that of a truth preternatural shapes were about him" and influencing "the witnesses . . . by irresistible power" (p. 236). Neal presents no actual apparitions, apart from what the people, in their terror, say they have witnessed, but so fully realized is the emotional intensity of the scene that their delusions strike the reader with the force of a perceived reality.

James Fenimore Cooper also used the Puritan belief in witchcraft to create an effective though much less lurid Gothic episode in *The Wept of Wish-ton-Wish* (1829). Like Neal, Cooper refuses to judge the New England colonists by nineteenth-century standards, but, reminding the reader that even the most learned men of the times believed in witchcraft, signs, and omens, he presents the experience of the Puritans as they lived it. Thus when Eben Dudley is hunting one day in the Connecticut wilderness, he encounters a series of strange phenomena. He sees a deer behave in an odd manner, hears a loud noise high in the air, and meets a man who tells him that the Powers of Darkness have been persecuting believers in the towns near the Bay. Dudley tells the story to his fellow colonists when he returns from the hunt, and as they discuss what he has seen and heard, they unwittingly prepare their minds for the mysterious events that follow. Outside the postern the Puritans have hung a conch that anyone seeking admission to the settlement may blow, and as the settlers prepare to set a guard for the night, they hear its melancholy sound.

Since none of the settlers is without the walls, the colonists are surprised at the signal, but they soon discover it is a mysterious stranger who visited Mark Heathcote, the leader of the community, once before. The sense of mystery his appearance occasions is further deepened, however, by more sounds from the conch which seem to echo precisely the way the stranger blew it. When the men go to the gate and ask who seeks admission, they get no answer, but the sounds are soon repeated in just the same tones. All the colonists, and especially Eben Dudley, are deeply affected by this fearful manifestation, and when Dudley and the stranger go outside the palisades through a secret sally port to watch the gate, they are amazed to hear the conch sound while no one is at the postern. Cooper brings the sense of Gothic mystery to a climax at this point, only to reveal through a flying arrow the true cause of the strange occurrence, a band of hostile Indians. Instead of the supernatural visitation their minds have led them to expect, the men scramble to safety to meet the assault of their physical enemies.

Such Gothic effects are not, of course, the main point of these books. They are merely the means through which Neal and Cooper examine the problems involved in the act of perception, especially the reasons why people misperceive the objective world and the serious consequences that can flow from their delusion. Puritan New England provided appropriate material for the development of this theme, for during the seventeenth century the mental disposition of a whole group of people caused them to perceive a reality that had no objective basis, and the nature of their delusion—belief in witchcraft—made the Gothic mode the perfect means for presenting it. Most American writers of the early nineteenth century explore the theme, however, not in terms of mass delusion but of the problems faced by the individual whose intellectual make-up is such that he takes the world he misperceives for the world as it is. This was the subject of Charles Brockden Brown's major romances, and his followers in the 1820s and 1830s made it their own. They examine the causes of such mental aberrations, suggest a possible cure, and explore the intellectual questions raised by the whole problem of perception.

In *Lionel Lincoln,* for example, Cooper finds the cause of mental aberration in the inability of his protagonist to shake off the pernicious influence of the past. A morbid sensibility has afflicted the Lincoln family for many generations, manifesting itself most particularly in the gloomy withdrawal of Reginald Lincoln, Lionel's great-grandfather, into a narrow religious bigotry, and in the insanity of Lionel's father, who has long been confined to a madhouse. An educated man (Lionel is an Oxford graduate, Member of Parliament, and major in the British army during the siege of Boston), he nonetheless feels the influence of the hereditary bias of his race. His mind can at times create realities out of shadows. He flees in near terror down Copp's Hill one night because he interprets the strange sounds he hears as the dead rising from their graves, and he carefully searches the church on the night of his wedding because the flickering shadows make him feel a presentiment of evil. Though Lionel is never deluded for any length of time, he possesses an imagination that sometimes plays him false.

Dudley Rainsford, in Paulding's *Westward Ho!* (1832), on the other hand, is so deeply affected by the past that he completely loses his hold on reality. His grandfather was cursed by a man he wounded during the Revolution, and events since that time have convinced young Rainsford that, like his grandfather, father, and brothers before him, all of whom have dwelled upon the curse, he will go mad by the time he reaches a certain age. A sense of impending catastrophe thus haunts his imagination, a presentiment that he cannot shake off. He feeds his mental disease by reading books on his mania, and he is finally driven over the edge of sanity by an itinerant preacher who so plays on his morbid sensibiity that Rainsford comes to believe he must sever all earthly ties if he is to be saved. His disturbed mind becomes convinced that he must kill Virginia Dangerfield, the girl he loves. Though he does not actually carry out the murder—he cannot at the last moment bring himself to stab her—he does go mad and at one point perceives Virginia as a devil determined to bring him to damnation.

Both Lionel Lincoln and Dudley Rainsford are saved from their delusions by the women who love them. When Lincoln leaves Boston with the mad Ralph on the night of the wedding, the deserted bride, Cecil, follows him into the American camp, keeps him from being seduced to the rebel cause, and, after the British are forced to withdraw by the American besiegers, accompanies him to England. During the voyage they discuss "the wanderings of intellect which had so closely and mysteriously connected" him with his "deranged father," descend "to the secret springs of his disordered impulses," and finally remove all "obscurity and doubt" from the incidents that have affected him.[25] In a similar fashion, Virginia Dangerfield never gives up on her lover. She cares for him when everyone thinks it is useless, and with the help of Father Jacques, who mingles "a rational philosophy with a rational religion,"[26] she brings him back to sanity. Both young men go out of themselves, accept the love and support of a faithful woman, banish the morbid fears that came to them from the past, and so are cured of the mental disease that has so grievously afflicted them.

Not every writer, of course, was so optimistic as Cooper and Paulding. Some, like Richard Henry Dana and Washington Allston, found the sources of mental delusion so deeply imbedded in the mind as to hardly admit of a cure. Dana and Allston were early admirers of Samuel Taylor Coleridge and became much interested in his work. Allston had met him in Italy on his first European tour and became his lifelong friend, and both he and Dana were among his earliest readers in the United States. They became especially interested in the romantic imagination, the creative force which allows the mind to come into contact with ultimate reality, and they use as the basis for their major works of fiction the reality that comes into being when mind and matter, the perceiver and the thing perceived, unite in the act of perception. The results, however, are not always positive. For Dana and Allston, as for others, the power of the imagination could sometimes be negative. If the darkness within the human mind controlled the act of perception, it created a vision not of beauty or truth but of madness and horror.[27]

In "Paul Felton" (1822), Dana presents such a case. The son of a widowed father who is often "lost in his own thoughts," Paul Felton grows up in almost complete isolation. He has no companions of his own class and education, and the uncouth, illiterate people of the neighborhood are so openly hostile that Paul comes to look "on strangers as in some sort enemies."[28] His insecurity fills him with self-doubts, and he spends his time alone, probing his thoughts and feelings. Though he meets, loves, and marries the cheerful Esther Waring, his early experience has given him a gloomy cast of mind. Esther is, of course, a healthy influence on Paul, but it soon becomes apparent that instead of curing his morbidity she runs the danger of succumbing to his melancholy. Even before they are married, she sees "something ominous . . . in his gloom; and though she knew it had been caused by long solitude and a mistaken estimate of the relation in which he might stand to others, still it was mysteriously foreboding to her, and there was an indistinct impression on the mind that some dreadful event, connected with it, awaited her" (p. 285).

Though Paul is happy with Esther, his state seems unreal to him, and he begins "to fear that his hopes and imagination had cheated him into" a visionary happiness. When, "in his saner moments," he cannot doubt its reality, he retains a vague notion that it will not be permanent. "A feeling, like those ill forebodings which sometimes come over us and then go off again," increasingly gains "possession of him, bringing back his old melancholy, troubling his reason, and distorting what he" perceives (pp. 295-96). Obsessive in his desire to be all in all to Esther, he does not know how to estimate justly the obvious pleasure she takes in society. When her old—and rejected—lover appears on the scene, Esther, in all innocence, enjoys his visits and takes delight in the village dance that all of them attend. Misreading her gaiety, however, Paul becomes jealous. He wanders alone into a wild and desolate tract that adjoins his property and falls under the influence of a mad boy named Abel, who believes he is haunted by devils. Though Paul knows the child is insane, he cannot "shake off the feeling, that the miserable wretch [is] the victim of a demon" (p. 318).

Once this idea occurs to him, Paul begins to think of his passions as ugly devils stirring within him. He takes "a perverse satisfaction in self-torture," and he even wants "to make certain" what his "jealousy and superstition had imaged" (p. 338). Paul finally goes mad, a process that Dana, like Brown in *Edgar Huntly,* projects through the action and setting: the deserted tract through which Paul wanders and the solitary hut, called the Devil's Haunt, that lies there.[29] When he enters the hut one night, Paul has a frightening vision that transforms him into a homicidal maniac. The hut seems to expand and shadows of terrible beings flit about him. His own form seems to undergo a change, "taking the shape and substance of the accursed ones" that surround him (p. 339). The ground pitches and rocks, darkness fills the hut, and Paul awakes to find his hand clutching a rusty dagger that has been stuck in the wall. Taking this as a sign, he cleans and sharpens it, and when fully—though mistakenly—convinced of his wife's infidelity, he enters her room one night, waits for a command that only he can hear, and plunges it into her heart.

Washington Allston's Monaldi[30] undergoes a similar experience. Like Paul Felton, he has spent his childhood among illiterate boors and has shrunk into himself, but, sent at age twelve to a proper school, he has escaped Paul's mental gloom. Monaldi becomes at last a successful painter, marries the beautiful and accomplished Rosalia Landi, and lives a happy life. His delusion, therefore, comes not from morbidity of mind.

It is deliberately caused by Maldura, whom Monaldi considers his best and oldest friend. Because he envies Monaldi's success and hates him for winning Rosalia, who had refused him, Maldura hires Fialto, a notorious seducer, to create the impression that he is having an affair with Monaldi's wife. So successful are Fialto's deceits that Monaldi becomes convinced his wife is unfaithful, and in a fit of jealous passion he stabs her and leaves her for dead. Yet, dupe though he may be of Fialto's deceptions, the evil that destroys Monaldi's happiness comes as much from within as from without. Like Paul Felton, he is predisposed by jealousy to misinterpret what he perceives in the external world, and as a result he attacks the woman who, in Cooper's and Paulding's view, might have helped him maintain his mental balance.

Monaldi's story, however, does not end here. Though he disappears for a time after the attempted murder, he is eventually found by the now remorseful Maldura, who, shocked at his madness, cares for him until he returns to sanity. When he finally reveals that Rosalia has survived and was innocent of any wrongdoing, Monaldi rejoices, but when Maldura goes on to confess that it was he who hired Fialto to deceive him, Monaldi again goes mad. The treachery of one he had trusted and admired since boyhood is more than he can bear, and in his insanity he perceives Maldura as a demon and his wife, who is powerless to help him, as a specter. Despite his madness, however, Monaldi retains his ability to paint. After a time he returns to his art and creates a ghastly canvas that reveals his vision of reality. Monaldi's imagination has always been active, combining and giving life to images that have come to him through the senses. But now his darkened mind projects a vision of the Prince of evil as he has seen him in this world, an image of deadly beauty that entices men to damnation.

Dana and Allston take a dark view of humanity. Evil lurks within all men, they seem to say, not merely the envious Maldura and the sensual Fialto, but even the upright if melancholy Paul Felton and the intelligent and urbane Monaldi. Because they hold this view, Dana and Allston create a kind of Gothic tale that is much more serious than those of many of their predecessors and contemporaries. For other Gothic writers mental delusion was most often an aberration of otherwise rational minds. It affected the ignorant and superstitious, the conscience stricken, and those who through misplaced reading exposed themselves to it. In all such cases, the imagination, always an untrustworthy faculty, was at fault, but the phantoms it raised could easily be dispelled through reason and common sense, the norms of all mental activity. With Dana and Allston, however, the imagination becomes the central means for leading men toward truth. When it is perverted, therefore, it creates not an aberration which can be corrected through reason but an alternate reality which, in the case of Paul Felton and Monaldi, displaces the common-sense order of things and totally absorbs the mind.

A variation on this idea appears in two stories by William Cullen Bryant in which he explores the problem faced by men whose vivid experience contradicts their reason.[31] In "The Indian Spring" (1829), the narrator has a frightening encounter with a spectral Indian who stares at him with burning eyes, pursues him through the woods, leaps at him, and leaves him unconscious in a forest glade. And in "Medfield" (1832), a man of strong passions who has promised his dying wife that he will control his temper feels himself restrained by ghostly hands whenever he is about to commit a violent act. Though their friends would explain these phenomena as "nothing but a dream" or "only a delusion of the imagination,"[32] the men themselves cannot dismiss them so easily. However convincing the rational explanations may seem to be, they have experienced the bizarre events as objectively real. They have seen or felt them with the same organs of sense that report to them the ordinary experiences of the everyday world, and they cannot reject the one without rejecting the other. Since both realities depend on the same kind of evidence, the men have no means for distinguishing between them.[33]

The imagination did not, of course, always lead to such an impasse. It was sometimes the means for discerning the truth behind deceptive appearance, the function it serves in Simms's *Martin Faber* (1833), a tale of the imagination in which a criminal is brought to justice through its agency. A man of undisciplined passion and unbridled will, Martin Faber murders Emily Andrews, a girl he has seduced, and throws her body into a cavity of a large rock in the forest. Because the crime took place in the heart of the woods, no suspicion fell on him for the girl's disappearance, and Martin Faber might have gone scot-free but for the strange compulsion he feels, the perverse desire to confess. Like Coleridge's Ancient Mariner,[34] he is impelled to tell his story to his lifelong friend, William Harding. Martin is careful, however, not to reveal the name of the victim, and he so changes the details of the crime that when William, unable to stand the terrible knowledge he possesses, accuses

Martin publicly, the facts as he has related them cannot be verified, Martin is released, and William is scorned for bringing false witness against his friend.

William is therefore determined to learn the truth. He accompanies Martin in his rambles about the countryside, staying so close to him as to become almost a second self, the conscience perhaps to Martin's will. His powerful imagination allows him to read in his companion's face the relation between a particular place or thing and Martin's guilty mind. In this way, William discovers the scene of the crime and the rock where the body is concealed. He even learns the identity of the victim. Imagination matches imagination, and William, who can paint, begins to depict in a series of canvases accurate representations of the murder, which, as he has observed, still haunts Martin's consciousness. He has read the mind and heart of his companion and projects what he has discovered for other men to see. To bring Martin Faber to justice, of course, William Harding must find the external evidence that a court of law will accept, but that part of the process is mere confirmation of what he has already learned. The imagination alone has allowed him to penetrate the secret soul of his companion to discover the truth that lay buried there.

Although Dana, Allston, and Bryant hold no important place in the history of American fiction and Simms is much better known for his historical and border romances than for his Gothic tales, they made an important contribution to the development of American Gothicism. Other American writers had also made significant use of the mode, adapting the techniques of the British and German romancers to the American scene to depict, in Cooper and Bird, the terrors of the American wilderness, or to laugh, like Paulding, at the follies of the superstitious and the inept; and some of them—Neal, Cooper, and Paulding—had begun to examine the psychological questions raised by the problem of misperception. But these four writers went further in their analysis to explore more deeply the nature of the human mind, the power of the imagination, its function in the act of perception, and its relation to the problem of knowledge. Their achievement was important. They foreshadowed the kind of fiction that would focus intensely on the problem of perceived realities and opened the way for the further development of the American Gothic in the works of Edgar Allan Poe and Nathaniel Hawthorne.

SEVEN

Edgar Allan Poe

When Edgar Allan Poe began to publish fiction in the early 1830s, he was well aware that the Gothic mode provided an important means for attracting and holding an audience. Among his earliest tales are "Metzengerstein" (1832), an imitation of the German, as he once called it,[1] in which a demonic horse, the reincarnation of his enemy, carries Frederick of Metzengerstein to his death; "The Visionary" (1834), later called "The Assignation," in whch Poe exploits the darkness and gloom of the Italian setting to tell a tale of double suicide; and "Berenice" (1835), his most horrible story, in which an obsessed protagonist draws the teeth of the prematurely interred Berenice while her body still lives. Poe knew what he was about. Though he admitted to Thomas W. White of the *Southern Literary Messenger* that "Berenice" was indeed "by far too horrible," it was the kind of story that is "invariably sought after with avidity," that is frequently reprinted in other periodicals and papers, and that takes firm "hold upon the public mind." Since in order to be appreciated one has to be read, Poe turned unabashedly to the popular Gothic tale in order to make his way as a writer of fiction.[2]

Poe was already well versed in the Gothic mode. Critics have discerned the influence of British Gothic fiction in his earliest published stories: *The Castle of Otranto* in "Metzengerstein" and *The Mysteries of Udolpho* in "The Assignation;" and "A Decided Loss" (1832), later expanded into "Loss of Breath" (1835), is an obvious satire on the horror stories in *Blackwood's Edinburgh Magazine*.[3] Poe further satirized such tales in "How to Write a Blackwood's Article" (1838), but he also borrowed from them for some of his most effective fiction and wrote in "The Pit and the Pendulum" (1842) a tale which derives in part from at least two *Blackwood's* stories, but which, as Thomas O. Mabbott has observed, is superior to its models.[4] As Poe's career developed, moreover, he revealed in both his critical essays and his tales his wide knowledge of British, American, and German Gothic writers. We cannot always be sure, of course, how early or how well he knew the many authors, books, and tales he mentions, but taken in the aggregate they certainly reveal that his interest in the Gothic mode was wide ranging and endured throughout his life.

In addition to Walpole and Radcliffe, Poe knew and admired the novels of William Godwin, especially *Caleb Williams* and *St. Leon,* and he quotes Godwin's *Mandeville* in "Loss of Breath." He borrowed a detail from Charles Robert Maturin's *Melmoth the Wanderer* for "The Pit and the Pendulum."[5] And he was familiar with the most Gothic romances of Sir Walter Scott: *The Antiquary; Anne of Geierstein,* from which he borrowed material for "Berenice," "The Pit and the Pendulum," "The Raven" (1845), and "The Domain of Arnheim" (1847); and *The Bride of Lammermoor,* which he calls "that most pure, perfect, and radiant gem of fictitious literature."[6] Among American writers, Poe greatly admired the works of Charles Brockden Brown. He thought at one time to write a critical study of Brown's novels, and he borrowed material from *Edgar Huntly* for both "The Pit and the Pendulum" and "A Tale of the Ragged Mountains" (1844). He considered Washington Irving's *Tales of a Traveller* as among the best in America, second perhaps only to Hawthorne's *Twice-told Tales* in merit, and he singled out for praise "The Story of the Young Italian." He seems to have been especially fond of William Gilmore Simms's *Martin Faber,* and he describes "Grayling; or, 'Murder Will Out'" as "an admirable tale," well conceived and well executed.[7]

The German influences on Poe's Gothicism are less easily traced. He probably knew Sir Walter Scott's "On the Supernatural in Fictitious Composition" with its long and important discussion of the works of E.T.A. Hoffmann, and he apparently borrowed details from Hoffmann's "The Entail," perhaps as he found it discussed in Scott, for both "Metzengerstein" and "The Fall of the House of Usher" (1839). We know that Poe was much taken with Fouqué's *Undine,* which he called "the finest romance in existence," and he especially liked the way the forms of the water sprites sometimes fade away "into shower and foam." But apart from these works and some mention of Ludwig Tieck,[8] Poe's knowledge of German and of German fiction has been a source of argument among scholars. Thomas O. Mabbott minimizes the influence of German tales on Poe and claims that his knowledge of German literature must have come through translation; Henry A. Pochmann, however, makes a persuasive case for Poe's knowledge of German and shows that Poe's interest in mesmerism and metempsychosis links him to Hoffmann, whose "Mesmerizer" Pochmann believes Poe directly echoes in "A Tale of the Ragged Mountains."[9]

The question is not a vital one. By the time Poe began to write fiction, American authors were drawing upon a large body of Gothic material that had been accumulating since the 1790s. It had become the common property of all writers of fiction, to be used by any who wished to do so. For this reason, it is best not to talk of sources but simply to show that some of the materials in Poe's tales had been current in Gothic writing for many years. In Karl Grosse's *Horrid Mysteries* (1797), for example, we find a series of incidents in which Elmira, the much loved and idealized wife of Don Carlos, seems to die three times in his presence only to turn up twice again alive and well, even after he once retains her body until decomposition has gone so far as to leave no doubt of her death. On one occasion, moreover, Elmira is buried alive and awakens in her coffin to find herself in a burial vault. Such passages cannot perhaps be considered sources for Poe's "Ligeia" (1838) or "The Premature Burial" (1844), but they certainly indicate that Poe was working in a long-established Gothic tradition.

In a similar fashion, what is important in "A Tale of the Ragged Mountains" is not that Poe may echo Hoffmann's tale but that, in the strange vision of Augustus Bedloe in the Virginia hills, Poe suggests the same kind of intersection of coterminous worlds that formed the staple of much German romantic fiction. The spirit world that Bedloe penetrates when he finds himself involved in a long-past insurrection in India recalls the strange experiences that characters in German fiction sometimes have—Anselmus, for example, in "The Golden Pot." Both characters suddenly perceive a world that bears no relation to their everyday realities, and both consider the bizarre events as actually happening. Like Hoffmann, too, Poe does not demand that we take the experience as real. Both include details that permit us to read the events as misperceptions, and Poe provides an explanation which, at the time, at least, would have been accepted as scientific: that Bedloe was mesmerized over a distance by Doctor Templeton,[10] who, at the time Bedloe has the experience, is writing an account of just the incident that Bedloe reports he has witnessed.

The point can be illustrated further. The famous scene at the end of "The Cask of Amontillado" (1846) in which Montresor walls up Fortunato and leaves him to die has many analogues: in *Count Roderic's Castle* (1794), where, behind a bricked-up door, a skeleton is found that, in the flesh, had been fastened to the wall by an iron waist-band and collar; in Godwin's *St. Leon* (1799), where Bethlem Gabor lures St. Leon into his dungeon and chains him to the wall; and in Maturin's *Melmoth the Wanderer* (1820), where a pair of lovers is led through a subterranean passage, ostensibly to escape a monastery, only to be left to die behind the nailed-shut door of a vault. The struggle between conscience and will in "William Wilson" (1839), moreover, has its analogue in Simms's *Martin Faber* (1833), especially in the early history of the two protagonists, both of whom escape the discipline of even their parents to do as they please. And Martin Faber's perverse desire to confess his crime to his friend parallels the use of perversity in many Poe stories, most especially "The Tell-Tale Heart" (1843), "The Black Cat" (1843), and "The Imp of the Perverse" (1845).

Because he drew so heavily on widely used Gothic materials, it was perhaps inevitable that some of Poe's tales—most often his weakest—should be direct imitations of the British and German schools. "Metzengerstein," for example, resembles the kind of tale that emanated from Germany and was occasionally picked up in Great Britain by writers such as Lewis and Maturin. It makes no attempt to explain away the demonic but presents its bizarre phenomena as real. "Life in Death" (1842), on the other hand (a tale later shortened and renamed "The Oval Portrait") is reminiscent in both atmosphere and content of the school of Ann Radcliffe, whom Poe mentions in passing. The tale takes place in a deserted chateau in the Apennines, where the protagonist, wounded by banditti, has taken refuge. Here he undergoes a strange experience with a mysterious painting—a staple of Gothic fiction. Though the story of the living picture can perhaps be taken at face value as a truly supernatural occurrence, there is a strong intimation, especially in the earlier version,[11] that the experience can be rationally explained. What the narrator perceives may be simply a delusion of the senses brought on by his wounds and the opium he has taken to ease his fever and let him sleep.

Poe also worked in the comic Gothic mode, but his tales of this type are also less than successful. He lacked the light touch of Irving, Paulding, and Kennedy, and to many readers today "The Premature Burial" and "The Sphinx" (1846) may appear to be rather heavy-handed attempts at humor. Yet both are much like other American comic Gothic tales in the psychological explanation Poe provides for the self-induced misperceptions of his protagonists. In "The Sphinx," for example, the narrator is obsessed with fear of death from cholera. Even though he lives up the Hudson, away from the source of contagion in New York, every breeze from the south seems to threaten him, and instead of allowing his rational friend to divert his thoughts, he feeds his latent superstition with ill-advised reading that only confirms him in his belief in omens. When he sees a monstrous creature appear on a distant hill, therefore, he considers the vision a warning of death or, worse, of approaching madness. What the narrator sees, however, is neither monster nor omen but merely a misperceived insect climbing a thread close to his eye. His overwrought mind projects the image into the external landscape where it assumes enormous size.

"The Premature Burial" presents a more frightening experience but resolves it in a similar way. The narrator fears that he may be buried alive, and he goes to extreme lengths to insure his escape from the coffin and vault should one of his cataleptic spells be mistaken for death and his friends prematurely inter him. His obsession is clearly revealed in a number of ways, not the least in the many tales he recounts—each more bizarre than the previous one—of people who have been buried alive, and in the wild dreams that, he informs us, haunt his sleep. So engrossing, indeed, are these tales that the unwary reader can be taken in by the final experience he records: he awakens one night in the dark to find himself surrounded by wooden boards and the air permeated with the odor of damp earth. He seems, in fact, to have been buried alive, but not in the coffin and vault that he had prepared for such a contingency. At this point, however, Poe gives his tale a comic turn. When the narrator screams in terror, he is answered at once by a group of workmen who seem rather annoyed at the sudden commotion.

Restored to memory by these voices, the narrator recalls where he is. Out hunting the night before with a friend, he took refuge from a sudden storm in a sloop loaded with garden mould. His coffin is thus only a bunk in the cabin, his premature burial merely the figment of his overwrought imagination. So real does the experience seem, however, that his terror is quite as great as if he had indeed undergone premature interment, and the very excess of his mental torture works a revulsion in him. He turns away from his preoccupation with death, discards his medical books, reads no more graveyard poetry, and disavows "bugaboo tales"—like the one he has been telling! "I dismissed forever my charnal apprehensions," he writes, "and with them vanished the cataleptic disorder, of which, perhaps, they had been less the consequence than the cause" (3: 969). Though the tale may lack the sprightliness of some by Irving and Paulding, it resembles theirs in its affirmation of reason and common sense and in the psychological causes it presents for the misperception of phenomena, especially those books, attitudes, and preoccupations that can give the mind an unhealthy cast and lead it to self-delusion.

But if Poe's tale is much like the work of Irving and Paulding in its major aspects, the final paragraph relates it to Dana's "Paul Felton" and Allston's *Monaldi.* Although Poe's narrator is cured of his mental and physical disorder, he has learned that there are parts of the human mind that are best left unprobed: "the imagination of man is no Carathis," he concludes, "to explore with impunity its every cavern. Alas! the grim legion of sepulchral terrors cannot be regarded as altogether fanciful—but, like the Demons in whose company Afrasiab made his voyage down the Oxus, they must sleep, or they will devour us—they must be suffered to slumber, or we perish" (3: 969). Poe's view of the imagination, like Dana's and Allston's, is a romantic one. Despite his recovery of mental tone and return to society, the narrator of "The Premature Burial" is well aware that there are other realities besides the common-sense one in which he finds himself again. The imagination can discover a world of terror far more sinister than simple misperception might suggest; there are mental journeys that can utterly destroy the mind that makes them.

This perception gave Poe a problem in writing that previous American Gothicists did not have. Since most American readers were thoroughly imbued with a fundamental rationalism, those writers could simply dismiss with a reasonable explanation whatever Gothic effects they had created to satisfy the literary taste of their audience. Though Richard Henry Dana had preceded Poe in his exploration of the darkened mind, he had never been a popular writer, his magazine, *The Idle Man,* had failed, and he withdrew in his middle years into private life. Poe, however, had to live by his writing. He needed to reach consistently a wide popular audience whose views, he knew, were not at all like his own. He abhorred, as he put it in his review of *Undine,* the "anti-romantic national character," that "evil genius of mere matter-of-fact, whose grovelling and degrading assumptions" work against romantic literature.[12] He had to devise, in other words, the kind of tale that would allow him to explore the dark reaches of the human imagination without doing too much violence to the rational predilections of his audience. He found that form in his best Gothic fiction.

He has left us, fortunately, a clear description of precisely what he was doing. In his review of Robert Montgomery Bird's *Sheppard Lee* (1836), a novel that makes its satiric points through the reincarnation of the protagonist's soul in a number of different bodies, Poe complains that Bird destroys his effect by explaining away the metempsychosis as only a dream; and he describes a second and, in his opinion, much superior method for handling such bizarre phenomena. Much, Poe believes, should be left to the imagination. The author should write as if "firmly impressed with the truth, yet astonished at the immensity, of the wonders he relates, and for which, professedly, he neither claims nor anticipates credence." The result is thus left "as a wonder not to be accounted for." Because the author "does not depend upon explaining away his incredibilities," he directs his attention "to giving them the character and the luminousness of truth, and thus are brought about, unwittingly, some of the most vivid creations of human intellect." The reader, on his part, "readily perceives and falls in with the writer's humor, and suffers himself to be borne on thereby."

Poe saw no harm in such practice. "What difficulty, or inconvenience, or danger can there be," he goes on to say, "in leaving us uninformed of the important facts that a certain hero *did not* actually discover the elixir vitae, *could not* really make himself invisible, and *was not* either a ghost in good earnest, or a bonâ fide Wandering Jew?"[13] There was precedent for this opinion. Even so thoroughgoing a rationalist as William Godwin saw no need to explain away the elixir of life and philosopher's stone through which St. Leon gains youth and wealth, Sir Walter Scott makes no attempt to provide a rational explanation for the White Lady of Avenel, and Charles Robert Maturin endows his protagonist with unequivocally supernatural powers. These British writers—and of course many of the Germans, too—simply ask the reader to make that willing suspension of disbelief that much romantic literature requires. But if Poe agreed with them in principle, his practice departs somewhat from theirs. He presents supernatural events as if they were real, carefully constructing his tales to win the reader's acceptance, but he sometimes instills a sense of ambiguity in his fiction by suggesting that alternative interpretations are possible.

"Ligeia," one of his favorite tales, provides a good illustration. There can be little doubt that we are intended to take literally the revivification of Rowena's corpse by the soul of Ligeia. Apart from Poe's letter to Philip P. Cooke, September 21, 1839, which makes quite clear that Ligeia has indeed possessed the body of her successor,[14] the action of the story fully supports the theme announced in the epigraph: that through strength of will, Ligeia has been able, at least for a moment, to triumph over death. She has been given the mental and moral attributes that make her volition plausible, and through the narrator's emphasis on her eyes, traditionally the path to the soul, her identity is rendered unmistakable. This does not mean that Poe intends us to accept the event as a possible occurrence in the real world. Like the return of Madeline in "The Fall of the House of Usher," through a screwed-down coffin lid and secured iron door, it is to be taken as an immense and astonishing wonder. Its credibility is not at issue. Indeed, Poe avoids even raising the question so as not to spoil the effect he has labored so hard to create.

Although Poe did not wish to explain away his wonders, he does include material that permits more than one interpretation of the phenomena. If our first understanding is that the Lady Ligeia returns by the force of her own will, a close look at the details of the story suggests that it may be the narrator's will which is decisive. He calls aloud for Ligeia long before there is any hint that she might return, and once Rowena dies, the corpse revivifies only when the narrator gives himself over to memories of Ligeia or dwells upon "passionate waking visions of" her (2: 327), and it sinks to death and dissolution when he turns his thoughts to Rowena. Lest we leap to the conclusion, however, that the narrator alone is responsible for Ligeia's return, Poe also reveals that the Lady Rowena, while still alive, is aware of Ligeia's unseen presence before the narrator is able to detect it. Twice she hears faint sounds and sees slight motions that the narrator does not notice. We are free to believe, therefore, that Ligeia's will, or the narrator's, or perhaps some combination of both is responsible for her temporary triumph over death.

This ambiguity opens the way for other interpretations, of course, especially those which see the tale as merely the hallucination of the distraught protagonist's disturbed or opium-influenced mind. For critics who refuse to suspend disbelief, Ligeia does not revive at all, and the point of the story is not the strength of her will but the abnormal psychology of the narrator, who only imagines that she has reanimated Rowena's corpse. [15] But such interpretations often take us far afield from the story, wrench it from its historical context, and even make it serve the *a priori* assumptions of the critic, who may use the tale to expound his own favorite theory. This is not to say that the psychological state of the narrator is irrelevant to both the story itself and the corpus of Poe's fiction. It is very much to the point of both [16] and has to be examined in some detail if we are to perceive not only the artistic effectiveness of Poe's Gothic tales but also the meaning he wished to express through them. In "Ligeia" that mind is best understood through the bizarre room the narrator prepares for the reception of his second wife.

From one point of view the room in "Ligeia" may be seen as merely the appropriate setting for the strange events that occur there, a room designed to enhance the effect of the dramatic conclusion, the reincarnation of Ligeia in Rowena's corpse. Like the slowly decaying house, subterranean vault, and gloomy chamber in "The Fall of the House of Usher," the castellated abbey with the seven bizarrely decorated rooms in "The Masque of the Red Death" (1842), or the labyrinthine catacombs lined with human bones and encrusted with nitre in "The Cask of Amontillado," it is designed to work on the imagination of the reader and dispose his mind to accept the strange and terrible occurrences that take place in them. Such a consideration must always have been in Poe's mind as he wrote, but artistic effect was not his only concern. As he writes in his second discussion of Hawthorne's tales (May 1842), truth is also "and in very great degree, the aim of the tale," [17] a truth he could most effectively express through the skillful handling of his physical settings.

That Poe used rooms and other types of enclosures for the symbolic development of theme is easily demonstrated. [18] In a letter to Rufus W. Griswold, May 29, 1841, he states explicitly: "by the Haunted Palace I mean to imply a mind haunted by phantoms—a disordered brain," [19] a view amply confirmed by even a casual reading of the poem, which, though originally published separately, eventually became an organic part of "The Fall of the House of Usher." In using a house or room as a symbol of mind, Poe was by no means original. In the major romances of Charles Brockden Brown, a temple, house, room, closet, or cave is often used to symbolize the mental state of a character, and in Richard Henry Dana's "Paul Felton," the protagonist goes completely mad in a hut called, appropriately, the Devil's Haunt. But if Poe resembles Brown and Dana in his use of such enclosures, he goes well beyond their practice in his treatment of the device and the use to which he puts it. Poe develops in his enclosures a consistent pattern of imagery, which, detailed and explicit, contributes markedly to our understanding of his characters and the themes he attempts to express through their bizarre actions.

Several such enclosures appear in "The Fall of the House of Usher": the house itself with its "vacant and eye-like windows" (2: 398); Roderick Usher's "large and lofty" study enveloped in darkness (2: 401); the vault beneath the house where Madeline is entombed; and the strange picture that Roderick paints, an enclosed room far below ground through which pours "a flood of intense rays" (2: 406). All of these suggest—as the poem explicitly states—the mental condition of one who has lost his hold on reason. Two elements are especially important: the utter isolation of the rooms and the strange light that plays through some of them. The windows in Roderick's study are so high as to be "altogether inaccessible from within," the walls and ceiling cannot be perceived in the darkness, and only "feeble gleams of encrimsoned light" enter "the trellised panes," merely enough to enable one to distinguish "the more prominent objects around" (2: 401). No clearer image could be drawn of a darkened mind, disoriented within itself and unable to establish a relation to the world without. Cut off from external light, it exists, as Roderick's painting suggests, in a lurid, self-engendered gleam.

The room in "Ligeia" bears a strong relation to those in the later story. Like Roderick Usher's study, it has no means for viewing clearly the outside world. The only window is a large sheet of Venetian glass, "tinted of a leaden hue, so that the rays of either the sun or moon, passing through it, fell with a ghastly lustre on the objects within." The only other source of light is a huge Saracenic censer, from which writhe, "as if endued with a serpent vitality, a continual succession of parti-colored fires" (2: 321). The ceiling is as lofty and the walls as obscured as those in Roderick's room. Set at obtuse angles (the room is a pentagon), the walls are covered "with a heavy and massive-looking tapestry" that is in constant motion, the "hideous and uneasy animation" caused by "a strong continual current of wind." These draperies are "spotted all over, at irregular intervals, with arabesque figures" that change in appearance as one approaches them (2: 322). In both rooms we find the same incoherence, the suggestion of disorientation, and the complete isolation from any direct relation to the external world.

Poe used the image of strangely appointed rooms in a number of different stories. Its first appearance—a chamber complete with vaulted ceiling, tapestries of crimson velvet, trellised windows, and arabesque lamp—is in the satiric tale "The Bargain Lost" (1832), but when Poe rewrote the story as "Bon-Bon" (1835), he changed the setting completely and left out all mention of the bizarrely decorated chamber. Poe had by that time included a similar room in "The Visionary," and since he continued to develop the image thereafter in his most important Gothic tales, the implication is strong that he had already determined to reserve the enclosure image to symbolize the disturbed minds of his Gothic protagonists. The room in "The Visionary" clearly foreshadows those in "Ligeia" and "The Fall of the House of Usher," and like them it reveals the distraught mental state of its occupant. The same lack of order and coherence is visible in its furnishings, and the rays of the sun pour in through windows "of crimson-tinted glass." The light glances "in a thousand reflections, from curtains which [roll] from their cornices like cataracts of molten silver" and mingle "at length fitfully with the artificial light" from censers that send out "tongues of emerald and violet fire" (2: 157-58).

This type of symbolic room appears again in "The Masque of the Red Death," where the imagery of the single chamber is expanded to include a suite of seven fantastic rooms located within a deeply secluded castellated abbey. Both images reflect the mind of Prince Prospero, who retires with his courtiers behind the "strong and lofty wall" of the "extensive and magnificent structure." When all have entered, the prince's retainers bring "furnaces and massy hammers" to weld shut the bolts of the iron gates, sealing the abbey off completely from the outside world (2: 670-71). The image thus becomes a rather complex one. The wall that surrounds the abbey is a symbol of enclosure, within which there is another, the abbey itself, within which there is yet another, the seven apartments where the main action of the story takes place. If the whole image reflects the mental isolation of the prince, the suite of rooms, enclosed on each side by a corridor and arranged in an irregular line that isolates each from the others, is an obvious symbol of the inner recesses of his mind.

The decoration of these rooms is as bizarre as that in "Ligeia" and "The Visionary," but it is different in one important aspect. There is no source of light in any of the rooms. That which enters through the Gothic windows derives from the dancing flames of braziers set in the corridors on either side of the suite. Six of the chambers are each decorated with a single color—blue, purple, green, orange, white, and violet—and the panes of glass in the windows match in tint the rooms into which they open. In the seventh and last, however, the light comes in through blood-red glass and, playing upon the black velvet drapes that fall from the ceiling to the black carpeted floor, creates an effect that is "ghastly in the extreme" (2: 672). The seven chambers are thus completely removed from even the distorted light of the external world that enters the room in "Ligeia." Prince Prospero, even more than Roderick Usher and other occupants of such fantastic chambers, has separated himself from reality and lives in a bizarre mental world inhabited by dreams, the wraithlike dancers who move through the rooms on the night of the masquerade ball.

Not all of Poe's rooms are so gaudy as these, nor do they all have the same characteristics. The room in "Berenice," for example, is neither chamber nor ballroom. It is a library that seems to have no windows or special source of light, but it too functions as a symbol of the protagonist's mental state. His mind is so enclosed by its own intellectuality, objectified by the room's function, that "the realities of the world" affect the protagonist "as visions only, while the wild ideas of the land of dreams" become not merely "the material of [his] every-day existence, but in very deed that existence utterly and solely in itself" (2: 210). In "The Man of the Crowd" (1840), on the other hand, the room is the lobby of a London coffee house. The protagonist sits in a "large bow window" looking "through the smoky panes into the street" (2: 507). As night falls, the light of the gas lamps throws "over every thing a fitful and garish lustre," and "the wild effects of the light," combined with the unclear glass, make the outside world appear to him like a rapidly changing spectacle (2: 511). Poe varies his enclosures in these two stories to fit the minds of the major characters.

In only one tale, "William Wilson," does Poe use a series of different enclosures to depict the developing mental state of his protagonist. The first of these images, Dr. Bransby's school, resembles the house of Usher and Prince Prospero's castellated abbey. It is "a large, rambling, Elizabethan house," enclosed by "a high and solid brick wall"—the symbolic equivalent of tarn and wall in the other stories—"topped with a bed of mortar and broken glass." The gate, set in "an angle of the ponderous wall," is "riveted and studded with iron bolts, and surmounted with jagged iron spikes." Within, the house itself resembles nothing so much as a labyrinth in which intricate passages wind through "incomprehensible subdivisions." No two rooms meet at the same level, and one can never be sure on which of the two stories he happens to be. The lateral branches are numerous and return so upon themselves that Wilson views the structure in much the same way as he ponders infinity (2: 427-29). The house is undoubtedly Poe's most convincing depiction of the human mind: its complexity, its hidden recesses, and the dark chambers where one's secret self lies concealed.

Wilson discovers that self one night by threading "a wilderness of narrow passages" to penetrate the dark recess in which his double, a fellow student with the same name and general appearance, is sleeping. Because he resents the presence of this student, the only one in the school who does not fall under his wilful and despotic sway, Wilson intends to play a trick on him. But when he throws the light of a lamp on his face, he is aghast to discover the perfect identity of the sleeping boy with himself (2: 437). He leaves the school the following day and meets his double thereafter only under unusual circumstances: in a dimly lighted room at Eton and a completely darkened chamber at Oxford. In both places the second William Wilson—an obvious symbol of conscience—appears unexpectedly to keep the protagonist from completing some dastardly act. They meet for the final time in a lighted anteroom at a masquerade ball, where Wilson, infuriated by his double's constant interference in his affairs, runs him through with his sword and discovers once again his identity with himself. Each of these rooms must represent, therefore, the mental state of Wilson as he struggles with a part of himself that he wants to escape or deny.

The obvious relation between mind and enclosure that Poe presents in "William Wilson" is most unusual in his fiction. The struggle between conscience and will that takes place in each of the rooms is so very explicit—it is even underscored in the title and epigraph of the tale—that

"William Wilson" must be read, at one level, at least, as an allegory, that class of fiction which Poe severely criticized Nathaniel Hawthorne for writing. As a form, Poe writes in his last review of Hawthorne's tales, allegory cannot be defended. Its meaning must always interfere with the fiction that embodies it to disturb "that unity of effect which to the artist, is worth all the allegory in the world." Poe does not mean to imply that theme is unimportant in fiction or that stories cannot be made the vehicles of truth. It is simply a question of expressing that meaning in the most appropriate manner. Fouqué's *Undine*, he goes on to say, provides the correct model. In it, Poe writes, the allegory is "judiciously subdued, seen only as a shadow or by suggestive glimpses, and making its nearest approach to truth in a not obtrusive and therefore not unpleasant *appositeness*." [20]

Since this critique was published in 1847, we may take it as representing Poe's mature thinking on the manner in which a tale should present its theme. Meaning must surely be present, but not the kind of obvious meaning that, eight years before, he had expressed in "William Wilson." In most of his fiction, of course, Poe had followed this dictum, his Gothic tales for the most part suggesting rather than explicitly stating their themes. The meanings lurk beneath the surface of the action, as much concealed as revealed by the symbolic expression. The stories thus invite the reader to look behind the fantastic settings and bizarre events to their fundamental significance. Since protagonist and enclosure are so closely identified in most of the Gothic stories, the meaning of the tales may be discovered through an analysis of their interrelation. The enclosures lead us back to the protagonists they symbolize, and they, on their part, reveal the themes that are embodied in their experience. We must therefore turn to his protagonists if we are to perceive the thematic thread Poe developed in his Gothic fiction.

They are a varied lot, and their tales are presented in a number of different ways. Some, like Egæus in "Berenice," narrate their own stories; others, like Roderick Usher and Prince Prospero, are the protagonists of tales told by another character or by an omniscient narrator. Some, like Montresor in "The Cask of Amontillado," seem to maintain complete intellectual control over the experiences they describe; others, like the narrators of "Ligeia" and "The Black Cat," are anything but rational, and the protagonist of "The Tell-Tale Heart" appears to be on the verge of hysteria. Most are afflicted with some degree of insanity, yet some vigorously deny the very madness that their actions indicate. Because so many of them are mentally unbalanced, twentieth-century critics have been quick to apply modern theories of psychology—usually Freudian—to Poe's fiction, and to discuss his protagonists as if they were case studies in abnormal psychology as the modern age understands it. Such interpretations, however, are always of dubious relevance and can only be maintained at the expense of the stories themselves, which make quite plain the sense in which the question of madness is to be understood.

Poe established that sense in "Morella" (1835), one of his earliest Gothic tales. In the long description of his and Morella's speculative studies, the narrator pauses to define what he means by personal identity, that which distinguishes one "from other beings that think." A person, he believes, is "an intelligent essence having reason, and since there is a consciousness which always accompanies thinking, it is this consciousness which makes every one to be that which he calls 'himself'" (2: 226). The narrator is not so concerned, however, with the problem of identity in the living person as with the question of whether or not that identity survives the moment of death. If it does not, or if the person believes it does not, the approach of death threatens one's identity, its loss necessarily involves the loss of reason, and the person, filled with terror at the prospect of psychic annihilation, goes mad. Reason and madness in Poe's tales, therefore, must not be taken in twentieth-century terms but in the frame of reference Poe himself provides. Reason, madness, terror, death, and loss of identity are all involved in the experience of his distraught narrators and their companions.[21]

A number of Poe's tales explore the relation among reason, personal identity, and psychic survival. The narrator of "Berenice," enclosed in the family library—a clear symbol of his rationality—has convinced himself of the soul's preexistence and will hear no argument in the matter. Faint memories "of aerial forms—of spiritual and meaning eyes—of sounds, musical yet sad," haunt his mind, and he is certain that he will not lose them "while the sunlight of [his] reason shall exist" (2: 210). His tenacious belief in the soul's preexistence, linked here with the reasoning mind, strongly suggests that identity transcends the limitations of the flesh. Other characters in Poe's tales focus their attention on the other extreme of life and become obsessed with the question of personal survival. Morella dies peacefully with the firm conviction that she will yet live,[22] and Ligeia faces her end, not in fear, but with so fierce a desire for life that only the weakness of her human will keeps her from resisting the power of death. Both of these intellectual ladies, moreover, succeed, if only temporarily, in clinging to life in the flesh: Morella in the body of her daughter and Ligeia in the corpse of Rowena, whom she reanimates.

Poe does not always develop the theme in so supernatural a fashion. In "A Descent into the Maelström" (1841) and "The Pit and the Pendulum," the narrators survive natural dangers, the threatened plunge into whirlpool or pit, through an exercise of reason. The old man who describes his experience in the Moskoe-ström would, like his terrified brother, have plunged to his death in the depths of the vortex had not his rational mind allowed him to cling to life and preserve his identity. He is terrified, of course, when he discovers that he is trapped in the Maelström, and he even has the "*wish* to explore its depths" (2: 589). But once within its power, his self-possession returns, and curiosity takes "the place of [his] original terrors" (2: 591). He soon observes that cylinders fall less rapidly than objects of any other shape, and lashing himself to a water cask, he throws himself into the sea. His by now irrational brother clings to the ring bolt in the ship and plunges with it "into the chaos of foam below" (2: 594). Only the rational narrator preserves his identity and survives.

The narrator of "The Pit and the Pendulum" has a similar experience. He is a man who retains, even when "sick unto death" and reduced by his captors almost to the point of unconsciousness, some spark of self-awareness. He insists that not even in death will it be lost (2: 681-82). With convictions like these and a mind disposed to cling to rationality even in the face of torture, he is, like the old sailor in "A Descent into the Maelström," a prime candidate for survival. When placed in the dungeon, he retains enough reasoning power to try to determine the size and shape of his pitch-black prison, and he even thwarts his tormentors by devising a means to escape his bonds just as the pendulum cuts into his flesh. His final escape does not result from the workings of his rational mind, of course, for at the end of the tale he is saved from the pit only by the timely arrival of rescuers. Yet without his reasoning powers and strong sense of personal identity, he would not have survived long enough to be rescued at all. Like "A Descent into the Maelström," the story is a parable of rationality, self-awareness, and survival.[23]

For some of the characters in Poe's Gothic tales, the death wish experienced briefly by the old man caught in the Maelström is more powerful than any desire for survival. This idea is developed most clearly in "The Imp of the Perverse," a tale that seems to present a theme directly opposed to that in "A Descent into the Maelström" and "The Pit and the Pendulum." Unlike the protagonists of those tales, the narrator does not try to avoid the plunge into the abyss but actively seeks it. He examines the propensity of human beings to do precisely what they should not, a trait he calls perversity, and in explaining his meaning he uses a significant illustration. He notes how people often react when standing upon "the brink of a precipice. We peer into the abyss—we grow sick and dizzy." Though we know we should turn away from the edge, we nonetheless remain, attracted by a desire to plunge from the height and feel the "rushing annihilation" of the fall (3: 1222-23). The implications are unmistakable. Perversity is the mad desire to plunge into the unknown, where, from the point of view of the living, psychic survival remains an open question.

The narrator's own experience confirms this interpretation. He has committed a perfect murder and is safe from all suspicion if, as he puts it, he "be not fool enough to make open confession!" No sooner does this idea occur to him than he experiences the perverse desire for self-destruction. Aware of the strain of perversity in his nature, he tries to shake off the suggestion. He begins to walk fast, then to run; and he feels "a maddening desire to shriek aloud" (2: 1225). He dares not think, he says, lest he be lost, but in turning away from thought he confirms his fate. He bounds "like a madman" through the streets, attracting the attention of others, who take the alarm, arrest him, and hear him blurt out his confession. Tried and convicted for the murder, he pens the tale the night before his execution, concluding with the words: "To-day I wear these chains, and am *here.* To-morrow I shall be fetterless!—*but where?*" (3: 1226). The narrator has, it seems, done exactly what his reason would tell him not to do. He has risked his personal identity by a mad plunge into the abyss of death.

Two other characters in Poe's tales undergo a similar experience: the narrators of "The Tell-Tale Heart" and "The Black Cat." By the time they tell their stories, they too are at the point of death, imprisoned for the hideous crimes they have committed and which they have in effect confessed by the way they have held the police near the spots where their victims are concealed until some extraordinary event—the beating of the heart or the scream of the cat—reveals what has happened there. Since the events occur within tight enclosures—the shuttered chamber of the old man in "The Tell-Tale Heart" and the cellar of the house in "The Black Cat"—we must see them as mental as well as physical experiences and interpret the sounds they hear as involuntary confessions of the crimes they have consciously sought to conceal. The truth will not lie buried beneath the floor or hidden behind the bricked-up wall because of the perverse desire of both men to reveal what they have done. In "The Tell-Tale Heart" the narrator confesses in the presence of the police; in "The Black Cat" the protagonist unburdens his soul by narrating the events on the eve of his execution.

How they tell their stories, moreover, reveals the underlying theme that Poe wants to develop. In "The Tell-Tale Heart" the protagonist is nervous to the point of madness, the very first words of the tale revealing his extremely distraught emotional state, yet he repeatedly insists that he is not mad, that the calm way he can recount the events proves his sanity. In "The Black Cat" the narrator seems less disturbed, but he too tries to deny his madness and presents his bizarre tale as "nothing more than an ordinary succession of very natural causes and effects" (3: 850). The attempts by both men to assume a rationality they no longer possess indicates their desire to cling desperately to a personal identity they are in imminent danger of losing; and the obvious madness they reveal behind the assumed façade of sanity makes unmistakably clear the rapid approach of death and its attendant fear of annihilation. Their tenuous hold on reason places them even beyond the point reached by the narrator of "The Imp of the Perverse," who can, at the end of the story, still ponder the question of where he will be "tomorrow."

The relation between madness and loss of identity is even more clearly presented in "The Masque of the Red Death," where symbolic expression renders the meaning unmistakable. The terrible plague that scourges the countryside is a fitting sign of the omnipresence of death, the withdrawal of Prince Prospero and his companions within a group of enclosures represents their attempt to escape its physical presence, and the masquerade ball reveals their desire to avoid even the thought of it. But the masque that Prince Prospero gives serves a second purpose: it also suggests a change of identity. And because the masque itself, the strange decor of the rooms, and even the grotesqueness of the revelers' costumes are all the prince's invention, they symbolize his state of mind: the growing madness that afflicts him as he tries to ward off death and its attendant horror of psychic annihilation. Prince Prospero fails, of course, in his mad attempt to hold death at bay. At the end of the tale he falls dead, the revelers die in despair, the clock stops, and the fires go out. "Darkness and Decay and the Red Death" have assumed dominion where the prince once ruled (2: 677).

A similar conclusion appears in "The Fall of the House of Usher," where family and family mansion both collapse into the dark waters of the tarn, leaving no trace behind. But there is one major difference. The first-person narrator escapes the debacle to tell the story. The presence of this character sets "The Fall of the House of Usher" off from Poe's other Gothic tales, for he provides a rational voice to counterbalance the mad Roderick Usher. From the very beginning the narrator is disposed to seek rational explanations for apparently supernatural occurrences. Though he feels the strange influence of the house when he first approaches it, he tries to dismiss the impression as mere superstition or the workings of his imagination, and he treats with contempt the belief of Roderick Usher that, as the result of their long continuance in a peculiar arrangement, the stones of the house have become sentient, have worked a "terrible influence" upon both Roderick and his family, and have turned him into the hypersensitive and nervous person he has become. "Such opinions," the narrator writes, "need no comment, and I will make none" (2: 408).

As time passes, however, the narrator is affected by his friend's actions and beliefs. "By slow yet certain degrees, the wild influences of [Roderick's] fantastic yet impressive superstitions" creep upon him, and as he lies in bed during his last night in the house, the narrator must struggle "to reason off the nervousness" he feels and to put down "an incubus of utterly causeless alarm." But "an intense sentiment of horror" at last overpowers him, and he tries to rouse himself from his distraught state "by pacing rapidly to and fro through the apartment" (2: 411-12). When Roderick comes to his room, both are appalled by the unnaturally lighted whirlwind that is blowing about the mansion, and the narrator tries to calm his friend by explaining the phenomena rationally and by reading to him from a book. Even when the strange sounds begin to be heard that herald Madeline's escape from her entombment, he retains sufficient presence of mind not to excite his friend. Though the narrator soon becomes "completely unnerved" (2: 415) and witnesses the final reunion and death of Roderick and his sister, his rationality preserves his identity and he escapes from the crumbling mansion.

There can be no escape, however, for Roderick Usher. Like the narrator of "The Tell-Tale Heart," he is already in a state of "excessive nervous agitation" when his friend first sees him (2: 402), and he reaches the point of hysteria on the night he dies. His phantasmagoric paintings reveal his growing insanity, and his poem, "The Haunted Palace," shows unmistakably, as the narrator observes, Roderick's own awareness of his faltering reason. That his mental state derives from his fear of death and possible loss of identity is revealed in his relation to Madeline, his identical twin. She is already deathly sick when the story opens, and though Roderick does not explicitly state the thought, he undoubtedly fears that he will die with her—a superstition involving twins that Charles Brockden Brown had used in *Edgar Huntly,* where Mrs. Lorimer is convinced that her fate is entwined with that of her twin brother, Wiatte, and that her death must occur with his.[24] For Roderick, then, the approaching death of Madeline fills him with terror, first of all for the death he fears is approaching and then for the threat of annihilation which that death might entail.

The dénouement of the story seems to imply that his fears are justified. While Roderick sits with rigid countenance, his eyes "bent fixedly before him" (2: 415), Madeline comes from the depths of the house, breaking through coffin lid and sealed doors, to claim him for death. In his hypersensitive state he claims to have heard her stirrings in the coffin, her step on the stair, and "that heavy and horrible beating of her heart." At this point the heavy doors of the room swing slowly open, Madeline totters a moment on the threshold, falls "with a low moaning cry . . . upon the person of her brother, and in her violent and now final death-agonies, [bears] him to the floor a corpse, . . . a victim of the terrors he had anticipated" (2: 416-17). As the narrator flees in horror across the causeway, the house of Usher begins to come apart. In the radiance of "the full, setting, and blood-red moon," the "fierce breath of the whirlwind" sweeps violently about the house, the walls rush asunder, and to "a long tumultuous shouting like the voice of a thousand waters," both house and family disappear beneath the surface of the tarn (2: 417).[25]

The end of the story is in many ways much like that of "The Masque of the Red Death." The darkness and decay that dominate the scene in the one tale are paralleled in the other by the sullen and silent closing of the waters over the house of Usher, and the blood-red moon that shines luridly thrugh the collapsing house is strongly suggestive of the Red Death. There are, however, two important differences: the survival of the narrator in "The Fall of the House of Usher" and the whirlwind or vortex that claims the house and family. Like the Norwegian seaman's terrified brother in "A Descent into the Maelström," Roderick Usher plunges into a whirling abyss, while the narrator, like the seaman himself, escapes with his life. "The Masque of the Red Death," in other words, seems to end in complete desolation, leaving only the unholy trinity of darkness, decay, and death to preside over a void. In "The Fall of the House of Usher," on the other hand, as in "A Descent into the Maelström," the vortex seems to provide a passage between two worlds, one that the narrator with his strong reason and sense of personal identity does not enter, but into which the mad Roderick Usher is plunged.

To pursue the line of thought suggested by this image, we must go beyond Poe's Gothic fiction to a pair of stories that end in a similar fashion: "MS. Found in a Bottle" (1833) and *The Narrative of Arthur Gordon Pym* (1838). Both of these tales of the sea are related in imagery to Poe's Gothic stories: in the enclosures, for example—the holds of the ships— into which the narrators descend in the course of their adventures, and in the cave in which Pym is briefly buried alive. Like several of Poe's Gothic protagonists, too, Pym is afflicted with sudden fits of perversity, the most important of which occurs near the end of the tale when he is descending a cliff. His imagination becomes excited "by thoughts of the vast depth yet to be descended," and he feels an "irrepressible desire" to look down. "With a wild, indefinable emotion, half of horror, half of a relieved oppression," he looks into the depths below and his "whole soul [is] pervaded with a *longing to fall.*" With a spinning brain, he lets go his hold, and had his companion not caught him, he would "have been precipitated into the abyss."[26]

But if Pym is saved at this point, it is only to undergo a final plunge at the conclusion of the story. Both he and his counterpart in "MS. Found in a Bottle" end their voyages caught in a strong current that carries them rapidly toward the antarctic pole. In "MS. Found in a Bottle" the narrator sees the ice suddenly open around him, and the ship begins to whirl "dizzily, in immense concentric circles, round and round the borders of a gigantic amphitheatre." The circles quickly grow smaller, and the ship, caught "within the grasp of the whirlpool," plunges madly, quivers, and goes down (2: 146). In a similar fashion Arthur Gordon Pym sees before him "a limitless cataract, rolling silently into the sea"; soundless winds rush about him; and in the increasing darkness, the canoe in which he rides plunges "into the embraces of the cataract, where a chasm [throws] itself open to receive [him]." [27] The relation between these descents and the fall of the house of Usher into the tarn is clear. All three protagonists have plunged into the abyss of death, but the narrators of the sea tales have approached their end in a manner quite different from the abject terror of Roderick Usher.

The experience is most clearly depicted in "MS. Found in a Bottle," the shorter and more direct of the two sea tales. The narrator, a rationalist with a predilection for science, embarks, in a fit of "nervous restlessness" (2: 135), on an ocean voyage. Struck by a violent storm, the ship he is on is blown through a chaos of wind and water, and the narrator alone survives a collision with another ship. He is thrown by the force of the blow onto a Flying Dutchman, whose crew takes no notice of him and where he feels "a new entity" has been added to his soul (2: 141). This ship, like the *Jane Guy* in the second half of *Pym*, is bound on a voyage of discovery, and though the narrator fears for a time that the Dutchman is "doomed to hover continually upon the brink of eternity, without taking a final plunge into the abyss" (2: 143), he eventually believes that he is "hurrying onwards to some exciting knowledge—some never-to-be-imparted secret, whose attainment is destruction" (2: 145). By this time the narrator has lost his original identity and now looks forward to the plunge into death, which will presumably reveal what lies hereafter.

The world beyond the grave which many of Poe's protagonists face with such terror is the subject of three dialogues: "The Conversation of Eiros and Charmion" (1839), "The Colloquy of Monos and Una" (1841), and "The Power of Words" (1845). In all three, the characters have acquired new identities suggested by the names they have received (2: 455); Una is "born again" into a new life (2: 608); and Eiros no longer hears "that mad, rushing, horrible sound, like the 'voice of many waters'" (2: 456)—the same sound that occurs when the house of Usher collapses—which he seems to have heard as he plunged into the abyss.

Of the three dialogues, "The Colloquy of Monos and Una" is probably the most important, for it suggests that death entails a progressive loss of sentience as the human being becomes at one with the material and spiritual universe. Monos describes to Una (both names mean "one") the gradual loss of the sense of being and the appearance in its stead of a sense of locality and duration as the body decays. The human being thus becomes identified with time and space, at one with the whole of the universe.

The metaphysical view suggested by this conclusion is most fully developed in Poe's *Eureka* (1848), a philosophic essay (Poe called it a prose poem) which describes a cosmos that was formed when a primordial particle, the manifestation of God, exploded in a series of immense pulsations to create the cosmos. In the process God differentiated himself into all the discrete objects of the physical universe, including, of course, each human being. With the passage of time, however, the process will be reversed and the entire cosmos will collapse once again into its original unity. The process will then be repeated again and again, a new universe expanding into being and collapsing into unity with each beat of the divine heart. The position of man in this cosmos is a difficult one. Though each person may have a strong sense of his individual identity, he feels nonetheless a natural desire to return to the original unity from which all things have come. Such a return is necessarily a threat to his personal identity, and he resists the urge, which he sees as perversity, to become once again identified with the spirit of the cosmos.

The relation between Poe's Gothic tales and his view of the universe is obvious. The cosmic vision explains both the abject terror the protagonists feel at the approach of death and the perverse desire of some of them to embrace the very death they dread. In some of the tales, moreover, one gets a sense that an even more general theme is being developed. "The Fall of the House of Usher" and "The Masque of the Red Death" are not only tales of terror depicting the plunge of individual characters into the abyss of death, but also parables of the destruction of an entire universe. "The Fall of the House of Usher" ends with the collapse of the whole world of the tale into the tarn;[28] and "The Masque of the Red Death" concludes with a phrase that suggests no limited application of its theme. Three of the last four words in the tale are absolutes: "Darkness and Decay and the Red Death held illimitable dominion over all" (2: 677). This certainly implies a great deal more than the destruc-

tion of a group of revelers in a castellated abbey, or even the personal de-
mise of Prince Prospero. This is the death of a world.[29]

To read Poe's Gothic tales in terms of this philosophy is to recognize
at once his important contribution to the developing Gothic mode.
Other writers, such as Charles Brockden Brown and Richard Henry
Dana, had made their Gothic effects indicative of the mental states of
their characters; some, such as William Godwin and Charles Robert
Maturin, had used conventional Gothic devices for philosophic purposes; and Brown himself had made his fiction the testing ground for
ideas. Poe learned from all these men but went far beyond them. He developed more fully than Brown or Dana the relation between details of
the Gothic setting, especially enclosures, and the disturbed minds of his
characters; and even more than Godwin and Maturin, he used the
Gothic mode as a vehicle for the expression of a consistently developed
theme. He did not, like Godwin, Maturin, or Scott, vacillate in his most
effective tales between the rationally explained and the frankly supernatural Gothic, but assumed a position that can best be called noncommit-
tal. Poe presents the phenomenal world as it is perceived by his protagonists and feels no need to explain away supernatural events or to insist
upon their reality.

In taking this stance, Poe freed the Gothic tale from the constricting
limits imposed on it by the naive rationalists who felt compelled to explain away their most telling Gothic effects. Poe was too fine an artist to
spoil a good tale in this way, and much too serious a thinker to make his
stories merely the source of meaningless titillation. Everything in his
tales had to tell for both effect and meaning, and in his best work the
Gothic devices, though effective in themselves, are also necessary elements in the exposition of the theme. The rationalist observer, who, in
another's work, might explain away the strange events that occur, plays
in Poe's tales an essential role in establishing the philosophic basis of the
story; and the terror-stricken or mentally disturbed characters are not
merely the victims of self-induced chimeras but major actors in a cosmic
drama played out in a series of garishly lighted and strangely furnished
enclosures that are the symbolic counterparts of their own minds. Until
Poe's time, no American writer had managed to forge so organic a bond
between Gothic device and symbolic meaning. None since has equalled
Poe in the skill with which he accomplished that feat.

EIGHT

Nathaniel Hawthorne

To turn from Poe to Nathaniel Hawthorne is to perceive at once how pervasive and important the Gothic mode had become in American fiction. The men were not much alike in mind or temperament, and they wrote quite different kinds of tales, but we recognize in both the strong influence of the Gothic mode and their skillful adaptation of its techniques to diverse intellectual and artistic ends. They knew and respected each other's work. Though Poe's critiques of Hawthorne's tales are not entirely favorable, Poe recognized in their author an important American artist, and his reviews contain for the most part a just and appreciative estimate of Hawthorne's talents. Less well known is Hawthorne's opinion of Poe. In 1846, when he sent Poe a copy of his latest book, *Mosses from an Old Manse,* Hawthorne acknowledged his awareness of Poe's review of *Twice-Told Tales,* demurred from some of his critical judgments, but also vowed his admiration for the "force and originality" Poe had exhibited in his fiction.[1] Each man was able to respond to something in the works of the other.

Hawthorne was, like Poe, thoroughly conversant with classic Gothic fiction. While a boy still in his teens in 1819, Hawthorne wrote his sister Louisa that he had read, among other books, *Waverley* and *The Mysteries of Udolpho,* and in the following year he mentioned an impressive group of novels that he had enjoyed: the recently published *Melmoth the Wanderer,* Godwin's *Caleb Williams, St. Leon,* and *Mandeville,* and all of Scott's romances published to that date, a list that must have included *The Antiquary, The Bride of Lammermoor, A Legend of Montrose,* and *The Monastery.*[2] During the years at Bowdoin College (1821–1825), we know that he read novels by John Neal, and we learn from later evidence that he knew both *The Castle of Otranto* and at least some of the novels of Charles Brockden Brown.[3] That he read other fiction is certain, novels that he borrowed from the Salem Circulating Library and which may have included other Gothic fiction. Even without a list of these books, however, we can be sure that Hawthorne, like most young men of the time, absorbed the Gothic fiction that was available, books that appealed to his temperament and which exerted a lifelong influence on his art.

From *Fanshawe* (1828), his first published but soon repudiated juvenile novel,[4] to the "American Claimant" and "Elixir of Life" manuscripts, which he left incomplete at his death, the influence of literary Gothicism is apparent in some of Hawthorne's best and most important work. His earliest stories are filled with Gothic devices. "The Hollow of the Three Hills" (1830) is an effective tale of witchcraft with a chilling conclusion, and such well known stories of the period as "My Kinsman, Major Molineux" (1832) and "Young Goodman Brown" (1835) are steeped in Gothic atmosphere and contain strong intimations of the demonic. In "Howe's Masquerade" (1838) we find the ghostly procession of Royal Governors who glide down the stairs and out the door of the Province House on the night of the British evacuation of Boston; and in "Edward Randolph's Portrait" (1838) the well known Gothic device of the mysterious painting. Indeed, in "The Prophetic Pictures" (1837) Hawthorne combines two such Gothic elements, the mysterious painting and the prophetic warning,[5] a device that had appeared as prophetic dreams in the romances of Charlotte Smith and Ann Radcliffe, and as the supernatural visions of Highland seers in those of Sir Walter Scott.

Most of Hawthorne's romances also contain conventional Gothic elements.[6] In "The Custom-House," the long introduction to *The Scarlet Letter* (1850), Hawthorne uses a number of such devices: the dusty manuscript found in the garret, from which the narrator, like the younger Melmoth in Maturin's *Melmoth the Wanderer,* learns the story which he then recounts; and the strange relic of cloth that is supposed to authenticate the narrative but which seems to possess preternatural qualities when the narrator places it against his breast. In *The House of the Seven Gables* (1851) he includes an ancestral curse laid on the usurper, Colonel Pyncheon, by the reputed wizard, Matthew Maule, who was cheated out of his land. The curse afflicts the Pyncheon family until, in a dénouement that recalls the oldest Gothic romances, the property is at last restored to its proper owner, the descendant of Matthew Maule, when he marries the last of the Pyncheon girls.[7] And in *The Marble Faun* (1860), he even employs so traditional an element as the sinister monk,

Miriam's model, who appears in the catacombs like a shade from the past, haunts the girl like a specter, and threatens her with some mysterious but never fully disclosed evil.

It is seldom easy, however, to determine the precise source of the Gothic material Hawthorne uses. The Germans seem to have had little influence upon him,[8] and the British writers of fiction left only a few specific marks on his work. Hawthorne's lifelong fondness for the elixir of life theme undoubtedly derives from his early reading of Godwin's *St. Leon,* and the tale of the knight and the water nymph that Donatello recounts to Kenyon in Chapter XXVII of *The Marble Faun* probably derives from a similar episode in Scott's *The Bride of Lammermoor.* The influence of Scott on Hawthorne, as Neal F. Doubleday has shown,[9] seems to have been pervasive, but we cannot always be certain that an incident in Scott is directly related to an analogous one in Hawthorne. The sign of Maule's curse on the Pyncheons, the gurgling noise sometimes heard in their throats, may owe something to the similarly inherited sign that appears, generation after generation, on members of the Redgauntlet family in Scott's novel of 1824: the horseshoe-shaped mark that appears on their foreheads when they become angry. But if Hawthorne was, in fact, influenced by this novel, he altered the device in such a way as to make it his own.[10]

We are on surer ground when we detect the influence of Maturin's *Melmoth the Wanderer* on "Ethan Brand" (1850).[11] We know, of course, that many of the details of Hawthorne's story derive from his trip to North Adams, Massachusetts, in the summer of 1838,[12] and the tale is filled with local characters and customs. But Brand himself is no indigenous type. He is, rather, an American version of Melmoth. The sin of both is, as Melmoth puts it, "the great angelic sin—pride and intellectual glorying," and both men announce their presence by, in Maturin's words, a "demoniac laugh," a "wild shriek of bitter and convulsive laughter that announces the object of its derision is ourselves."[13] Hawthorne used this kind of laugh in other stories—"My Kinsman, Major Molineux" and "Young Goodman Brown," among them[14]—but nowhere is he so close to his source as in "Ethan Brand." Both Melmoth and Brand recognize the evil that lies in their hearts, and both go to their deaths without regret or remorse. Hawthorne avoids the supernatural conclusion of Maturin's book, the intimation that Melmoth, like Lewis's Monk, is carried away by a demon, but in his despairing suicide,

Ethan Brand is consistent with the mental and moral attitude of his literary forebear.

Examples like these could be multiplied to include the possible influence of John Neal's *Rachel Dyer*[15] or even James Fenimore Cooper's *The Wept of Wish-ton-Wish* on Hawthorne's use of New England witchcraft as a version of American Gothic, but such influences, even if they could be well established, would tell us little about Hawthorne's Gothicism or the use to which it was put. Hawthorne borrowed only a few specific elements or incidents from his predecessors, but he made good use of what might be called the general ambience of the mode: the darkness in which the Gothic experience most often takes place; the flickering light of candle, lamp, or hearth which, projecting moving shadows, renders the vision uncertain; or the pale glow of moonlight, which, bathing the surroundings in a soft light, transforms even the commonplace into what seems to be a completely different world. This Gothic environment had, of course, been the common property of romancers since the days of Charlotte Smith and Ann Radcliffe, whose heroines, candle in hand, walk the halls of ancient manors at night or penetrate the darkness of subterranean vaults, but the device had, over the years, undergone a considerable development.

Although Radcliffe and Smith had shown that the imagination, stimulated by deceptive light, could lead a distraught character to misperceive reality, they had laid primary stress on the terror of the moment to elicit from their readers an appropriate emotional response. The Americans altered that purpose. Charles Brockden Brown focused his attention on the misperception itself, probed the moral nature of man, and stressed the philosophical aspects of the problem; and Washington Irving, assuming the intellectual position of the Common Sense realists, used the device of deceptive light and misapprehended reality as a source for humor. But Irving had adapted the technique to an additional end. In *Bracebridge Hall*, he introduced the silver "streaks of dewy moonshine" into a garden scene and suggested that such lighting can arouse, not feelings of Gothic terror, but a sense of supernatural solemnity that leads the observer, for the moment at least, to entertain the possibility of reunion with his beloved dead.[16] The ghosts thus raised are no creatures of terror, nor is the experience one to unnerve the observer. Whether real or not, these ghosts are objects of deep and solemn interest.

Nathaniel Hawthorne was strongly attracted to this kind of Gothic

setting. In a well known passage, dated October 13, 1848, in *The American Notebooks*—a passage later rewritten for the introduction to *The
Scarlet Letter*—he describes the effect of uncertain light in his dark sitting
room. A coal fire diffuses a "scarcely visible" but "mild, heart-warm influence" throughout the room, while moonlight from the window
"produces a very beautiful effect." It makes all the furnishings visible
but bathes them in a cold spirituality that is only partly offset by the
"faint ruddiness" from the fire. All the familiar objects of the room "are
invested with something like strangeness and remoteness," as if one
were viewing them after the passage of years. Between these two lights,
Hawthorne goes on to say, "such a medium is created that the room
seems just fit for the ghosts of persons very dear, who have lived in the
room with us, to glide noiselessly in, and sit quietly down, without af-
frighting us. It would be like a matter of course, to look round, and find
some familiar form in one of the chairs" (8: 283-84).[17]

The conditions under which these friendly ghosts appear are not in-
herently different from those which produced the terrifying phenomena
in Radcliffe's romances. The difference lies in the way one views the
imagination. Gothic romancers in general distrusted the imagination as
a deceptive faculty that could frighten one with chimeras, and they saw
in the power of reason, operating in the light of common day, the force
necessary to offset its baleful influence. Most American writers, including Irving and Hawthorne, were also distrustful of the imagination, but
even so confirmed a realist as Irving allowed it some positive value when
playing across the moonlit garden, and Hawthorne carried the device
one step further to make the uncertain light of his study, not a source of
mental delusion, but the condition under which the mind might perceive a world neither wholly fanciful nor wholly real. He created in his
softly lighted room "a neutral territory," as he calls it in *The Scarlet Letter,* a place "somewhere between the real world and fairy-land, where
the Actual and the Imaginary may meet, and each imbue itself with the
nature of the other" (1: 36).

Hawthorne's skill in walking "that difficult and narrow line between
the Natural and Supernatural" was recognized in his own day and suggested to at least one reviewer of *Mosses from an Old Manse* his relation
to such writers as Sir Walter Scott and the Baron de la Motte Fouqué.[18]
More important, however, is Hawthorne's belief that this neutral territory provided the basis for much of his work. In *The House of the Seven*

Gables, for example, he includes a brief description of the house and garden at twilight that expresses perfectly the atmosphere he needed for his fiction. The glow of the moon softens and embellishes "the aspect of the old house," while shadows fall "deeper into the angles of its many gables, and [lie] brooding under the projecting story, and within the half-open door." The garden grows increasingly picturesque. "The common-place characteristics—which, at noontide, it seemed to have taken a century of sordid life to accumulate—were now transfigured by a charm of romance" (2: 213). Such conditions provided him with the proper medium for the introduction of the marvelous which he defends in his preface to the book and which plays so important a role in all of his best work.

Hawthorne's use of the marvelous includes apparitions of many different kinds. The old regicide who opposes Sir Edmund Andros in "The Gray Champion" (1835) is a real man perceived by some as a ghost, while Mary Goffe, who pleads with Richard Digby to return to human fellowship in "The Man of Adamant" (1837), may be taken as either an actual apparition or "a dreamlike spirit, typifying pure Religion" (11: 168). Both appear, nonetheless, in that uncertain light which Hawthorne saw as the proper medium for the manifestation of such phenomena. Other phantoms appear in dimly lighted rooms or in the reflected light of mirrors. The specters who are said to haunt the Province House in "Old Esther Dudley" (1839) are apparitions of those who were once reflected in the mansion's clouded mirror, and those that Arthur Dimmesdale sees during his nighttime vigils in *The Scarlet Letter* appear "by a faint light of their own, in the remote dimness of the chamber, or more vividly, and close beside him, within the looking-glass" (1: 145). Hawthorne, of course, does not insist on the reality of these ghosts. Those in the Province House are presented as merely a legend, while the ones that Dimmesdale sees are only a delusion of the senses.

Even with such explanations, however, Hawthorne knew that he had to use supernatural phenomena with discretion: "to mingle the Marvellous rather as a slight, delicate, and evanescent flavor, than as any portion of the actual substance of the dish offered to the Public" (2: 1). When he went beyond the brief suggestion of ghostly phenomena, therefore, to include an extended Gothic scene in *The House of the Seven Gables,* he used the old device of the fictional voice who disavows belief in the story he tells. The incident is that in which the dead Judge Pyn-

cheon sits in the patriarchal chair before the picture of Colonel Pyncheon, the founder of his family. The narrative voice pretends to put no
faith in the scene he describes, but he also makes it clear that the Judge
himself, whose materialism he has mercilessly attacked, also "believes in
no such nonsense" (2: 278). This narrative voice, in other words, is not
to be trusted. Despite his insistence on the fanciful nature of the episode,
he manages the Gothic atmosphere so well as to render entirely credible
the ghostly company of Pyncheons who once had lived in the house and
now reappear in it as phantoms.

The scene is most effectively drawn. The night is at first windy and
dark, with an "inscrutable blackness" that annihilates sight, and we
hear only the blast of the wind, the creaking of the old house, and all
those kinds of noises that suggest the presence of apparitions (2: 276-
77). But the night soon clears, and little by little the moonbeams appear
in the room: "they dance hand-in-hand with shadows, and are reflected
in the looking-glass, which," the narrator states, "is always a kind of
window or door-way into the spiritual world" (2: 281). In this evanescent light, the ghosts materialize. Each approaches the portrait of Colonel Pyncheon, tries the picture frame, and turns away, angered, dis-
tressed, and frustrated by something about it. Even Judge Pyncheon's
son, thought still to be alive, appears in the scene, and the Judge himself, whose corpse can be discerned in the room "as plainly as the flickering moonbeams can show us anything" (2: 280-81), walks among the
other spirits to probe unsuccessfully the mystery of the ancestral portrait. At this point the narrative voice dissolves the scene and returns the
reader to actuality as the first light of dawn begins to show in the room.

By presenting the episode in this way, Hawthorne suggests that another kind of reality has superseded that of the material world, which,
in the sudden death of Judge Pyncheon, has been shown to be as insub-
stantial as the ghosts that seem to materialize in the transient moonbeams. These uneasy spirits are in many ways more real than the corpse
of the dead Judge, for they represent the ongoing pride, guilt, and frus-
tration that has beset the Pyncheon family ever since the Colonel
cheated Matthew Maule out of his land and established his dynasty on a
great wrong that has reproduced itself in successive generations. The
House of the Seven Gables is haunted by ghosts that cannot be laid until
the wrong done the Maules is righted and the pride of the Pyncheons,
best expressed through the wealth and power they expect to receive

when they recover the lost deed to some eastern lands, is at last humbled. Both these conditions are met when the Judge and his son die, the deed to the now worthless land is discovered behind the portrait, and the family possessions devolve on young Phoebe Pyncheon, who marries the last of the Maules and so restores the land to a new, legitimate line.

Hawthorne's ghosts are thus effective representations of the pervasive influence of the past. If, as Holgrave suggests at one point, the past is a grave from which dead men, through social institutions, exert their will on the living, and if, as is suggested elsewhere, memory is a sepulchre, it does not really matter whether the ghosts are perceived as real, imagined, or figurative. The effect, in any case, is the same. The ghost of Colonel Pyncheon haunts the House of the Seven Gables whether he is seen as a spectral manifestation or the historical cause of the Pyncheon woes. In a somewhat different fashion, Clifford and Hepzibah Pyncheon—and even Hester Prynne and Arthur Dimmesdale in the forest scene of *The Scarlet Letter*—are depicted as living ghosts because, blighted by sin or sorrow, their lives have been destroyed by events that occurred long before. Not all of Hawthorne's ghosts are negative, of course—the apparition of the Gray Champion reappears at moments of national crisis to keep alive the spirit of freedom—yet, whatever their function, all of them represent the effects of a past that seems dead but which, in their ghostly forms, is nonetheless still living.

Hawthorne also used the device of deceptive light to develop a related but, in his hands, quite different strain of the Gothic: the demonic. This aspect of the mode, familiar from British and German literature, came to him from a number of different sources: *Melmoth the Wanderer,* of course, but also the many books he read in seventeenth-century New England history, where devils and witches play an important role. American writers had not been quick to develop this aspect of the Gothic mode. Washington Irving, John Pendleton Kennedy, and Edgar Allan Poe had written some amusing devil stories,[19] and James Fenimore Cooper and Robert Montgomery Bird had employed significant devil imagery to express the darkness and violence of the American frontier. But no American writer before Hawthorne had made such extensive use of the demonic or drawn so heavily on Puritan sources. Though, in "The May-Pole of Merry Mount" (1836), Hawthorne may dismiss as superstition the Puritan belief that the wilderness was filled with "devils and ruined souls" (9: 56), he put the concept to excellent use in some of his tales and romances: *The Scarlet Letter,* for example, where the Black Man in the forest provides a locus for the sense of evil that pervades the book.

"Young Goodman Brown" is the classic example of Hawthorne's use of the concept. Brown leaves his home and his wife, Faith, in Salem village just at sunset to encounter in the dim light of the forest a demonic figure. Brown speaks of the devil and he appears. Since it is "deep dusk in the forest, and deepest in that part of it where these two were journeying," Goodman Brown can barely discern his companion or what is going on about him. The staff of his fellow traveler, formed in the shape "of a great black snake," seems "to twist and wriggle itself, like a living serpent," but, we are told, this "must have been an ocular deception, assisted by the uncertain light" (10: 76). Goody Cloyse, who taught Brown his catechism, the minister, and Deacon Gookin all seem to appear, but these, in Puritan belief of the time, may be only their specters, intent on deceiving him.[20] Indeed, Brown does not see the latter two at all, but, like the lady in "The Hollow of the Three Hills," merely hears some sounds that suggest to him their presence.

Though dismayed by what he has seen and heard in the deceptive light, Goodman Brown nonetheless stands "firm against the devil" (10: 82). When he hears some sounds, however, which seem to indicate that the whole town, including his Faith, is in the forest, he plunges in the madness of despair through the haunted woods, laughing wildly. Himself demoniac now, he has become the most frightful figure there. Brown arrives at last at the witches' meeting, where lurid flames from supernatural fires, "blazing high into the night," fitfully illuminate "a numerous congregation" (10: 84). In "the sudden gleams of light" that flash "over the obscure field," Brown thinks he sees the pious folk of his community consorting with the most dissolute (10:85), and he feels "a loathful brotherhood" with them "by the sympathy of all that [is] wicked in his heart" (10: 86). Yet Brown is not totally lost. When Faith appears at his side to join him as a convert to the dark assembly, he calls on her to "look up to Heaven, and resist the Wicked One" (10: 88). All at once the vision disappears, the fires vanish, and Young Goodman Brown finds himself alone in the calm night.

When Brown returns to Salem village the next morning, he sees the town and its people in a new way. Although everyone seems engaged in innocent activity, Brown shrinks from them as if they were indeed the black sinners he perceived them to be in the forest. He even turns away from Faith, and though he lives what seems to be a long and fruitful life, "they carved no hopeful verse upon his tomb-stone; for his dying hour was gloom" (10: 90). Like the characters in William Cullen Bryant's "Medfield" and "The Indian Spring," Brown is faced with alternate realities, each of which is based on the same kind of evidence. His senses tell him one thing in the forest, and, if he would believe them, quite another in the town. But unlike Bryant's characters, who reach an impasse, Brown accepts as true the bizarrely lighted scene he has witnessed in the forest. It is a bad decision however one looks at it. If the vision is real, Brown has been taken in by the arch deceiver, but if it is not, Brown has deceived himself by surrendering to that part of his nature which can not only generate such a delusion but also prevent him from dispelling it.[21]

We know from the story that Brown has deliberately sought his encounter with the devil. He "kept covenant by meeting" him in the forest. Brown does not, to be sure, intend to become completely involved with evil. After that single night, he tells us, he expects to cling to his wife's "skirts and follow her to Heaven" (10: 75-76). In his one attempt to experience evil, however, Brown falls into the devil's snare by seeking it in others: his father and grandfather, his teacher, his minister, indeed the whole town. And of course he finds what he seeks. But there is one place where he does not look for it—in his own breast. Had he done so, his vision of others might have been brighter. Not that the world he sees in the forest is entirely false. There is indeed, as he learns, evil in everyone, but Brown has no business looking for it in his fellows. With a deeper sense of his own guilt he would not have gone into the forest, and instead of shrinking from his fellow men he would have discovered a parallel truth: the good that can be perceived in Salem village in the light of day.

Young Goodman Brown's experience resembles in many ways that of Richard Henry Dana's Paul Felton and Washington Allston's Monaldi. All three begin as honest and upright men, but the evil that lurks within them, as it does in everyone, causes them to misperceive the external world. Because their imaginations are controlled by their dark inner beings, they project a vision of madness and terror. Brown is perhaps more culpable than either Paul Felton or Monaldi, for he makes a deliberate choice to experience evil, but the point is much the same in all three tales. The source of evil lies in the human heart, a point that Hawthorne makes abundantly clear in "Earth's Holocaust" (1844). In this allegorical tale, he satirizes the favorite reforms of the time—reforms designed to bring about a better, indeed, a perfect future. In a general conflagration all things that men call evil are destroyed, but just as they are about to congratulate themselves on what they have done, "a dark-complexioned personage" with glowing eyes (an obvious devil figure) assures them that unless the human heart is cleansed, all of the old evil—and worse—will return (10: 403).

This idea formed the basis of "Ethan Brand," a tale of the demonic which resembles "Young Goodman Brown" in the use Hawthorne makes of uncertain light, but which differs from it in the diabolism of the central character. The sun has already sunk behind the encircling mountains when Ethan Brand, returning from his quest for the Unpardonable Sin, approaches the lime kiln where a man named Bartram has succeeded him as lime burner. Although some rosy light still shines in the upper sky, the scene below is illumined only by "the tender light of the half-full moon" and, when the door of the kiln is opened, by the lurid glare of the fire that quivers "on the dark intricacy of the surrounding forest" (11: 85). Since Ethan Brand arrives after night has fallen, his face cannot be seen by the other characters except in the intense light from the kiln. Bartram throws the door open first to get a good look at his visitor, and when others come from the village to see the man who has been absent for some eighteen years, he sets the door ajar "that the whole company might get a fair view of Ethan Brand, and he of them" (11: 91).

That light has, however, some unusual properties. Although this fire, unlike the lurid flames that Brown sees in the forest, is a natural one, Hawthorne associates it with a number of suggestive images. When he first describes the kiln with "smoke and jets of flame issuing from the chinks and crevices of [its] door," he likens it to "the private entrance to the infernal regions, which the shepherds of the Delectable Mountains were accustomed to show to pilgrims" in John Bunyan's *The Pilgrim's Progress* (11: 84). This image of the kiln as a kind of hell is further suggested by a popular superstition of the neighborhood: that when Ethan Brand began to contemplate his quest for the Unpardonable Sin, "he had been accustomed to evoke a fiend from the hot furnace of the limekiln, night after night, in order to confer with him." Then, "with the first gleam of light upon the mountain-top, the fiend crept in at the iron door, there to abide in the intensest element of fire, until again summoned forth" by Ethan Brand (11: 89). Though Hawthorne presents the tale as merely a local tradition, the suggestion is strong that Ethan Brand has, in some sense, had an experience of evil by the light of this fire.

If so, it was not apparent to him at first. He began his quest for the Unpardonable Sin as "a simple and loving man" who looked with reverence into the hearts of others. In time, however, his intellectual development so far surpassed the moral as to destroy his heart and turn him into a cold observer who made mankind "the subject of his experiment" (11: 98-99). Instead of recoiling from others because of their presumed frailties, as Brown had done, Brand exerts his will upon them, loses all "sense of brotherhood with man, and reverence for God," and sacrifices everything to the claims of his mighty intellect (11: 90). Like Goodman Brown, who, laughing wildly, plunges into the forest toward the witches' meeting "with the instinct that guides mortal man to evil" (10: 83), Ethan Brand becomes demoniac as a consequence of his even more relentless and cold-blooded search for evil. His terrible laugh, like Brown's and Melmoth's; his fiery eyes, like those of countless demons in Gothic fiction; and his kinship with the Wandering Jew, present here in the old German with his show-box—all indicate the devilish qualities that Brand has acquired in the course of his quest.

The great irony of Ethan Brand's experience is that after years of probing into the hearts of others to find the Unpardonable Sin, he discovers it in his own. Despite the absurdity of his long search, however, and the serious harm he has done to others, Brand feels neither regret nor remorse. He proudly states that, given the opportunity, he would incur the guilt again, and he unshrinkingly accepts the retribution. Unlike Goodman Brown, a deeply troubled man who lives his life in unmitigated gloom yet still retains his hold on humanity, Ethan Brand turns himself into a devil and ends his life in despair. His task done, and, as he believes, well done, nothing remains for him in this world. He climbs the mound of earth that partly encompasses the kiln and looks into the dancing flames that rise and fall as from a magic circle. The last we see of him, the blue flames play about his face, imparting "the wild and ghastly light which alone [can suit] its expression . . . that of a fiend on the verge of plunging into his gulf of intensest torment" (11: 100).

A man may turn "himself into a devil," Hawthorne writes in *The Scarlet Letter,* "if he will only, for a reasonable space of time, undertake a devil's office" (1: 170). This is what Ethan Brand has done in his search for the Unpardonable Sin, and it is what Roger Chillingworth accomplishes when he probes the heart of Arthur Dimmesdale in that romance.[22] Chillingworth enters the book already cast in the role of Gothic villain: the learned doctor, perhaps a necromancer, whose body reflects the deformity of his character. He carries one shoulder higher than the other, and his eyes, though "dim and bleared" from poring over books, have "a strange, penetrating power" whenever it is his "purpose to read the human soul" (1: 58). When Chillingworth arrives in Boston, moreover, and discovers that Hester Prynne, his young wife, is an adulteress with an illegitimate child, he reacts in such a way as to suggest that there is indeed a demonic aspect to his nature. "A writhing horror [twists] itself across his features, like a snake gliding swiftly over them," and his face darkens "with some powerful emotion" that he instantly controls (1: 61).

Despite these demonic qualities, however, Hawthorne makes it clear that Chillingworth, like Ethan Brand, once possessed a number of fine attributes. Although he was always a rather cold man who spent many years in improving his own knowledge, he also faithfully worked "for the advancement of human welfare" and lived a life that was "peaceful and innocent." Chillingworth even calls on Hester Prynne to witness that, in their life together, he had shown himself to be an unselfish man, thoughtful of others, and of "kind, true, just, and . . . constant, if not warm affections." Hester agrees that he was "all this, and more" (1: 172). Even as he begins his search for Hester's partner in sin, moreover, Chillingworth acts with something less than a totally evil purpose. He thinks that he can conduct the investigation "with the severe and equal integrity of a judge, desirous only of truth" (1: 129). But Chillingworth forgets one all-important thing. Unlike Goodman Brown and Ethan Brand, he has a personal motive for seeking evil in the heart of the man who wronged him, and as he pursues his quest, he becomes so absorbed in the process that he loses his basic humanity and transforms himself into a fiend.

The effects are apparent even in his physical being. Three years after his arrival in Boston, Hester is startled to see the change that has already come over him. His features have become much uglier, his complexion more dark, and his body more misshapen than she had remembered them. Over the years his eyes grow increasingly bright: sometimes "burning blue and ominous, like the reflection of a furnace, or, let us say, like one of those gleams of ghastly fire that darted from Bunyan's awful door-way in the hill-side" (1: 129); at other times shining with "a glare of red light," as if to reveal the fire that burns in his soul (1: 169). Even the people of Boston recognize the change that takes place in Chillingworth's aspect, especially after he goes to live with Arthur Dimmesdale, whom he identifies as Hester's partner in sin. "Something ugly and evil" appears "in his face, which they had not previously noticed, and which grew still the more obvious to sight, the oftener they looked upon him." They come to believe that their beloved minister, whom they consider a person of special sanctity, is for that reason "haunted either by Satan himself, or Satan's emissary, in the guise of old Roger Chillingworth" (1: 127-28).

They are not far wrong in their estimate of the old man's character. When, after much probing of the minister's heart, Chillingworth finds him asleep one day and, throwing aside the vestment that covers his breast, sees a mark that he takes as a sign of the sin, the old man reacts with "ghastly rapture." He throws his arms in the air and stamps his foot on the floor. Had anyone seen him then, Hawthorne comments, "he would have had no need to ask how Satan comports himself, when a precious human soul is lost to heaven, and won into his kingdom" (1: 138). From this point on, the old man probes the minister's heart with active malice and becomes so much a devil that, in the final scaffold scene, he assumes the role of the tempter himself. When Dimmesdale, about to mount the scaffold, summons Hester and Pearl, his daughter, to him, Chillingworth rushes forward with a look "so dark, disturbed, and evil" that he seems to have risen "up out of some nether region" (1: 252). He tries to dissuade the minister with promises to save him, but Dimmesdale, seeing him now for the devil he is, refuses to listen.

When Arthur Dimmesdale confesses his sin and dies on the scaffold, Roger Chillingworth undergoes a remarkable transformation. "All his strength and energy—all his vital and intellectual force—[seem] at once to desert him," and the old man withers up and shrivels away "like an uprooted weed that lies wilting in the sun." He has made "the pursuit and systematic exercise of revenge" the sole "principle of his life," and, having carried it to "its completest triumph and consummation," he no longer has any reason for living. Left without any devil's work to do on earth, the dehumanized old man can only die (1: 260). In the life of Roger Chillingworth, as in that of Ethan Brand, Hawthorne affirms his belief in the reality of devils. Though the Black Man in the forest may be only a Puritan superstition and Goodman Brown's vision merely a self-created delusion, Ethan Brand and Roger Chillingworth are neither. They are, rather, the flesh-and-blood embodiments of a principle of evil that can so possess the mind and heart as to change what was once a kind and decent human being into an incarnate fiend, capable of performing the most appalling acts against his fellow men.[23]

To express those qualities of intellect and heart that can so seriously affect the well-being of men, Hawthorne sometimes uses a familiar Gothic device—the house, room, cave, or some other type of enclosure—that writers such as Charles Brockden Brown and Richard Henry Dana had turned to good purpose before him and that Edgar Allan Poe was also using at about the same time. Like all of these writers, Hawthorne occasionally turns an enclosed space into a symbol of mind. In an early sketch, "The Haunted Mind" (1835), for example, a common bedroom late at night becomes a place where the mental state of the narrator may be projected into the external world. It is two o'clock of a winter morning, the room is filled with soft light, and once during the sketch the hearth-fire in the adjoining room flares up to add a ruddier glow. This is, in other words, the neutral territory that Hawthorne was so fond of, the place where ghosts may appear in the deceptive light and shadow. The man who awakes at such an hour, therefore, may expect to encounter those spirits and demons that do not appear in the light of common day.

He may awaken so suddenly, for example, as to surprise the creatures of his "dream in full convocation round [his] bed, and catch one broad glance at them before they can flit into obscurity" (9: 304). But others will come to take their place. Ghosts of the past may glide by the bed as the "things of the mind become dim spectres to the eye," and should the watchful one be so unfortunate, "a fiercer tribe," those "devils of a guilty heart, that holds its hell within itself," may come to torment him. Yet even without such guilt, the "nightmare of the soul," a "heavy, heavy sinking of the spirits," a "wintry gloom about the heart," and an "indistinct horror of the mind" may blend "itself with the darkness of the chamber" (9: 306-07). The sleeper may shake off this dreadful mood and "on the borders of sleep and wakefulness" (9: 308) enjoy more pleasant visions before falling off once more to sleep, but from our point of view the significance of the sketch is clear. A room or other enclosure may become an index to the mind and reveal the mental state of whatever character is associated with it.

A number of such enclosures appear in Hawthorne's fiction, usually associated with a Gothic figure and containing some ominous intimations. In "The Birth-mark" (1843) there are two, both the creations of Aylmer, a scientist who, in his projection of optical illusions and interest in the universal solvent and elixir of life, reminds one of the necromancers who had long appeared in Gothic fiction. When Aylmer attempts to remove the birthmark, the sign of human imperfection, from the cheek of Georgiana, his newly married wife, he isolates her in a series of Poe-like rooms, lighted by "perfumed lamps, emitting flames of various hue" and "hung with gorgeous curtains" that, falling in heavy folds from ceiling to floor, appear "to shut in the scene from infinite space" (10: 44). These bizarre rooms indicate how far Aylmer has isolated himself and his bride from both common humanity and the sight of heaven. His second apartment, moreover, the laboratory where he prepares the potion for her to drink, suggests—in the intense heat of the furnace, the close, oppressive atmosphere, and the gaseous odors that taint the air—the hellish aspect of Aylmer's purpose to make his wife the subject of an experiment.

The garden of poisonous flowers in "Rappaccini's Daughter" (1844) is another such enclosure. Within its confining walls the pale emaciated doctor—lineal descendant of many Gothic scientists—has kept Beatrice, his child, in an isolation as complete and an environment as bizarre as Georgiana's strange apartment, and he has made her the subject of an even more terrible experiment. A man of penetrating mind but little warmth of heart, Rappaccini has not only reared Beatrice in a garden filled with exotic poisonous plants but has also trained her to care for even the most dangerous of them. As a result he has rendered her as poisonous to others as the most deadly plant in his garden. He even fills Giovanni, her lover, with the same kind of poison, intending to send them together into the world, like a new Adam and Eve, "most dear to one another, and dreadful to all besides" (10: 127). In the arrogance of his intellectual pride, Rappaccini has asumed godlike powers, and shows, in the creation of his inverted Eden, the kind of world such a mind would produce and the race of terrible people with which he would fill it.

In some of his fiction, however, Hawthorne made a departure from the usual Gothic practice and created a number of enclosures that are symbols not of mind but of heart. In "Ethan Brand," for example, the lime kiln functions at first as the projection of Brand's intellect, for, before he began his quest, we are told, "he had thrown his dark thoughts into the intense glow of its furnace, and melted them, as it were, into the one thought that took possession of his life" (11: 84). After his return, however, the lime kiln functions consistently as a heart image. Ethan Brand has looked, he states, "into many a human heart that was seven times hotter with sinful passions than yonder furnace is with fire" (11: 90), and by a series of associations the furnace is linked to both prison-house and hell.[24] By this means Hawthorne creates a complex image in which the human heart, its own private hell, can hold its possessor prisoner to his own dark passions. If we follow the image to its logical extreme, therefore, when Ethan Brand plunges into the furnace near the end of the story, he is consumed in the flames of his own demonic heart.

Hawthorne was fond of the heart image and used it to depict a wide variety of human types.[25] The human heart, he knew, was capable of both great good and great evil, a belief he symbolized in a well-known passage in *The American Notebooks* that sketches out an idea for an unwritten tale. The heart is like a cavern with sunshine and flowers at its entrance. Step but inside, however, and you "find yourself surrounded with a terrible gloom, and monsters of divers kinds; it seems like Hell itself." Though you may "wander long without hope" in this region, press on and you will find another "that seems, in some sort, to reproduce the flowers and sunny beauty of the entrance, but all perfect. These are the depths of the heart, or of human nature, bright and peaceful; the gloom and terror may lie deep; but deeper still is this eternal beauty" (8: 237). Hawthorne presents an optimistic picture of human nature in this passage, but in most of the heart images in his fiction, he focuses on that middle area of gloom where ghosts and devils trouble those whose hearts have been in some way blighted.

Not every heart burns with the fire that consumes Ethan Brand. Gervayse Hastings in "The Christmas Banquet" (1844) is just the opposite. Though he attends for many years the holiday banquet given in a grotesque, Poe-like room for the world's most miserable people, he is so cold of heart that he remains completely unaffected by their plight. Utterly inhuman in his lack of sympathy, he cannot relate to them as real people, but perceives them as shadows flickering on the wall. Though Gervayse Hastings is a successful man as the world counts success, he is, in the final analysis, the most miserable of all the guests. Also different is Richard Digby, the religious fanatic in "The Man of Adamant" (1837). Convinced that he alone has the key to salvation, he hurls anathemas at his fellows; and, lest his true faith be contaminated by others, he retires to a cave, a tomblike enclosure that, "hung with substances resembling opaque icicles" (11: 163), drips with mineral waters that change everything to stone. So pleased is the hard-hearted Digby with his retreat, however, that he refuses to heed even a messenger from heaven, but remains in his self-imposed prison until he too turns to adamant.

In Hawthorne's longer fiction, such images of heart and mind can become extremely complex, for a single object may serve a number of different purposes. In *The House of the Seven Gables,* for example, the old Pyncheon mansion becomes at different times the physical embodiment of both mind and heart as it reflects, over the hundred and sixty years of its history, the changing fortunes of the family. When it is first built, it is clearly a head symbol, the external manifestation of Pyncheon family pride, and it embodies over the years that sense of their own importance which makes the Pyncheons stand apart from their fellows in a self-appointed position of superiority. With the passage of time, however, such varied human experience takes place within its walls that the house, filled with "rich and sombre reminiscences," begins to resemble "a great human heart, with a life of its own" (2: 27). Various parts of it also serve a similar function: "the great kitchen-fireplace," for example, which becomes, during an especially dreary storm, a fitting "emblem of the mansion's heart, because, though built for warmth, it was now so comfortless and empty" (2: 224).

Since the House of the Seven Gables is most closely associated with

Hepzibah Pyncheon and, after his return from prison, her brother Clifford, its condition reveals the desolate state of their hearts. Before Clifford's return, for example, a "waste, cheerless, and dusky chamber" is said to resemble "nothing so much as the old maid's heart; for there was neither sunshine nor household-fire in one nor the other, and, save for ghosts, and ghostly reminiscences, not a guest, for many years gone-by, had entered the heart or the chamber" (2: 72). But it is not only the room that reveals Hepzibah's heart. The entire house, where "for above a quarter of a century" she "has dwelt in strict seclusion" (2: 31), aptly reflects the loneliness and gloom that have afflicted her heart throughout those years. Both house and heart are brightened somewhat with the arrival of Phoebe, her sprightly young cousin, and when Clifford returns home, Hepzibah's tender heart at last has something on which to dote. But Hepzibah, like the house, has been blighted by time, and when Clifford pays most attention to the bright and sunny Phoebe, his heart-sick sister is left to make the best of her grief.

For Clifford, the house becomes both heart and prison. After years of loneliness in jail for a crime he did not commit, he longs for companionship, and though repulsed by the near-sighted Hepzibah's scowling looks and her clumsy attempts to help him, he finds that cheerful sympathy in Phoebe which turns the old house and its decaying garden into something resembling a home. But Clifford, like Hepzibah, remains isolated from the outside world. Though he sometimes sits in the great arched window on the second floor to watch the passing life in the street below, neither he nor his sister is able to rejoin that stream of humanity. When they try to attend church one Sunday morning, they find that they cannot reenter the society of their fellow men. As soon as they step across the threshold, they are filled with so great a fear that they retreat at once, like the ghosts they have become, into the depths of an oppressive house that seems ten times more dismal to them for the brief "glimpse and breath of freedom" they have just had. They cannot escape. As Hawthorne explicitly states, they are trapped in the dungeon of their own hearts (2: 169).

For Judge Jaffrey Pyncheon, on the other hand, the enclosure image has a different meaning. It is the symbol of his character. The cold and sagacious spirit of the Judge has constructed "a tall and stately edifice" of reputation which, in his own view and in the view of others, appears to be a palace. The windows seem to "admit the sunshine through the most transparent of plate-glass," and the whole is painted and gilded in a magnificent fashion. But, despite the glittering splendor of the Judge's figurative mansion, there is something hidden deep within that is not reflected in the imposing exterior: "in some low and obscure nook— some narrow closet on the ground floor, shut, locked, and bolted, and the key flung away [lies] a corpse, half-decayed, and still decaying, and diffusing its death-scent all through the palace!" The Judge himself no longer notices it, nor do the visitors who come to flatter the man of wealth and power. "They smell only the rich odors which the master sedulously scatters through the palace, and the incense which they bring, and delight to burn before him!" (2: 229-30).

The image is an appropriate one for the ambitious politician. To retain his respected position in society, Jaffrey Pyncheon has robbed the unfortunate Clifford of his inheritance and allowed him to go to prison for the murder of their uncle, a crime of which Jaffrey, who was present at the old man's death, knew him to be innocent. Because the palace of his reputation is founded upon this great wrong, the Judge's experience epitomizes that of the entire family. The House of the Seven Gables was also built "over an unquiet grave" (2: 9), and the corpse—the original wrong done Matthew Maule by Colonel Pyncheon—has tainted both house and family throughout their long history. Indeed, Judge Pyncheon becomes himself the physical manifestation of this concept when, after his sudden death, he is left alone, sitting in the ancestral chair, throughout an entire day and night. If the deserted house represents in this scene the collective character of the Pyncheon family, the dead Judge has assumed the role of the festering corpse. Sitting unheeded in the mansion's parlor, he embodies the terrible reality that lies concealed behind the proud façade of the House of the Seven Gables.

Hawthorne developed this kind of imagery more fully in *The Marble Faun*, where many of the enclosures are subterranean and suggest death and the grave. Here the festering corpse is Imperial Rome itself, a dead "giant, decaying for centuries, with no survivor mighty enough even to bury it, until the dust of all those years has gathered slowly over its recumbent form and made a casual sepulchre" (4: 110).[26] Hawthorne uses this figure several times in the book to keep before the reader a sense of the past—dead, decaying, yet still somehow alive, both in the ghosts and specters that arise out of it to haunt the living, and in the numerous relics that, unearthed from these graves, forever remind us of its continuing influence on the present. The book is punctuated with such enclosures: the Catacomb of St. Calixtus, into which the characters descend with such unfortunate consequences to both Miriam and Donatello; the cemetery of the Capuchins, where Miriam's model is buried after they have murdered him; and the excavation into which Kenyon descends in the Roman Campagna, an area that Hawthorne associates with columbaria and richly frescoed Etruscan tombs.

Of these enclosures, the most important is the first, the catacomb in which Miriam encounters the model who thenceforth haunts her path until, at a glance from the distraught girl, Donatello hurls him from the Tarpeian Rock to his death. The "Spectre of the Catacomb" (4: 30, 31), as he is called, is a ghost from Miriam's shadowy past, a sign that she cannot escape its pernicious influence. But he is also associated with a number of figures who suggest the dark side of human experience: not only such common malefactors as the robber or assassin who might hide in the catacomb to escape the police, but also the legendary Memmius, the "man, or demon, or Man-Demon" who, stealing into the catacomb to betray the early Christians, remains to haunt it (4: 32), and the Gerasene demoniac, the man, possessed by devils, who lived among the tombs and "whose awful cry," Hawthorne comments, "echoes afar to us from Scripture times" (4: 35).[27] By this range of association, Hawthorne suggests that the spectral figure represents something beyond his relation to Miriam, and that the Gothic drama which unfolds from this scene has far-ranging significance.

At one point, moreover, Hawthorne suggests that the catacomb, a place of bones and dusty death, is an image of human life. As the characters stand in a small chapel carved out of the red sandstone, "their collected torches" illuminate only the "small, consecrated spot," while around them "the great darkness" spreads "like that immenser mystery which envelopes our little life, and into which friends vanish from us, one by one" (4: 26-27). The image of human life as all but engulfed by mortality is fully developed here and repeated elsewhere in the book, most notably in the description of the cemetery of the Capuchins. For just as the remains of the early Christians are visible in the niches along the many passageways of the catacomb—human shapes resolved to dust, crumbling bones, and grinning skulls—so too are the skeletons of the dead monks in the modern cemetery, each disinterred in turn to make room for a successor to lie in the consecrated earth, and placed around the walls and niches of the vault to create a house of death. Both cata-comb and cemetery, separated in time by nearly two millenia, present a chilling image of the human condition.

A dark view of human fate is further suggested by the experience of the major characters and the enclosure imagery through which it is pre-sented: not only that of the unfortunate Miriam, who evokes a terrible ghost from the past in the Catacomb of St. Calixtus, but also that of her friends, who had gone "joyously down" with her "into that vast tomb" (4: 24), and are indelibly stained as a consequence of what hap-pens there. Donatello becomes a murderer, and even the innocent Hilda is somewhat changed by the crime, which she inadvertently witnesses. The most seriously affected is, of course, Donatello. The sylvan faun who had danced so gaily in the Borghese Grove shuts himself up behind the bolted gates of his ancient tower in Tuscany. Within, the tomblike rooms, dark prison chambers, and deserted chapel bespeak the isolation to which his crime has driven him. The tower, therefore—like so many similar structures in Poe's tales—reflects the moral and psychological state of the Count of Monte Beni after the murder has stripped him of his faunlike innocence and before his transformation into a man has been completed.[28]

Kenyon, who visits him at the tower, observes the change that is tak-ing place in Donatello, an experience that is described in terms of yet an-other enclosure. The young count has "had glimpses of strange and sub-tile matters in those dark caverns, into which all men must descend, if they would know anything beneath the surface and illusive pleasures of existence." Not everyone draws an abiding lesson from such a descent, but Donatello does emerge with "truer and sadder views of life" (4: 262). Reunited with Miriam in Perugia, the two have a brief interlude together. Then, filled with remorse for his deed and willing to accept the retribution, he allows himself to be taken by the police during the carnival in Rome. He disappears thereafter into a Roman dungeon, but despite the gloom of his final imprisonment, Hawthorne makes clear that Donatello has become a better and truer man for his experience. Through sin and sorrow the carefree young count has acquired a depth of feeling and intelligence that he would not otherwise have had, and he even seems to possess a higher beauty than that of the innocent faun he had once appeared to be.

The ethereal Hilda also undergoes an experience that renders her more human. Her relation to the faunlike Donatello is established early in the book by the revulsion they both feel at the death and decay they encounter in the Catacomb of St. Calixtus, but unlike Donatello, whose isolation in his ancestral tower results from guilt, this daughter of the Puritans has separated herself from common humanity by the high moral stand she invariably takes. Her state, like his, is well represented by the lofty tower in which she lives. Rising above all other structures in Rome except the domes of some of the churches and the statue of St. Paul on the column of Antoninus, it isolates her from the dark realities of life. Hilda is shocked into a perception of them by the murder she witnesses, and she sins herself in her cold rejection of Miriam, who comes to her for help. Remorseful at how she has acted, however, Hilda fulfills a promise she had made to deliver a package for Miriam to the gloomy Cenci palace. There Hilda vanishes for several days, to reappear during the carnival in exchange for the surrender of Miriam and Donatello to the police.

Though somewhat softened by her brush with evil and her passage through that dark enclosure, Hilda has not been greatly changed by her experience. Her eyes may fill with tears when she thinks of Miriam's plight, but she still maintains her high moral stand and remains as optimistic about the human condition as she has ever been. She will not accept Kenyon's suggestion that the faunlike Donatello was inevitably destroyed by the "sadly serious" business of life, and although she perceives the growth that all have seen in him, she rejects the interpretation that Miriam and Kenyon have considered: that sin, "like Sorrow," is "merely an element of human education, through which we struggle to a higher and purer state than we could otherwise have attained" (4: 459-60). She even wins Kenyon over to her opinion. He abandons his speculation at once when she voices her disapproval, and he wants her to be his polestar and guide him home. Hilda comes down from her tower to marry him, and the two young people, turning away completely from the dark view of humanity that their experience in Italy has everywhere thrust upon them, return to the United States to live out their lives, presumably, in domestic happiness.

Such a conclusion seems at first to be a complete reversal not only of the apparent theme of *The Marble Faun* but, since it is Hawthorne's last completed work of fiction, of all the dark tales and romances that he had previously written. The Gothic world of Italy seems to dissolve in the sunlight that Hilda, with her "hopeful soul," sees shining "on the mountain-tops" (4: 462). But this kind of conclusion is not that unusual in Hawthorne. "Young Goodman Brown" ends, after all, with a view of Salem village by daylight that directly contradicts what Brown has seen in the forest, and the morning after Ethan Brand's death, the sunrise is depicted in such glorious terms as to suggest the union of heaven and earth in a kind of paradise. Indeed, even in *The Marble Faun* Hawthorne suggests, in the magnificent landscape seen from Donatello's tower, the glory of God and his Providence for men. Thus the dark view expressed through Gothic imagery is only part of Hawthorne's vision of reality, and any conclusion one may draw about his beliefs must include the light as well as the dark.

In a similar fashion, other women besides Hilda lead, or try to lead, their men from moral and intellectual positions that seem unhealthy. Like the heroines of Paulding's *Westward Ho!* and Cooper's *Lionel Lincoln,* both Rosina in "Egotism; or, The Bosom-Serpent" (1843) and Phoebe in *The House of the Seven Gables* draw their men back to the bounds of common life. Others, such as Mary Goffe in "The Man of Adamant," fail completely; some, including Elizabeth in "The Minister's Black Veil" (1836) and Faith in "Young Goodman Brown," remain with them throughout their lives, and try, unsuccessfully, to help them; and a few, such as Georgiana in "The Birth-mark" and Esther in "Ethan Brand," are simply destroyed by the men who dominate them. Other women, of course—Hester, in *The Scarlet Letter,* and Miriam, in *The Marble Faun*—serve no such function: they lead their men to tragic ends. But these few aside, Hilda is one of a whole sisterhood in Hawthorne who, in affirming the social virtues of hearth and home, provide an alternative to the often misdirected intellectuality of those men who probe the dark side of human experience.

And yet, when all is said and done, the Gothic world of darkness and uncertain vision, of ghosts and specters that rise from the past, and of devils that possess the minds and hearts of men, seems more real to many a reader of Hawthorne than does the brighter vision he sometimes includes in his tales and romances. The dark curse in *The House of the Seven Gables* outweighs the cheeriness of the sunny Phoebe, and the gloomy vision of life in "Young Goodman Brown" and "Ethan Brand" dominates those tales in a way that the brighter episodes do not. Even in *The Marble Faun,* Donatello and Miriam seem more alive than the cold

Kenyon and Hilda. The Faun, through sin and suffering, finds a soul and becomes a man, while the persecuted Miriam comes to love him with a depth of feeling she had never before experienced. Their young American friends, however, do not fully appreciate what has happened. Both are bewildered by the dark mysteries of life that the experience of Miriam and Donatello seems to reveal, and, rather than confront the implications of what they have seen, the sculptor and his bride flee to their trans-Atlantic home where such problems do not exist.

Seen in these terms, the conclusion of *The Marble Faun* is profoundly ironic. It does not controvert but rather gives added validity to the dark vision of reality that Hawthorne had projected through the decaying world of time-drenched Italy. Americans like Kenyon and Hilda, it seems to say, refuse to accept reality. Their vision is at best a partial one. Although the spaciousness and light of their native land bespeak one kind of truth, the darkness and decay they leave behind teach their lessons, too. As long as Americans turn their backs on the total experience of mankind, fail to perceive the significance of the past, and refuse to accept the reality of those ghosts and devils that emerge from its gloomy depths or lurk in the human heart, they will not achieve the insight that can only come, as it does to Donatello and Miriam, from a full awareness of the dark underside of life.[29] The Gothic world of Hawthorne's fiction serves, therefore, an important thematic purpose. It provides the appropriate vehicle for expressing those somber truths which Hawthorne believed Americans of his generation needed most to know.

NINE

Conclusion

The publication of *The Marble Faun* in March 1860[1] brought to a close the major phase of American Gothicism. The book appeared just on the verge of the Civil War, a conflict which began with a great sense of elan on each side and much romantic panoply in the two armies, but which by 1864 had become a bitter and disillusioning war of attrition. The Civil War left an indelible mark on the American psyche, erasing the historical memories of the antebellum days and ushering in an age that was utterly different from the one that had gone before. The victory of the northern states enabled them to determine the course of American society for the better part of a century. Their rapid industrialization, spurred by the needs of the Federal armies and the accelerating growth of technology, led to a process of urbanization that profoundly transformed the American consciousness. The city replaced the landscape as the locus of interest in both literature and art, and a renewed sense of realism began to dominate American critical theory. The fundamental rationalism of the American mind could only have been reinforced by these developments, leaving little room for the kind of Gothicism that had pervaded the works of Poe and Hawthorne.

The effects of these developments are apparent throughout late nineteenth-century literature, even in those areas where, at first glance, there would seem to be little change. Consider, for example, Henry James's statement on the paucity of materials for the American novelists, a statement that was stimulated by Hawthorne's complaint in his preface to *The Marble Faun,* and which is often treated by critics with Hawthorne's and Cooper's opinions as if they were all the same. They are not. What James enumerates in *Hawthorne* (1879) as "absent from the texture of American life" are "items of high civilisation, as it exists in other countries." America has: "No State, in the European sense of the word, and indeed barely a specific national name. No sovereign, no court, no personal loyalty, no aristocracy, no church, no clergy, no army, no diplomatic service, no country gentlemen, no palaces, no castles, nor manors, nor old country-houses, nor parsonages, nor thatched cottages, nor ivied ruins; no cathedrals, nor abbeys, nor little Norman churches; no great Universities nor public schools—no Oxford, nor Eton, nor Harrow; no literature, no novels, no museums, no pictures, no political society, no sporting class—no Epsom nor Ascot!"[2]

James knew he was overstating the case, for whatever an Englishman or Frenchman might think (and they would have been appalled by his list) a good deal was left for the American author to use, as witness the career of Nathaniel Hawthorne, whose works James admired. What is important in James's indictment is not what he says but what he does not say. Unlike Cooper he does not mention the lack of obscure fictions and dark passages in the annals of the country; unlike Hawthorne he does not regret the absence of mystery and sense of gloomy wrong in the American scene. His primary interest lies not in the traditional elements that were for Cooper and Hawthorne the essence of romance but in the kind of actuality that *did* exist: the cold, thin, blank American scene, as opposed to the "denser, richer, warmer European spectacle." He even cites passages from Hawthorne's *American Notebooks,* "accounts of walks in the country, drives in stage-coaches, people he met in taverns," as illustrations of the "general vacancy" that presented itself to Hawthorne's "field of vision."[3] James's position is that of the literary realist, concerned with the quality of the social world that is available for his use.

In his discussion of Hawthorne's work, the same bias appears. "Hawthorne," James insists, "was not in the least a realist—he was not to my mind enough of one." This opinion colors his treatment of Hawthorne's romances. James objects to "a want of reality and an abuse of the fanciful element" in *The Scarlet Letter,* and though he sees in *The House of the Seven Gables* "more literal actuality than" in the other American novels, he makes no great claim for the book on that score. Hawthorne "never attempted to render exactly or closely the actual facts of the society that surrounded him"; hence "the reader must look for his local and national qualities between the lines of his writing." Even *The Blithedale Romance* is not, in James's opinion, realistic enough. "As the action advances," he observes, "we get too much out of reality, and cease to feel beneath our feet the firm ground of an appeal to our own vision of the world." In *The Marble Faun,* on the other hand, though Hawthorne, to his credit, attempts "to deal with actualities more than he did in" his previous works, "the element of the unreal is pushed too far" and the book wavers between the actual and the fanciful.[4]

James's opinion of Hawthorne in 1879 is a fair indication of the change that had taken place in American taste over the preceding twenty years. Literary realism had again come to the fore, and American writers felt free to criticize what they saw as deficiencies in the works of their predecessors. The break, however, was by no means complete. Though the best American writers in the new generation were committed realists who put into practice new theories and created a basically different kind of fiction, they nonetheless maintained their links with the past. Both Henry James and William Dean Howells, for example, owe obvious debts to Hawthorne, and Ambrose Bierce was deeply influenced by Poe. Their realistic predilections, moreover, did not prevent them from using materials which one might suppose were greatly at odds with their theories. They did not entirely eschew the Gothic mode. Henry James wrote a number of ghostly tales and produced in "The Turn of the Screw" (1898) a classic of Gothic fiction; Ambrose Bierce instilled both terror and horror into the stories that appeared in his best book, *In the Midst of Life* (1892);[5] and even that archrealist William Dean Howells produced both novels and tales that are based on occult phenomena.

There are, nonetheless, important differences between the generations. Hawthorne and Poe, after all, were born in the first decade of the nineteenth century, right after the appearance of Radcliffe's and Brown's romances, and they grew to manhood just at the time when the works of Maturin, Scott, and the German romantic writers were current fiction. They absorbed the works of these Gothic writers, made them their own, and used the mode as an organic part of their literary expression. Later generations of American writers felt the influence less strongly. Even Herman Melville, born in 1819 and drawing his inspiration from his early experience at sea, was only lightly touched by the Gothic, primarily in *Moby Dick* (1851). Fedallah's burning eyes mark him as the devil figure of conventional Gothic fiction, and certain scenes in the romance, most notably that in Chapter XCVI, "The Try-Works," use typical Gothic devices. But aside from elements like these and his satire on Gothic fiction in Isabel's story in *Pierre* (1852), Melville makes relatively little use of the mode.[6] It was never so central to his fiction as it was to the works of Poe and Hawthorne.

The next generation of writers, those born in the 1830s and 1840s, were even less strongly influenced by Gothic fiction. Growing to manhood just on the verge of the Civil War, they experienced the trauma of that conflict (Bierce, indeed, as a Union soldier) and many turned as models for their writing to a new generation of European authors—Balzac, Flaubert, Turgenev, and others—more closely attuned to the kind of fiction they wished to write. Important changes had taken place, moreover, in the popular attitude toward the supernatural during the 1840s and 1850s, changes that were to turn even their limited use of the Gothic in new directions. The wide interest in mesmerism, or, as it was sometimes called, animal magnetism, during the 1840s was the first of a series of phenomena that was soon to transform the mode.[7] Poe took up the subject in some of his fiction. In "Mesmeric Revelation" (1844), for example, he used the device as a means for presenting some of the theories he was to develop at length in *Eureka*, while in "The Facts in the Case of M. Valdemar" (1845), perhaps his most gruesome story, he created one of his most successful hoaxes.

Hawthorne, on his part, treated the phenomenon with deep suspicion because it seemed to provide a means by which the mesmerist could violate the integrity of another human soul. This is the use to which it is put by Matthew Maule in *The House of the Seven Gables* (1851), when he takes control of the proud and unfortunate Alice Pyncheon to make her do his will. The process is almost repeated several generations later when Holgrave, telling the story of Alice to Phoebe Pyncheon, perceives her about to fall under his hypnotic influence, but Holgrave resists the temptation to assume dominion over her spirit and sets Phoebe free. In *The Blithedale Romance* (1852), however, another young girl, Priscilla, falls under the influence of the devil-like Westervelt and is made to appear veiled on a public platform to exhibit supposedly supernatural powers. Though she too is eventually set free by Hollingsworth, Hawthorne's attitude is clear. Mesmerism is a sinister power that in the hands of the wizard Maule or the devilish Westervelt can be used for evil purposes. As such, it fit in well with the other Gothic devices that Hawthorne used to develop the themes of his most effective fiction.

Though mesmerism could be made to fit conveniently into the Gothic fiction created by Poe and Hawthorne, new developments in popular culture could not. The advent of spirit rapping in the late 1840s and the widespread growth of spiritualism in the succeeding decade could only have a deleterious effect on the Gothic mode.[8] The spirits of the dead, long a source of supernatural terror in literature, were in a sense domesticated. Summoned at will by a medium to participate in a séance, they lost much of their power to frighten. The result was, in effect, to trivialize the supernatural, especially when the supposed spirits were made to perform silly tricks or were asked to respond to inane questions. An aura of scientism was also added to the subject as spiritualistic investigators attempted to provide empirical evidence for the existence of an afterlife and clothed their activities in pseudoscientific language. Spiritualism was of course fraught with deception, and in the course of time its many frauds were exposed. It had done, meanwhile, great damage to the Gothic mode, which could not long survive in the intellectual climate that the spiritualist movement had created.

The decline of American Gothic fiction can be easily traced in Howells's *The Undiscovered Country* (1880) and James's *The Bostonians* (1886), both of which derive from *The Blithedale Romance.* All three novels depict the experience of an ethereal young girl who, placed in a trance by a mesmerist or spiritualist, exhibits supposedly supernatural powers, but as we move from book to book, the Gothic influence weakens. Hawthorne played down the spiritualistic basis for Priscilla's performance to concentrate on the evil power of Westervelt and link him to the traditional Gothic villain. When Coverdale first encounters him on the wood-path at Blithedale, Westervelt's black eyes are sparkling, his teeth are "remarkably brilliant," and he carries "a stick with a wooden head, carved in vivid imitation of that of a serpent." Though Coverdale feels "as if the whole man were a moral and physical humbug," it seems to him, nonetheless, "as if the Devil were peeping out of" his sparkling eyes (3: 92, 95, 94). His control over Priscilla is therefore sinister, and though she, like the Lady in Milton's *Comus,* remains untouched in her inner being by the power of the sorcerer, the point of the experience, in Hawthorne's view, is that she has been in real danger.

Howells and James, on the other hand, make their entrancers rather ordinary human beings, caught up, for one reason or another, in the spiritualist excitement. Howells turns the devilish Westervelt into the rather pitiful Doctor Boynton, a well meaning physician-spiritualist who joined the movement to communicate with his dead wife and who anxiously wants to prove that there is life after death. The dupe of fraudulent spiritualists and the butt of a skeptic's prank, Doctor Boynton is hardly a sinister figure. Though he dominates his daughter, Egeria, who serves as a medium for communication with the spirits, he is a rather ineffectual man who must admit at last the futility of his quest. There is little room for the Gothic in the experience of such a character. Though Howells does briefly create a sense of the eerie in his description of a séance and provides one "physical manifestation" of the spirits that the doctor believes he sees during a thunderstorm,[9] most of the book takes place in the rural quiet of a Shaker village, where much attention is given to the quaint spirituality that the doctor and his daughter perceive in that strange sect.

James transforms the character even more drastically in *The Bostonians* to make him an object of satire. Selah Tarrant, the entrancer of his daughter, Verena, cuts a ludicrous figure as he moves through the book in "his eternal waterproof" in pursuit of personal aggrandizement.[10] Possessing neither the sinister villainy of Westervelt nor the ineffectual honesty of Doctor Boynton, Selah Tarrant is a venal fraud. A former spiritualist, he has been exposed as a fake by some scientific investigators and has had to become instead a mesmeric healer. Tarrant is so corrupt that he wants to profit from the talents his daughter possesses as a trance lecturer, and he even sells her to Olive Chancellor, who wants to use her to further feminist causes but who soon finds herself in a bitter struggle with Basil Ransom for control of the pliant girl. All kinds of strange people appear in the book, "witches and wizards, mediums, and spirit-rappers and roaring radicals," as one character calls them,[11] but James makes no attempt to create a Gothic atmosphere with their presence. His book is a satire upon the gross excesses of much nineteenth-century popular thought in America. Its mode is the comic.

Though the rise of spiritualism in the United States led to the decline of American Gothic fiction, the advent of psychical research as a respectable discipline helped bring about its partial rejuvenation. Men of indisputable integrity both here and in Europe brought the hard light of science to bear on occult phenomena in an attempt to determine whether or not such manifestations had a basis in reality, and they founded the Society for Psychical Research to pursue their investigations. The society began in England in 1882, and two years later an American branch was established. Although these researchers studied both physical and psychical phenomena, it was the latter investigations that had the most important influence on literary artists.[12] Scientific research into the occult, including such phenomena as mental telepathy and the perception of apparitions, inevitably led to an interest among writers in the psychological basis for strange and uncanny manifestations, in the kind of consciousness that perceives them, and in the nature of the reality they represent. To develop such ideas, American writers turned once again to the Gothic and began in the 1890s to produce a small body of fiction based upon a growing interest in human psychology.

The reaction of human beings to apparently supernatural phenomena had of course been a major element in Gothic fiction since the days of Radcliffe and Brown, both of whom were interested in the psychological causes of a misperceived reality, and the many Gothic writers who followed them in the first half of the nineteenth century were well aware of the psychological implications of the mode. Late nineteenth-century writers, however, lived in a much altered intellectual environment, and their handling of the psychological Gothic differs in important ways from that of their predecessors. For one thing, literary fashion had changed. Authors now presented their apparitions in a realistically depicted setting, usually densely social, and they wrote in a style that had little of the romantic suggestiveness of their literary forebears. William Dean Howells used his normal straightforward prose and conversational idiom in writing his tales of the uncanny; Ambrose Bierce wrote a clear, precise, and simple style even when depicting his most gruesome horrors;[13] and Henry James, approaching his major phase, wrote his ghostly tales in his usually highly nuanced fashion. The style of the Gothic fiction of these three men differs in no essential way from that which they used in their most realistic writing.

Though all of these writers employ some of the paraphernalia of Gothic fiction—presentiments, prophetic dreams, the haunted house, the mysterious picture, and assorted apparitions—these elements are seldom given the prominence they had previously had in Gothic writing. Usually underplayed and made subordinate to the predominant realism of the stories, they serve as suggestive hints that the occult is at least possible. But the main focus of attention is most often the character who has the unusual experience, and the major interest in the tale is in his psychological condition. Howells, in "His Apparition" (1903), concentrates his attention not on the figure Hewson sees but on his psychological reactions after he has perceived it; Bierce is deeply concerned, in tales like "One of the Missing" (1892), with the nature and consequences of psychological time; and James, in "The Jolly Corner" (1908), is most deeply interested in the consciousness of Spencer Brydon, his major character. Though all these tales may be called Gothic, they differ sharply from the kind of fiction written by Brown, Poe, and Hawthorne, both in the themes the authors develop and in the manner of presentation.

As one might expect, William Dean Howells least resembles the earlier Gothic writers. He makes no attempt to create the shadowy atmosphere of darkness and uncertain light that typifies American Gothic writers from Brown to Hawthorne, nor does he invoke the sense of mystery that gives their work its characteristic tone. For Howells, uncanny events are material for case studies in abnormal psychology. Though Faulkner may have what turns out to be a prophetic dream in *The Shadow of a Dream* (1890), it is caused by his own delusion and mania. His madness makes him dream that his wife, Hermia, and their friend Nevil are in love and waiting for him to die so that they may marry. And after Faulkner's death, the dream has a blighting effect on the lives of his wife and friend only because of "their own morbid conscientiousness" and "exaggerated sensibility."[14] In some of his occult tales, indeed, Howells includes a psychologist, Wanhope, who either recounts the strange incident himself, as in "The Eidolons of Brooks Alford," or comments upon a tale told by another, as in "A Case of Metaphantasmia," stories of strange occurrences that Howells included in *Between the Dark and the Daylight* (1907).

In most of the tales, moreover, the reader perceives not the vision the characters have but the characters having the vision. In *Questionable Shapes* (1903) Howells includes three ghostly tales, in only one of which, "His Apparition," is the appearance even described, and then only as "that weird figure seated at his table." In "The Angel of the Lord," we see only the change of mood, from gloomy apprehension to sense of solemn joy, that Ormond experiences after he perceives a vision; and on the day he meets his death we merely perceive him running into the woods "calling joyfully, 'Yes, I'm coming!'" before he falls over a boulder and is killed. We also see Alderling in "Though One Rose from the Dead" rush joyfully to the shore with shouts of "I am coming" in answer to a mysterious call from his dead wife.[15] He rows out into the fog and vanishes forever. Howells makes no attempt to create a Gothic mood, to work on the reader's emotions and make him see or feel what the characters experience. The technique can only be described as clinical, as if the uncanny episode were merely a natural phenomenon to be examined rationally.

Ambrose Bierce was also interested in the psychology of his characters, but unlike Howells he often creates a real sense of horror or terror in the tales he included in his two main collections, *In the Midst of Life* and *Can Such Things Be?* (1893). Strongly influenced by Poe, Bierce sometimes outdoes his master in horror, especially in such war tales as "The Coup de Grâce," where the wounded Sergeant Halcrow has been chewed by hogs, or in "Chickamauga," where a deaf child witnesses the horrors of battle unaware of what is really happening. His tales of terror also include a group in which the protagonists actually die of fright. Bierce apparently believed that a superstitious fear of the dead, derived from primitive man, was so deeply ingrained in human beings as to be considered hereditary.[16] Given the proper conditions for the play of the imagination, one could literally succumb to terror. This is what happens to Henry Brentshaw in "The Famous Gilson Bequest" when he perceives the specter of Milton Gilson—real or imagined—in a cemetery at night, and to Willard Marsh in "The Suitable Surroundings" when, reading a ghostly tale at night in a reputedly haunted house, he sees the face of a curious boy look in at the window.

Not all of Bierce's tales are so naturalistic. In some he allows considerable room for those experiences that cannot be rationally explained. In "The Secret of Macarger's Gulch," for example, he uses the occult idea that a violent act may so affect the environment in which it takes place as to influence those who enter it a long time later. Elderson, who narrates the tale, goes into the gulch on a quail hunt and spends the night in a ruined cabin. Overtaken by causeless apprehension, he dreams about the people who had lived there, and after he awakens he hears in the dark the reenactment of a murder. Only later does he learn that his dream was accurate, down to such details as the name of the family, their ancestral home in Edinburgh, the shawl the woman wore, and the appearance of her husband. Other tales are even more patently supernatural. In "A Diagnosis of Death" the ghost of Doctor Mannering appears to a character twice to give him a sign which indicates his approaching death; and in "Staley Fleming's Hallucination" the protagonist is found with teeth marks in his neck after seeing the ghost of a dog that belonged to his murdered enemy.

Though each of these tales is in its own way effective, Bierce is best when he uses the Gothic mode to explore human psychology. In "The Death of Halpin Frayser," for example, he creates what is probably his most terrible dream: a vision of horror in a haunted wood, dripping with blood, in which Frayser confronts the soulless body of his mother, who strangles him with her bare hands. In the world of actuality Frayser has been murdered in his sleep by a madman named Branscom, while in the world of psychological realities Frayser has indeed encountered his mother, who throughout his early life had threatened to smother him with her love. But Bierce adds another twist to the tale. The dream occurs in California years after Frayser left his home in Tennessee. His widowed mother had come west to find him, married Branscom, and, having been killed by her new husband, lies in the grave to which Frayser has been unaccountably and unknowingly drawn. Here he has his terrible dream and here he is murdered. "The Death of Halpin Frayser" is among Bierce's most impressive tales, a mixture of the realistic and the occult with a strong undercurrent of psychological meaning. [17]

Neither William Dean Howells nor Ambrose Bierce, however, was able to express in his Gothic tales the psychological subtleties to be found in those of Henry James. As realistic as Howells in his depiction of society, and as interested as Bierce in the strange and uncanny, James was able to blend the real and the fanciful more successfully than they to create more effective and more meaningful Gothic fiction. Unlike Howells, he allows the reader to see the apparitions his characters perceive and to experience with them the terror they feel, but he never indulges in the overwrought descriptions of grisly phenomena that characterize the work of Bierce. James relies on suggestion to create his Gothic effects. By keeping the objects of terror significantly vague and merely suggesting the sinister qualities they possess, he creates the kind of impression which stimulates the reader to conjure up in his own imagination a greater sense of horror than could ever be attained through a detailed description of the objects that suggest it. [18] For this reason, James's ghostly tales are much superior to those of Howells, who describes too little, and those of Bierce, who describes too much.

James's treatment of the ghost in "Sir Edmund Orme" (1891) provides a good example. He is manifest first only in the reactions of Mrs. Marden, who alone sees him, but even when he becomes visible to the narrator of the tale, he seems at first to be only a pale young man dressed in a somewhat old fashioned style. When the narrator learns, however, that the ghost of Sir Edmund Orme haunts Mrs. Marden's daughter, Charlotte, whom the narrator loves, and that the way the young girl treats him will determine whether or not she will see the ghost, Orme's presence becomes increasingly sinister. Charlotte has tendencies toward coquetry, a fault which, in her mother, had led to Orme's death, and as Charlotte toys with the narrator's affections, the ghost hovers about her in a most ominous fashion, much to the concern of her mother and her lover, who alone perceive what is happening. In the final scene, when Mrs. Marden is dying, Charlotte, on the point of making her choice to accept or reject the narrator, sees at last the ghost of Sir Edmund Orme and, throwing herself into the arms of her lover, escapes the sinister apparition by whom she has been haunted.

Though James was less interested in the ghosts themselves than in the way they are perceived by a human consciousness, he had nonetheless to make them appropriate agents for the terror they instill in those who perceive them. Because they were so inactive, he had little use for the unexpressive and undramatic ghosts that had been certified as real by psychical research. Their largely negative quality unsuited them to play a role in an action, and James dismissed them as proper figures for his Gothic tales.[19] He turned instead to the more lively ghosts of the Gothic tradition, and, realist though he may have been in most of his fiction, he placed them in contexts and environments that had been the stock in trade of Gothic writers since the days of Ann Radcliffe. James had read widely in their works[20] and he borrowed extensively from them. He often employs the frame device to lend distance to his tales and represents some of them as having been found in an old manuscript. He even includes the mysterious portrait that seems to come alive, the ghostly chamber, and the haunted castle.

James made excellent use of these Gothic devices to express the psychological state of those who confront the ghosts or enter the haunted precincts. The glowering ancestral portraits in "Owen Wingrave" (1892) express the deep sense of family disapproval that Owen feels when he abandons the military career which all of his forebears have pursued; and the night he spends in the haunted chamber, his confrontation with the ghost of his most forbidding ancestor, and his death in that room—all reveal unmistakably the personal bravery that he, no less than they, truly possesses. The haunted study in "The Real Right

Thing" (1899), like many enclosures in American Gothic fiction, represents the mind of a dead author whose wife and whose biographer not only sense his presence but also become acutely aware that he does not want the biography to be written. In a similar fashion, the house in "The Jolly Corner" becomes in effect the mind of Spencer Brydon, who wanders the labyrinth of its halls and chambers in search of the self he might have become had he spent the productive years of his life at work in New York instead of living freely in Europe.

The best example of James's technique is without question "The Turn of the Screw," a tale which draws heavily on traditional Gothic devices. Bly is the haunted castle, and the unnamed governess plays the role of the traditional Gothic heroine. Like most of her literary forebears, she ventures alone at night into the dark halls to confront the horrors they contain, the ghosts of Peter Quint and Miss Jessel. She has no one to turn to for help but an old housekeeper, Mrs. Grose, and she even has an adventure during a stormy night when she is frightened by a mysterious blast, "a gust of frozen air and a shake of the room as great as if, in the wild wind, the casement had crashed in." When she leaps to her feet, however, she sees "the drawn curtains unstirred and the window still tight." James is deliberately playing a variation upon the traditional Gothic romance, and he even provides the reader with a clue as to his source. When the governess first sees a strange man standing on the tower at Bly, she wonders if the house contains "a mystery of Udolpho" or some insane relative "in unsuspected confinement."[21]

This reference serves a double purpose. It makes clear to the reader the context in which the tale should be read, and it reveals as well the state of mind of the governess, who, even before she identifies the stranger as the ghost of Peter Quint, perceives her experience in terms of Gothic fiction. From this point on, the apparitions come thick and fast, and though James provides us with no definitive evidence by which we may determine their authenticity, neither does he explain the ghosts away as so many Gothic writers before him had done.[22] The governess simply perceives them, and that perception is the donnée of the tale. What happens thereafter is controlled to a large extent by her reactions as she tries to protect the children, Miles and Flora, from the frightening apparitions that she believes are attempting to get at them, and the manuscript she writes is the record of a mind that has been through a genuinely harrowing experience. She creates for the reader a profound sense of the terror she has felt, and she evokes an apprehension of evil that was for her as real as the walls of Bly, the commonplace Mrs. Grose, and the children themselves.

For all the effectiveness of his ghostly tales, however, James cannot be called an American Gothicist in the sense that the term is applied to earlier writers. For Brown, Hawthorne, and Poe, the Gothic mode was the primary means of expression; for James it was hardly more than a technique to be used in a small amount of his short fiction. There are Gothic incidents in some of his major novels—the ghost of Ralph Touchett in *The Portrait of a Lady* (1881), for example, and the grave and enclosure imagery used to describe the feelings of Isabel Archer after she marries Gilbert Osmond—but by and large the Gothic never became for him a major mode of expression.[23] James was a realist who was primarily concerned with the consciousness of his characters as they experienced life in a dense social world. When he turned to the ghostly tale, therefore, it was only to express certain elements in human consciousness that could not be so effectively treated in any other way, and he used the ghosts of the Gothic tradition only because they alone could provide him with effective agents for the psychological themes he wished to develop.

The brief reappearance of the Gothic mode in the serious fiction of the late nineteenth century was, we must conclude, a phenomenon of only minor importance in the history of American Gothicism. Writers such as Howells, Bierce, and James might use the techniques of the mode to exploit the current interest in psychical phenomena, but Howells and James in particular had already committed themselves in their major work to the new theories of literary realism, a practice soon to be followed by ensuing generations of writers. This is not to say that the Gothic died with the works of Poe and Hawthorne, or even with those of Howells, Bierce, and James. Writers from Edith Wharton to William Faulkner have made occasional use of it in their fiction, and Shirley Jackson has shown that serious Gothic romances can be written in the twentieth century. The mode has become a minor one, however, suited to only a narrow range of subjects. No one today could express through its use the broad philosophic themes of Poe or the great moral ones of Hawthorne. The American Gothic reached its peak in their work. After their passing it ceased to play a significant role in major American fiction.

BIBLIOGRAPHICAL NOTE

When this book was prepared for the press, the CEAA/CSE editions of American authors were not yet complete. Some books had been published with their edited texts, while others by the same author existed only in their nineteenth-century forms. This situation created a problem in documentation, especially in those chapters in which volume and page references are included in the text. For some authors the problem was minimal. The Centenary Edition of Hawthorne's works was approaching completion. The romances, tales, and *American Notebooks*, among others, had already appeared. Hence, I had to use an older edition only for *The English Notebooks*. Cooper also presented no problem. Among his novels, new editions of only *The Pioneers* and *The Pathfinder* had been published. Since I quote from neither and cite only the latter, it seemed best to document all of Cooper's novels from the same source, the Mohawk edition, published between 1895 and 1900. I used the new editions of Simms and Howells where available.

Poe, Brown, and Irving presented more serious problems. I have used the Thomas O. Mabbott edition of Poe's tales, cited as *Collected Works* in the notes, and the James A. Harrison edition, cited as *Complete Works*, for items by Poe not included in the Mabbott volumes. For Brown, I have used the modern texts for *Wieland* and *Arthur Mervyn* (volumes 1 and 3 respectively of the Bicentennial Edition of *The Novels and Related Works of Charles Brockden Brown*), but nineteenth-century texts of *Ormond* and *Edgar Huntly* (volumes 6 and 4 respectively of the 1887 edition of *Charles Brockden Brown's Novels*). Most of the works I cite by Irving appear in the new edition of the *Complete Works* published by the University of Wisconsin Press and Twayne Publishers. For *Tales of a Traveller* and *The Alhambra*, however, I have used the Author's Revised Edition of 1856; for *A History of New York*, both the 1809 and 1812 editions. Other works by Irving are identified in the notes.

For the many other British, German, and American novels and tales discussed here, I have turned to a variety of texts. I have used modern editions in many cases not because the texts are of any special value but because the editions often contain useful introductions and the books themselves may be relatively easy of access. For others, however, I have had to turn to older editions, such as Mrs. Barbauld's *The British Novelists,* to collected sets, to first editions, and to early American imprints as they appear on the Readex microcards. These may be located through the Evans and Shaw-Shoemaker numbers. See the appropriate bibliographies. Early American magazines cited here may be found on microfilm in the American Periodicals series for both the eighteenth and nineteenth centuries.

I have been very sparing in the use of secondary sources. Basic works on the Gothic mode—Eino Railo, *The Haunted Castle,* Edith Birkhead, *The Tale of Terror,* and Montague Summers, *The Gothic Quest*—are, of course, cited. But other books not directly related to the mode are also important to an understanding of the Gothic in America and must also be mentioned, especially Terence Martin, *The Instructed Vision;* Howard Kerr, *Mediums, and Spirit-Rappers, and Roaring Radicals,* a discussion of spiritualism in American literature; Maria M. Tatar, *Spellbound: Studies on Mesmerism and Literature*; and Martha Banta, *Henry James and the Occult.* I have cited books and articles on particular authors only when the reference has specific relevance to the point under discussion.

NOTES

ONE: Introduction

1. Nathaniel Hawthorne, *The Marble Faun; or, The Romance of Monte Beni*, in *The Centenary Edition of the Works of Nathaniel Hawthorne* (Columbus, O., 1968), 4: 3.

2. James Fenimore Cooper, *Notions of the Americans: Picked Up by a Travelling Bachelor* (Philadelphia, 1828), 2: 108-12.

3. James Kirke Paulding, "National Literature," *Minor Knickerbockers, Representative Selections*, ed. Kendall B. Taft (New York, 1947), pp. 15-17.

4. *Novus Ordo Seclorum*, the motto on the Great Seal of the United States.

5. A good discussion of the rise and prevalence of Scottish Common Sense philosophy in America is Terence Martin, *The Instructed Vision: Scottish Common Sense Philosophy and the Origins of American Fiction*, Indiana University Humanities Series, no. 48 (Bloomington, Ind., 1961). See especially his initial chapter, "Common Sense Philosophy in America: Provenience and Purpose."

6. This material is discussed in Martin's second chapter, "American Fiction and the Metaphysics of Actuality," especially pp. 60-84.

7. James Fenimore Cooper, *Early Critical Essays (1820-1822)*, with Introduction and Headnotes by James F. Beard, Jr. (Gainesville Fla., 1955), pp. 97-98. For the tentative attribution of this review to Cooper, see pp. xiii-xiv.

8. Ibid., p. 100.

9. [William Cullen Bryant,] "A Pennsylvanian Legend," *New York Review and Atheneum Magazine*, 2 (Dec. 1825): 49.

10. *Complete Works of Edgar Allan Poe*, ed. James A. Harrison (New York, 1902), 10: 30-31, 38-39.

11. William Gilmore Simms, *The Wigwam and the Cabin*, new and rev. ed. (New York, 1856), p. 1. "The Old Woman of Berkeley," a ballad by Robert Southey, recounts the fate of an old witch who, at her burial, is carried off by the devil. Simms no doubt intends the irony which results from the juxtaposition of Goethe's *Faust* with Southey's poem.

12. Simms, *Wigwam and the Cabin*, p. 36.

13. Paulding, "National Literature," p. 15.

14. [James Kirke Paulding,] *Westward Ho! A Tale* (New York, 1832), 1: 177.

15. William Gilmore Simms, "The Last Wager, or the Gamester of the Mississippi," *Wigwam and the Cabin*, pp. 71-72. Cf. the preface to *The House of the Seven Gables* where, in discussing the romance as opposed to the novel, Nathaniel Hawthorne makes a similar point.

16. Eino Railo, *The Haunted Castle: A Study of the Elements of English Romanticism* (London, 1927), pp. 168-71. Another discussion of American Gothicism in a European context is Edith Birkhead, *The Tale of Terror: A Study of the Gothic Romance* (London, 1921), pp. 197-220.

17. See, for example, the odd mixture of Marxist, Freudian, and Jungian principles used by Leslie Fiedler in *Love and Death in the American Novel* (New York, 1960).

18. Of many examples, the most noteworthy perhaps is Marie Bonaparte, *The Life and Works of Edgar Allan Poe: A Psycho-Analytic Interpretation* (London, 1949).

19. Henry James, *The Art of Fiction and Other Essays*, introduction by Morris Roberts (New York, 1948), p. 14.

Two: Early Gothic Imports

1. [Royall Tyler,] *The Algerine Captive; or, The Life and Adventures of Doctor Updike Underhill* (Walpole, N.H., 1797), pp. vi-ix.

2. The information in succeeding paragraphs is drawn from the catalogues of the following libraries and booksellers: William P. Blake, Boston, 1793, 1796, 1798; Thomas Bradford, Philadelphia, 1796; Robert Campbell, Philadelphia, 1791, 1796, 1797; Samuel Campbell, New York, 1794, 1799; Mathew Carey, Philadelphia, 1792, 1793, 1794, 1795; Hocquet Caritat, New York, 1799; Michael and John Conrad, Philadelphia, 1799; John Dabney, Salem, 1791, 1794; Hanover Bookstore, Hanover, N.H., 1799; Library Company, Baltimore, 1797, 1798; Library Society, Boston, 1797; Joseph Nancrede, Boston, 1796, 1798; Thomas Stephens, Philadelphia, 1795; Isaiah Thomas, Worcester, 1792, 1796, Boston, 1793.

3. That *The Italian* arrived earlier, however, is evidenced by the two American editions of the book published in 1797.

4. The dates of the German novels in this and later paragraphs are those of the English translations, and I have provided throughout the real names of the authors rather than the pseudonyms sometimes given on the title pages.

5. For a good discussion of this press and a list of its publications, see Dorothy Blakey, *The Minerva Press, 1790–1820* (London, 1939).

6. The dates in this paragraph are all of the American editions.

7. Although the title page describes it as the second American edition, there seems to be no record of an earlier one in this country.

8. See Sister Mary M. Redden, *The Gothic Fiction in the American Magazines, 1765–1800* (Washington, D.C., 1939). [Gottfried August Bürger,] "The Lass of Fair Wone," *American Universal Magazine*, 1 (Feb. 6, 1797): 211-15; "Lenora," *Weekly Magazine of Original Essays, Fugitive Pieces, and Interesting Intelligence*, 1 (March 17, 1798): 221-23; and "The Chase," *Weekly Magazine*, 2 (July 28, 1798): 413-14.

9. For *Herman of Unna*, see *New-York Magazine; or, Literary Repository*, n.s. 1 (Feb. 1796): 76-82; and *Literary Museum, or Monthly Magazine*, 1 (Feb. 1797): 80-88. For *The Ghost-Seer*, see *New-York Magazine*, 6 (Aug. 1795): 496-501; and *Literary Museum*, 1 (May 1797): 253-60. For *The Italian*, see *New-York Magazine*, n.s. 2 (July 1797): 340-41, and *Philadelphia Minerva*, 3 (Oct. 21, 1797): [4]. For *The Children of the Abbey*, see *Time Piece and Literary Companion*, 2 (Feb. 19 and 21, 1798): [1]; and *Philadelphia Minerva*, 4 (Mar. 24, 1798): 32. For the reviews, see *American Monthly Review*, 2 (June 1795): 174-76; (Aug. 1795): 386-87, 388; 3 (Nov. 1795): 298-99; (Dec. 1795: Appendix): 485, 486-87.

10. "Matthew Gregory Lewis, Esq. M.P.," *Weekly Magazine*, 4 (Apr. 13, 1799): 20-21. See also a review of *The Monk* in *American Universal Magazine*, 4 (Dec. 5, 1797): 53-58. "Mrs. Radcliffe," *New-York Weekly Magazine; or, Miscellaneous Repository*, 2

(Apr. 5, 1797): 318. See also "Mrs. Ann Radcliffe," *Weekly Magazine,* 4 (May 11, 1799): 138.

11. *New-York Weekly Magazine,* 1 (Apr. 20, 1796): 329.

12. *Weekly Magazine,* 2 (June 30, 1798): 278.

13. Horace Walpole, *The Castle of Otranto: A Gothic Story,* in vol. 22 of Mrs. Barbauld's *The British Novelists* (London, 1810), p. 183. See Walpole's apology for his use of the miraculous in the preface to the first edition, ibid. p. 178. Many of the romancers who followed him also set their stories in the distant past: *The Old English Baron,* for example, is set in the fifteenth century, *The Haunted Priory* in the fourteenth, and *Netley Abbey* in the late thirteenth and early fourteenth centuries.

14. Clara Reeve, *The Old English Baron: A Gothic Story,* in vol. 22 of Mrs. Barbauld's *The British Novelists,* p. 5. This book was entitled *The Champion of Virtue: A Gothic Story* when it first appeared in 1777. The edition of 1778 carried the present title.

15. Although prophetic dreams occur in *The Castle of Otranto,* they are not so central to the action as those in the other books. Both Ricardo, the murderer of Alfonso, and Frederic, the supposed heir, receive prophecies in their sleep that are eventually fulfilled.

16. [Stephen Cullen,] *The Haunted Priory; or, The Fortunes of the House of Rayo. A Romance, Founded Partly on Historical Facts* (Philadelphia, 1794), p. 39.

17. Similarities such as these suggest the influence the writers had on each other. For the influence of Radcliffe on Parsons, see Devendra P. Varma, introduction to *The Mysterious Warning, A German Tale,* by Eliza Parsons (London, 1968), p. xii. For the mutual influence of Radcliffe and Smith, see Florence M.A. Hilbish, *Charlotte Smith, Poet and Novelist (1749–1806)* (Philadelphia, 1941), pp. 522-27.

18. Ann Radcliffe, *A Sicilian Romance* (Baltimore, 1795), pp. 44-45.

19. Regina Maria Roche, *Clermont, A Tale,* introduction by Devendra P. Varma (London, 1968), p. 366.

20. Ann Radcliffe, *The Italian; or, The Confessional of the Black Penitents, A Romance,* ed. with introduction by Frederick Garber (London, 1971), p. 35.

21. One truly prophetic dream of the kind to be found in the works of Walpole and his followers does appear, however, in Eleanor Sleath, *The Orphan of the Rhine, A Romance,* introduction by Devendra P. Varma (London, 1968), pp. 351-52. In a pair of dreams, Laurette's grandfather is told to hasten to the Castle of Elfinbach, since it depends on him not only to restore her to her inheritance, but also "to save her from misery and from death."

22. Ann Radcliffe, *The Romance of the Forest: Interspersed with Some Pieces of Poetry,* in vols. 43 and 44 of Mrs. Barbauld's *The British Novelists,* 1: 12, 65-66.

23. Ann Radcliffe, *The Mysteries of Udolpho: A Romance, Interspersed with Some Pieces of Poetry,* ed. with introduction by Bonamy Dobrée (London, 1970), p. 343.

24. Charlotte Smith, *The Old Manor House,* in vols. 36 and 37 of Mrs. Barbauld's *The British Novelists,* 1: 64.

25. Matthew Gregory Lewis, *The Monk,* introduction by John Berryman (New York, 1952), p. 349.

26. For a discussion of this and other sources of *The Monk,* see Montague Summers, *The Gothic Quest: A History of the Gothic Novel* (London, 1938), pp. 223-28.

27. Only in *A Sicilian Romance* did Radcliffe even approach this kind of horror, but she did not exploit it as Lewis did. See the brief episode (p. 192) in which Julia and Hippolitus are trapped in a vault with the decaying bodies of the victims of some banditti.

28. [Cajetan Tschink,] "The Victim of Magical Delusion; or, Interesting Memoirs of Miguel, Duke of Ca*i*a, Unfolding Many Curious Unknown Historical Facts," *New-York Weekly Magazine*, 2 (Aug. 17, 1796): 54.

29. Cf. the four principles discussed in the translator's note at the end of "The Victim of Magical Delusion," *New-York Weekly Magazine*, 2 (Apr. 19, 1797): 330-31; (Apr. 26, 1797): 338-39.

30. Schiller's was the first of these romances to appear in German. First published in separate parts in the German magazine *Thalia* between 1785 and 1789, *The Ghost-Seer* appeared as a separate volume in German in 1789.

31. [Johann Christoph Friedrich von Schiller,] *The Ghost-Seer; or, Apparitionist: An Interesting Fragment, Found among the Papers of Count O*****(New York, 1796), p. 116. The passage may also be found in the text of the novel published in *New-York Weekly Magazine*, 1 (Nov. 18, 1795): 157.

32. [Karl Grosse,] *Horrid Mysteries: A Story Translated from the German of the Marquis of Grosse by Peter Will*, introduction by Devendra P. Varma (London, 1968), p. xv. Further evidence of interest in the society may be found in John Robison, *Proofs of a Conspiracy against All the Religions and Governments of Europe, Carried On in the Secret Meetings of Free Masons, Illuminati, and Reading Societies*. First published in Edinburgh in 1797, it was reprinted in both Philadelphia and New York in 1798.

33. Toward the end of the book, however, there are some hints of social purpose. Volkert, for example, feels justified in robbing a group of monks because of the wrongs he claims they have committed, and in the confession of Wolf, which ends the book, the robber chief claims he was turned into a complete rogue because of "the too great severity of the laws" under which he was punished. See [Karl Kahlert,] *The Necromancer; or, The Tale of the Black Forest, Founded on Facts; Translated from the German of Lawrence Flammenberg by Peter Teuthold*, introduction by Devendra P. Varma (London, 1968), pp. 111-17, 135-37.

THREE: Charles Brockden Brown

Throughout this chapter, text citations of *Wieland* and *Arthur Mervyn* are to volumes 1 and 3 respectively of the Bicentennial Edition of *The Novels and Related Works of Charles Brockden Brown* (Kent, Ohio, 1977, 1980). Citations of *Ormond* and *Edgar Huntly* are to volumes 6 and 4 respectively of *Charles Brockden Brown's Novels* (Port Washington, N.Y., 1963), a reprint of the edition of 1887.

1. See David Lee Clark, *Charles Brockden Brown: Pioneer Voice of America* (Durham, N.C., 1952), where this aspect of Brown's work is emphasized.

2. A study of Brown's novels in relation to British Gothic fiction is Robert D. Hume, "Charles Brockden Brown and the Uses of Gothicism: A Reassessment," *ESQ*, 18 (1st Quart. 1972): 10-18. Hume minimizes the influence of the Gothic novel, however, and does not really analyze the sources of Brown's Gothicism. The influence of Schiller's romance on *Wieland* was noticed by John Keats as early as 1819. See Hyder E. Rollins, ed., *The Letters of John Keats, 1814-1821* (Cambridge, Mass., 1958), 2: 173. Recent scholars have stressed the influence of Tschink; see Harry R. Warfel, "Charles Brockden Brown's German Sources," *Modern Language Quarterly*, 1 (Sept. 1940): 357-65; and Henry A. Pochmann, *German Culture in America: Philosophical and Literary Influences, 1600-1900* (Madison, Wis., 1957), pp. 361-62. On Radcliffe's influence see espe-

cially Fred Lewis Pattee, introduction to *Wieland; or, The Transformation, together with Memoirs of Carwin, the Biloquist, a Fragment* (New York, 1926), pp. xxxviii-xl; and Harry R. Warfel, *Charles Brockden Brown: American Gothic Novelist* (Gainesville, Fla., 1949), pp. 109, 129, 138-39, 156.

3. See Chapter 2, notes 31 and 32, above.

4. *Diary of William Dunlap (1766–1839)* (New York, 1930), pp. 338-39. The *Diary* is paged continuously throughout its three volumes.

5. The latitude and longitude he gives would, however, place it just inside the east coast of Australia.

6. These aspects of Constantia's character are stressed throughout, her only weakness being her lack of training in religion, which places her in danger of succumbing to Ormond's radical arguments (6: 175).

7. *Arthur Mervyn* was published in two parts, the first in Philadelphia in 1799, the second in New York in 1800.

8. Because he copied the details of the elder Wieland's death from the account of a supposedly real occurrence reported in *Literary Magazine, and British Review,* 4 (May 1790): 336-39, Brown clearly intended the event to be a completely natural one, and he signaled his intention to the reader by providing a footnote to additional sources (1: 19). But for the elder Wieland's children, Theodore and Clara, he deliberately leaves unresolved the question of supernatural influence, and they are left to interpret the nature of the event for themselves.

9. "The Man Unknown to Himself" had been the subtitle of Brown's now-lost first novel, *Sky-Walk,* parts of which, William Dunlap believed, were later incorporated into *Edgar Huntly* and other works. See William Dunlap, *The Life of Charles Brockden Brown: together with Selections from the Rarest of His Printed Works, from His Original Letters, and from His Manuscripts Before Unpublished* (Philadelphia, 1815), 1: 259.

10. The material in this and the two following paragraphs I have discussed in greater detail in "Charles Brockden Brown," in *Major Writers of Early American Literature,* ed. Everett Emerson (Madison, Wis., 1972), pp. 280-88. See also Arthur Kimball, *Rational Fictions: A Study of Charles Brockden Brown* (McMinnville, Ore., 1968), pp. 49-74.

FOUR: New European Developments

1. Cecil S. Emden argues "that the main body of the novel was written in about 1794, and that the sections burlesquing horror-novels, and Mrs. Radcliffe's *The Mysteries of Udolpho* in particular, were added some four years later." See "The Composition of *Northanger Abbey,*" *Review of English Studies,* n.s. 19 (Aug. 1968): 279.

2. *The Novels of Jane Austen,* Winchester ed. (Edinburgh, 1911), 9: 271. Although *The Mysteries of Udolpho* is the focus of attention, Austen also mentions *The Italian* and echoes incidents from *A Sicilian Romance* and *The Romance of the Forest.* Other Gothic novels included are *The Monk* and the seven famous "horrid novels" that Isabella Thorpe recommends to the heroine. For their titles, see *Novels of Jane Austen,* 9: 39.

3. *The Novels of Thomas Love Peacock,* introductions and notes by David Garnett (London, 1948), p. 419.

4. American editions of these books are: *St. Leon, A Tale of the Sixteenth Century* (Alexandria, 1801); *Mandeville, A Tale of the Seventeenth Century in England* (New York,

1818; Philadelphia, 1818); *Fatal Revenge; or, the Family of Montorio* (New York, 1808); *Melmoth the Wanderer* (Boston, 1821).

5. Dennis Jasper Murphy [Charles Robert Maturin], *Fatal Revenge; or, The Family of Montorio, A Romance* (New York, 1808), 2: 241.

6. Cf. Dale Kramer, *Charles Robert Maturin* (New York, 1973), p. 27.

7. William Godwin, *Mandeville, A Tale of the Seventeenth Century in England* (Edinburgh, 1817), 1: 28-29.

8. Ibid., p. x.

9. Quoted in Elton Edward Smith and Esther Greenwell Smith, *William Godwin* (New York, 1965), p. 91.

10. Charles Robert Maturin, *Melmoth the Wanderer, A Tale,* introduction by William F. Axton (Lincoln, Neb., 1961), pp. 118-19.

11. For a full discussion of these relations, see Kramer, *Maturin,* pp. 96-100.

12. Ibid., pp. 96, 102, 124-25.

13. Harold Bloom, "Afterword" to *Frankenstein; or, The Modern Prometheus,* by Mary Shelley (New York, 1965), pp. 213-15.

14. See B.Q. Morgan and A.R. Hohlfeld, *German Literature in British Magazines, 1750-1860* (Madison, Wis., 1949), especially p. 53; and V. Stockley, *German Literature As Known in England, 1750-1830* (London, 1929).

15. The dates are those of the English translations. *Undine* was published in German in 1811; *The Devil's Elixirs* in 1816. An American edition of *Undine* appeared in 1824.

16. For the appearance and influence of German literature in the United States, see Scott Holland Goodnight, *German Literature in American Magazines prior to 1846* (Madison, Wis., 1907), especially pp. 33-43; and Pochmann, *German Culture in America,* pp. 327-35.

17. See also Tieck's well known fanciful tales, "The Fair-Haired Eckbert" and "The Trusty Eckart," both of which contain dark undercurrents of fate and compulsion.

18. *The Works of Thomas Carlyle,* Centenary edition (London, n.d.), 22: 114.

19. Ibid., p. 20.

20. Sir Walter Scott, "On the Supernatural in Fictitious Composition; and particularly in the Works of Ernest Theodore William Hoffmann," printed in Ioan Williams, *Sir Walter Scott on Novelists and Fiction* (London, 1968), p. 348. Hoffmann himself changed the "William" in his name to "Amadeus."

21. All of these essays and reviews may be found in Williams, *Scott on Novelists and Fiction.* The dates are those of Scott's reviews.

22. "Horace Walpole" in ibid., p. 89.

23. For a full discussion of Scott's early Gothic works, see Coleman O. Parsons, *Witchcraft and Demonology in Scott's Fiction* (Edinburgh and London, 1964), pp. 49-57. See also Railo, *The Haunted Castle,* pp. 106-08, 141-43, 252-53; and F.W. Stokoe, *German Influence in the English Romantic Period, 1788-1818* (Cambridge, 1926), pp. 61-88.

24. *Waverley; or, 'Tis Sixty Years Since,* Border edition, ed. Andrew Lang (London, 1898), p. 2. All references to Scott's romances are to volumes in the Border edition.

25. Parsons, *Witchcraft and Demonology,* pp. 51-52. Scott mentions the Vehmic courts and their appearance in German fiction, including *Herman of Unna,* in his 1799 introduction to his translation of *Götz von Berlichingen,* reprinted in *Dramatic Works of Goethe* (London, 1850), pp. 403-04.

26. Scott presents this account of the naiad as "the generally received legend," but

also includes two other interpretations. Some people consider the story merely a lingering remnant of "ancient heathen mythology," while others believe it to be the veiled account of the fate that befell a beautiful plebeian girl who was killed in a fit of jealousy by her noble lover (p. 65).

27. Scott used this device in a number of his romances, the most striking use perhaps being the supposed apparition of Henry Morton in Chapter 38 of *Old Mortality* (pp. 513-16).

28. A number of other seers and crones in Scott's romances have the ability to predict approaching death. In *Waverley* a Scottish seer prevents a soldier from shooting a British colonel because he says the officer's time is not yet up. The seer perceives him with his winding sheet wrapped high on his breast and knows that he is fated to die the following day. And Ailsie Gourlay, an old crone in *The Bride of Lammermoor*, correctly predicts an early death for Lucy Ashton, for she sees that "her winding sheet is up as high as her throat already" (p. 435).

29. Scott used a similar technique in a specter tale that did not appear in one of his romances but was published separately in *The Keepsake for 1829* and may be found in *Chronicles of the Canongate*. In this tale, "The Tapestried Chamber," the major characters are converted from skepticism to belief in the supernatural by the appearance of a specter. The tale was told to the author, however, by a Miss Seward, who claimed to have it from an authentic source but concealed the names of the people concerned in it.

FIVE: Washington Irving

Throughout this chapter, text citations of *The Sketch Book* and *Bracebridge Hall* are to volumes 8 and 9 respectively in *The Complete Works of Washington Irving* (Madison, Wis., 1969–1970; Boston, 1976–1981), cited in the notes as *Complete Works*. Text citations of *Tales of a Traveller* are to volume 7 in *The Works of Washington Irving*, Author's Revised Edition (New York, 1856), cited in the notes as *Works* (1856).

1. See Henri Petter, *The Early American Novel* (Columbus, Ohio, 1971), pp. 321, 324-26, 330.

2. Isaac Mitchell, *The Asylum; or, Alonzo and Melissa. An American Tale, Founded on Fact* (Poughkeepsie, 1811), 2: 67-86. The mystery is explained at the end of the book (2: 258-67). For Mitchell's opinion of Mrs. Radcliffe, see 1: xviii. Mitchell's book had previously been serialized in a Poughkeepsie newspaper as "Alonzo and Melissa" in 1804. See Petter, *Early American Novel*, p. 328.

3. See Washington Irving, *Letters of Jonathan Oldstyle, Gent.*, in *Complete Works*, 6: 3-35; and *Washington Irving's Contributions to "The Corrector,"* introduction and attribution by Martin Roth (Minneapolis, Minn., 1968).

4. Pierre [M.] Irving, *The Life and Letters of Washington Irving* (London, 1908), 1: 22; Stanley T. Williams, *The Life of Washington Irving* (New York, 1935), 1: 390.

5. The best evidence for Irving's knowledge of Brown's work is a notice of William Dunlap's biography of Brown in the *Analectic Magazine*, which Irving was editing at the time. The notice, announcing the preparation of the book, contains a paragraph reviewing the strengths of Brown's works and estimating his accomplishment. It fails to mention *Edgar Huntly*, however. See *Analectic Magazine*, 4 (Dec. 1814): 520.

6. *Complete Works*, 1: 55-56, 489, 505.

7. Williams, *Life*, 2: 288. In Irving's fiction, mention of Mrs. Radcliffe may be

found in *Tales of a Traveller* (1824), and the epigraph of *The Mysteries of Udolpho* is quoted in the revised edition of *The Alhambra* (1850). See *Works* (1856), 7: 309; 15: 99.

8. *Complete Works*, 6: 248. Although we cannot always be sure which of the three authors wrote any given passage, their consistency of attitude toward the Gothic makes the problem of attribution here a minor one. For various attributions of this passage, see ibid., pp. 329-30, 332.

9. [Washington Irving,] *A History of New York, From the Beginning of the World to the End of the Dutch Dynasty*, by Diedrich Knickerbocker (New York, 1809), 1: 147.

10. Ibid., 2: 225-26.

11. *Complete Works*, 2: 34.

12. James Beattie, *Dissertations Moral and Critical* (London, 1783), pp. 207-30, 89-95.

13. *Complete Works*, 2: 9, 23, 29. While writing this notebook Irving was preparing his biography of Thomas Campbell, who, Irving knew, had been associated with Dugald Stewart in Edinburgh. See Washington Irving, *Biographies and Miscellanies*, ed. Pierre M. Irving (New York, 1866), p. 148. Stewart discusses the problems caused by an ill-regulated imagination in *Elements of the Philosophy of the Human Mind* (London, 1854), pp. 272-79.

14. *Complete Works*, 2: 34.

15. *Analectic Magazine*, 2 (Nov. 1813): 391-95; 3 (Feb. 1814): 164-68; 4 (Oct. 1814): 313-26.

16. This represents a major change from the edition of 1809. The whole latter part of Book II was rewritten to introduce the character of Oloffe and the sportive Gothic experience he goes through.

17. [Washington Irving,] *A History of New-York, From the Beginning of the World to the End of the Dutch Dynasty*, by Diedrich Knickerbocker, 2nd ed. with alterations (New York, 1812), 1: 88, 93, 94, 102.

18. *Complete Works*, 2: 36.

19. Walter A. Reichart, *Washington Irving and Germany* (Ann Arbor, Mich., 1957), pp. 19-20, 25-32; Pochmann, *German Culture in America*, pp. 367-72.

20. Reichart, *Irving and Germany*, pp. 146-47; Pochmann, *German Culture in America*, p. 377.

21. Reichart, *Irving and Germany*, pp. 21, 38-39. See also *Complete Works*, 2: 273.

22. *Complete Works*, 2: 34-37.

23. Irving may have learned this technique from Scott. He had read *The Antiquary* with its interpolated tale of "The Fortunes of Martin Waldeck" before he met Scott in 1817, for in his account of that meeting he mentions the novel several times. See *Complete Works*, 22: 132, 151, 162.

24. This is of course a direct reference to Gottfried August Bürger's famous ballad "Lenore," which had been current in the United States since at least 1798. See Chapter 2, note 8, above.

25. For the relation of this story to Musäus's "Dumb Love," see Reichart, *Irving and Germany*, pp. 38, 156.

26. For the influence of madness in distorting perception, see Stewart, *Elements*, pp. 78, 183. The madman mistakes imagined objects for realities.

27. Although Irving had been working on "Strange Stories by a Nervous Gentleman" since February 1824, and sent part of the manuscript to John Murray, his publisher, on June 18, 1824, he heard the story that became "The Adventure of the German Student" from Thomas Moore on June 17, wrote the story June 23-24, and forwarded it

to the publisher with instructions to insert it after "The Bold Dragoon." See *Complete Works*, 3: 352-54; and *Memoirs, Journal, and Correspondence of Thomas Moore*, ed. Lord John Russell (London, 1853), 4: 208.

28. Possible sources for this story are discussed in Reichart, *Irving and Germany*, pp. 150-51.

SIX: Further American Developments

1. [James Kirke Paulding,] *Salmagundi*, 2nd ser. no. 7 (Nov. 6, 1819): 43-44. Paulding, both realist and nationalist, objects of course to this attitude of his country-men.

2. Paulding greatly admired and imitated Fielding, and both he and John Pendleton Kennedy were influenced by Sterne.

3. Intended for Richard Henry Dana's *The Idle Man*, *Monaldi* was left in manuscript when the journal ceased publication.

4. William Gilmore Simms, *Martin Faber, the Story of a Criminal, and Other Tales* (New York, 1976), 2: 85. This is a reprint of the 1837 edition. As J. Wesley Thomas has shown, Simms drew heavily on German sources for some of his tales and novels, including (in addition to Bürger and Goethe) Schiller, Fouqué, Hoffmann, and others. See "The German Sources of William Gilmore Simms," *Anglo-German and American-German Crosscurrents*, 1 (1957): 127-53.

5. Cf. James Fenimore Cooper's use of the Gothic, especially the motifs of the Wanderer and the Wild Huntsman, in *The Heidenmauer* (1832), a tale of early sixteenth-century Germany, and his variation on the Secret Tribunal, or Vehme, in the Venetian Council of Three in *The Bravo* (1831). See especially *The Heidenmauer; or, The Benedictines: A Legend of the Rhine*, Mohawk edition (New York, 1896), pp. 213-14, 372-74, 384. Hereafter, all references to Cooper's novels are to this edition.

6. John Pendleton Kennedy, *Rob of the Bowl: A Legend of St. Inigoe's*, ed. William S. Osborne (New Haven, Conn., 1965), p. 355. The text is that of the 1854 edition. See also James Fenimore Cooper's *The Water-Witch* (1830), where optical deceptions and other tricks are used at sea by a smuggler to protect his trade.

7. John Pendleton Kennedy, *Horse-Shoe Robinson, A Tale of the Tory Ascendency*, ed. Ernest E. Leisy (New York, 1937), p. 82. The text is that of the 1852 edition.

8. William Gilmore Simms, *Guy Rivers, A Tale of Georgia* (Chicago, 1890), p. 363.

9. Cf. the similar experience of Virginia Fairfax on her night visit to the Recluse of Jamestown in the early chapters of William Alexander Caruthers's *The Cavaliers of Virginia* (1834).

10. William Gilmore Simms, *Katharine Walton; or, The Rebel of Dorchester* (Chicago, 1890), pp. 306-07. Cf. Simms's use of the sleeping-waking state in *Woodcraft; or, Hawks About the Dovecote*, introduction by Richmond Croom Beatty (New York, 1961), pp. 460-61. This edition of *Woodcraft* is a reprint of the revised edition of 1854. M'Kewn cannot distinguish between dream and reality, the living and the dead, when he confronts Bostwick, whom he supposed drowned.

11. His conclusion is reinforced by the experience of his cousin, Edith, who has a recurring dream "that has always been followed by evil." She dreams of their persecutor, Richard Braxley, just before the events occur that place the characters in a desperate sit-

uation. Robert Montgomery Bird, *Nick of the Woods; or, The Jibbenainosay. A Tale of Kentucky*, ed. Curtis Dahl (New Haven, Conn., 1967), p. 116. The text is that of the 1853 edition, somewhat modernized.

12. For a much more successful use of the device by Simms, see *Eutaw, A Sequel to The Forayers* (New York, 1856), pp. 81-91. Harricane Nell, like Allan M'Aulay in Scott's *A Legend of Montrose*, seems to be gifted with second sight, but Mother Ford, who herself believes that she and her mother saw her father's second self just before he died, provides a possible explanation of Nell's vision of her brother's death: it may have begun as a dream that her active mind now brings before her waking eyes. If so, it is a prophetic one, for her brother is hanged, just as Nell foresaw. For the German source of this character in Goethe's *Wilhelm Meister*, see Thomas, "German Sources," pp. 142-43.

13. See Barton Levi St. Armand, "Harvey Birch as the Wandering Jew: Literary Calvinism in James Fenimore Cooper's *The Spy*," *American Literature*, 50 (Nov. 1978): 348-68.

14. See, for example, *The Pathfinder*, pp. 110-11, 180; and *The Deerslayer*, pp. 33, 71, and passim.

15. For a full discussion of Bird's position, see James C. Bryant, "The Fallen World in *Nick of the Woods*," *American Literature*, 38 (Nov. 1966): 352-64. Cf. R.W.E. Lewis, *The American Adam: Innocence, Tragedy, and Tradition in the Nineteenth Century* (Chicago, 1955), pp. 105-09.

16. Bryant's tale may most conveniently be found in *William Cullen Bryant, Representative Selections*, ed. Tremaine McDowell (New York, 1935), pp. 224-39; Paulding's in *Minor Knickerbockers*, pp. 42-52.

17. See Charles H. Brown, *William Cullen Bryant* (New York, 1971), p. 166. The story may be found in *The Talisman for MDCCCXXVIII* (New York, 1827), pp. 229-88.

18. William S. Osborne, introduction to *Swallow Barn; or, A Sojourn in the Old Dominion*, by John Pendleton Kennedy (New York, 1962), pp. xxviii-xxxiv. This is a reprint of the 1853 edition.

19. The essay may most conveniently be found in *Minor Knickerbockers*, pp. 15-19. See especially p. 15.

20. James Kirke Paulding, *Koningsmarke; or, Old Times in the New World* (New York, 1971), 1: 29. This is a reprint of the revised edition of 1834–1835.

21. James Kirke Paulding, *The Dutchman's Fireside, A Tale*, ed. Thomas F. O'Donnell (New Haven, Conn., 1966), pp. 171-73. The text is that of the 1831 edition, somewhat modernized. The captain's inability to get beyond the first line of his story echoes Corporal Trim's similar experience in Book VIII, Chapter 19 of Laurence Sterne's *Tristram Shandy*.

22. [E.T. Channing,] "The Life of Charles Brockden Brown," *North American Review*, 9 (June 1819): 58-77; James Kirke Paulding, "National Literature," *Minor Knickerbockers*, p. 19; John Neal, *American Writers: A Series of Papers Contributed to Blackwood's Magazine (1824–25)*, ed. Fred Lewis Pattee (Durham, N.C., 1937), pp. 56-68, 213-15, 238-41; Richard Henry Dana, "The Novels of Charles Brockden Brown," *Poems and Prose Writings* (New York, 1850), 2: 325-43. The full reference to Dunlap's biography may be found in Chapter 3, note 10, above.

23. Discussions of Neal's aesthetics may be found in Benjamin Lease, *That Wild Fellow John Neal and the American Literary Revolution* (Chicago, 1972), pp. 69-80; and Donald A. Sears, *John Neal* (Boston, 1978), pp. 29-33.

24. John Neal, *Rachel Dyer,* introduction by John D. Seelye (Gainesville, Fla., 1964), p. 37. This is a reprint of the 1828 edition.

25. *Lionel Lincoln,* p. 432. For a full discussion of the Gothic in *Lionel Lincoln,* see my article, "Cooper's *Lionel Lincoln*: The Problem of Genre," *American Transcendental Quarterly,* no. 24 (Fall 1974): 24-30.

26. Paulding, *Westward Ho!,* 2: 172.

27. For a discussion of Dana's and Allston's relation to Coleridge and the artistic problems that the new thought created, see Doreen Hunter, "America's First Romantics: Richard Henry Dana, Sr., and Washington Allston," *New England Quarterly,* 45 (Mar. 1972): 3-30. See also my article, "Early American Gothic: Brown, Dana, and Allston," *American Transcendental Quarterly,* no. 19 (Summer 1973): 3-8.

28. *Poems and Prose Writings,* 1: 273, 271.

29. These are, of course, the symbolic equivalents of the Norwalk region and Edgar Huntly's cave.

30. See p. 103 and note 3 to this chapter.

31. Bryant had read "Paul Felton" when it first appeared, and defended it against critical attack in a letter to the Boston *Columbian Centinel,* November 27, 1822. See *The Letters of William Cullen Bryant,* ed. William Cullent Bryant II and Thomas G. Voss (New York, 1975–1981), 1: 133-35.

32. "The Indian Spring," *William Cullen Bryant, Representative Selections,* p. 257; "Medfield," *Tales of Glauber-Spa,* by Several American Authors (New York, 1832), 1: 275.

33. For a full discussion of these two tales in relation to Bryant's other short stories, see my article, "Bryant's Fiction: The Problem of Perception," to be published by AMS Press with other papers presented at the William Cullen Bryant Centennial Conference held at Hofstra University, October 1978.

34. Simms himself suggests the comparison. See *The Writings of William Gilmore Simms,* Centennial edition (Columbia, S.C., 1974), 5: 57.

SEVEN: Edgar Allan Poe

1. This story bore the subtitle "A Tale in Imitation of the German" when it was reprinted in the *Southern Literary Messenger* in January 1836. The subtitle was omitted in later printings. See *Collected Works of Edgar Allan Poe,* ed. Thomas O. Mabbott (Cambridge, Mass., 1978), 2: 17-18. Hereafter, all text citations will be to this edition, cited in the notes as *Collected Works.*

2. *The Letters of Edgar Allan Poe,* ed. John Ward Ostrom (New York, 1966), 1: 57-58. This view is contested, of course, by those who consider some or most of Poe's Gothic tales to be parodies, burlesques, or hoaxes. See, for example, Richard P. Benton, "Is Poe's 'The Assignation' a Hoax?" *Nineteenth-Century Fiction,* 18 (Sept. 1963): 193-97; G.R. Thompson, "Poe's 'Flawed' Gothic: Absurdist Techniques in 'Metzengerstein' and the *Courier* Satires," *Emerson Society Quarterly,* no. 60 (Fall 1970): 38-58. Thompson's view is most fully presented in his *Poe's Fiction: Romantic Irony in the Gothic Tales* (Madison, Wis., 1973). For an opposing view, see Benjamin F. Fisher, "Poe's 'Metzengerstein': Not a Hoax," *American Literature,* 42 (Jan. 1971): 487-94.

3. *Collected Works,* 2: 16-17; Celia Whitt, "Poe and *The Mysteries of Udolpho,*" *University of Texas Studies in English,* 17 (1937): 124-31. The relation to *Blackwood's Edin-*

burgh Magazine was noticed at once by James Kirke Paulding. See his letter to Thomas W. White, March 3, 1836, in *The Letters of James Kirke Paulding,* ed. Ralph M. Aderman (Madison, Wis., 1962), p. 174.

4. *Collected Works,* 1: 678-79 and footnote. The *Blackwood's* stories are "The Man in the Bell," *Blackwood's Edinburgh Magazine,* 10 (Nov. 1821), 373-75; and "The Iron Shroud," idem, 28 (Aug. 1830): 364-71. A third possible source is "The Involuntary Experimentalist," idem, 42 (Oct. 1837): 487-92. For a discussion of Poe's relation to British magazines, see Michael Allen, *Poe and the British Magazine Tradition* (New York, 1969).

5. *The Complete Works of Edgar Allan Poe,* ed. James A. Harrison (New York, 1902), 8: 92; *Collected Works,* 2: 55, 64, 698. The Harrison edition will hereafter be cited in the notes as *Complete Works.*

6. *Complete Works,* 8: 63-64, 233-34; John Robert Moore, "Poe's Reading of *Anne of Geierstein,*" *American Literature,* 22 (Jan. 1951): 493-96; Donald A. Ringe, "Poe's Debt to Scott in 'The Pit and the Pendulum,'" *English Language Notes,* 18 (June 1981): 281-83.

7. *Collected Works,* 3: 936; David Lee Clark, "The Sources of Poe's 'The Pit and the Pendulum,'" *Modern Language Notes,* 44 (June 1929): 349-56; Boyd Carter, "Poe's Debt to Charles Brockden Brown," *Prairie Schooner,* 27 (Summer 1953): 190-96. *Complete Works,* 10: 50; 11: 102, 109-10; 12: 248-49; 13: 95, 97, 153-54.

8. Thompson, *Poe's Fiction,* pp. 35-36, 110-11. *Complete Works,* 10: 37-39. For a full discussion of Poe's interest in and use of *Undine,* see Burton R. Pollin, "*Undine* in the Works of Poe," *Studies in Romanticism,* 14 (Winter 1975): 59-74.

9. *Collected Works,* 2: xxiii-xxiv; Pochmann, *German Culture in America,* pp. 388-408. For a list of German works in translation "available to Poe," see Thompson, *Poe's Fiction,* pp. 205-07. It will be remembered, however, that, as Poe himself said, the terror in his tales "is not of Germany, but of the soul." See *Collected Works,* 2: 473.

10. Sidney E. Lind, "Poe and Mesmerism," *PMLA,* 62 (Dec. 1947): 1082.

11. See *Collected Works,* 2: 667 for the material Poe excised in his revision of the story. For a discussion of Poe's revision, see Richard W. Dowell, "The Ironic History of Poe's 'Life in Death': A Literary Skeleton in the Closet," *American Literature,* 42 (Jan. 1971): 478-86.

12. *Complete Works,* 10: 30.

13. Ibid., 9: 138-39.

14. *Letters of Poe,* 1: 118.

15. These views are well summarized and answered in James Schroeter, "A Misreading of Poe's 'Ligeia,'" *PMLA,* 76 (Sept. 1961): 397-406. The argument still continues. See Thompson, *Poe's Fiction,* pp. 77-87.

16. A good discussion of the issue may be found in James W. Gargano, "The Question of Poe's Narrators," *College English,* 25 (Dec. 1963): 177-81, reprinted in *The Recognition of Edgar Allan Poe,* ed. Eric W. Carlson (Ann Arbor, Mich., 1966), pp. 308-16.

17. *Complete Works,* 11: 109.

18. Cf. Richard Wilbur, "The House of Poe," Library of Congress Anniversary Lecture, May 4, 1959, reprinted in *Recognition of Edgar Allan Poe,* pp. 255-77; and Nina Baym, "The Function of Poe's Pictorialism," *South Atlantic Quarterly,* 65 (Winter 1966): 46-54. Although both discuss many of the same elements as I, they come to quite different conclusions.

19. *Letters of Poe*, 1: 161.

20. *Complete Works*, 13: 148-49.

21. Darrel Abel first suggested an opposition of Life-Reason to Death-Madness in his treatment of "The Fall of the House of Usher," but he did not extend the discussion beyond that tale. See "A Key to the House of Usher," *University of Toronto Quarterly*, 18 (Jan. 1949): 176-85, especially p. 179.

22. That Morella feels no terror at her approaching death is more clearly expressed in the earliest version of the tale, the unfinished manuscript, than it is in the one Poe published. See *Collected Works*, 2: 228, 232.

23. "The Cask of Amontillado" may also belong to this group of stories. Montresor plans the murder of Fortunato with careful thought, and he retains his individual identity by concentrating on his personal revenge for fifty years.

24. Though William Bysshe Stein mentions "the Gothic convention of the common fate of twins" in "The Twin Motif in 'The Fall of the House of Usher,'" *Modern Language Notes*, 75 (Feb. 1960): 109, he cites no evidence for the statement.

25. Cf. Charles Feidelson, Jr., *Symbolism and American Literature* (Chicago, 1953), p. 42.

26. *Complete Works*, 3: 229-30.

27. Ibid., pp. 241-42.

28. The relation between *Eureka* and "The Fall of the House of Usher" has been discussed by a number of scholars. See Maurice Beebe, "The Fall of the House of Pyncheon," *Nineteenth-Century Fiction*, 11 (June 1956): 3-6; E. Arthur Robinson, "Order and Sentience in 'The Fall of the House of Usher,'" *PMLA*, 76 (Mar. 1961): 73-74; and John F. Lynen, *The Design of the Present: Essays on Time and Form in American Literature* (New Haven, Conn., 1969), pp. 229-36. For a more general discussion of the relation of *Eureka* to Poe's work, see Joseph J. Moldenhauer, "Murder as a Fine Art: Basic Connections between Poe's Aesthetics, Psychology, and Moral Vision," *PMLA*, 83 (May 1968): 289-90.

29. Cf. Joseph P. Roppolo, "Meaning and 'The Masque of the Red Death,'" *Tulane Studies in English*, 13 (1963): 59-69.

EIGHT: Nathaniel Hawthorne

1. J. Donald Crowley, "Historical Commentary," *Mosses from an Old Manse*, in *The Centenary Edition of the Works of Nathaniel Hawthorne* (Columbus, O., 1974), 10: 534. Hereafter, text citations are to this edition.

2. Randall Stewart, *Nathaniel Hawthorne: A Biography* (New Haven, Conn., 1948), p. 8.

3. Neal F. Doubleday, *Hawthorne's Early Tales: A Critical Study* (Durham, N.C., 1972), pp. 35-36. Hawthorne mentions Brown in *Mosses from an Old Manse*, *Works*, 10: 174, 380; and Walpole's *Castle of Otranto* in *The English Notebooks*, ed. Randall Stewart (New York, 1941), p. 552.

4. For discussions of Hawthorne's use of the Gothic in *Fanshawe*, see Jesse Sidney Goldstein, "The Literary Source of Hawthorne's *Fanshawe*," *Modern Language Notes*, 60 (Jan. 1945): 1-8 (the source is *Melmoth the Wanderer*); and Nina Baym, "Hawthorne's Gothic Discards: *Fanshawe* and 'Alice Doane,'" *Nathaniel Hawthorne Journal* (1974), pp. 105-15.

5. For a discussion of Hawthorne's use of such mysterious paintings, see Millicent Bell, *Hawthorne's View of the Artist* (New York, 1962), pp. 78-83, 122-25.

6. Hawthorne's use of traditional Gothic materials is discussed in Jane Lundblad, *Nathaniel Hawthorne and the Tradition of Gothic Romance, Essays and Studies on American Language and Literature*, 4 (1946). See also William Bysshe Stein, *Hawthorne's Faust: A Study of the Devil Archetype* (Gainesville, Fla., 1953), pp. 35-50, where Gothic influences are presented in terms of Hawthorne's interest in and use of the Faust legend.

7. Cf. Ronald T. Curran, "'Yankee Gothic': Hawthorne's 'Castle of Pyncheon,'" *Studies in the Novel*, 8 (Spring 1976): 69-80. Curran sees *The House of the Seven Gables* as an American adaptation of the traditional Gothic romance.

8. Pochmann, *German Culture in America*, p. 388. Hawthorne does, however, mention Tieck and Hoffmann in *The Marble Faun* as if he were familiar with their fiction. See *Works*, 4: 32. See also Hubert I. Cohen, "Hoffmann's 'The Sandman': A Possible Source for 'Rappaccini's Daughter,'" *ESQ*, 18 (3rd Quart. 1972): 148-53.

9. Doubleday, *Hawthorne's Early Tales*, pp. 42-49.

10. A closer relation can perhaps be made between *The House of the Seven Gables* and *The Bride of Lammermoor*. The likeness between the old Puritan, Colonel Pyncheon, and his descendant, the Judge, may derive from a similar resemblance between the Master of Ravenswood and his ancestor, Malise of Ravenswood, in Scott's novel. See *The Bride of Lammermoor*, pp. 247, 250, 414.

11. This relation was noted in Neal F. Doubleday, "Hawthorne's Use of Three Gothic Patterns," *College English*, 7 (Feb. 1946): 258-59. Since "Ethan Brand" is a late story, the material is not included in Doubleday's book, cited above.

12. See *The American Notebooks*, July 27-Aug. 11, Aug. 31, Sept. 7, 1838, in *Works*, 8: 89-109, 129-36, 144-45.

13. *Melmoth the Wanderer*, pp. 380, 29, 244.

14. See my article, "Hawthorne's Night Journeys," *American Transcendental Quarterly*, no. 10 (Spring 1971): 30. A full discussion of Hawthorne's use of laughter is Robert Dusenbery, "Hawthorne's Merry Company: The Anatomy of Laughter in the Tales and Short Stories," *PMLA*, 82 (May 1967): 285-88.

15. See John D. Seelye's introduction to *Rachel Dyer*, p. xii.

16. See above, pp. 90-91.

17. In this connection, it might be well to observe that Hawthorne himself was greatly interested in ghosts and was prepared, apparently, to accept their reality. His notebooks contain the record of ghosts he had heard about and the ghostly tales he had shared with others. He records in *The American Notebooks* the strange sounds that he and especially Sophia, his wife, had heard in the Old Manse in 1842 (*Works*, 8: 325), an experience that he somewhat playfully treats in the introductory sketch to *Mosses from an Old Manse* (*Works*, 10: 17-18); and he mentions in the notebooks an apparition that both of them, independently and repeatedly, saw entering their front yard at Salem in 1847. "I have often," he writes, "while sitting in the parlor, in the day-time, had a perception that somebody was passing the windows—but, on looking towards them, nobody is there. The appearance is never observable when looking directly towards the window, but only by such a side-long or indirect glance as one gets while reading, or intent on something else. But I know not how many times I have raised my head, or turned towards the window, with the certainty that somebody was passing" (*Works*, 8: 279).

18. [Charles W. Webber,] "Hawthorne," *American Review: A Whig Journal of Politics, Literature, Art and Science*, 4 (Sept. 1846): 311.

19. According to James J. Lynch, the devil is most often treated humorously in American literature "and almost never as the grand figure." See "The Devil in the Writings of Irving, Hawthorne, and Poe," *New York Folklore Quarterly*, 8 (Summer 1952): 112. Hawthorne seems to be an exception to this rule.

20. David Levin, "Shadows of Doubt: Specter Evidence in Hawthorne's 'Young Goodman Brown,'" *American Literature*, 34 (Nov. 1962): 344-52.

21. For a discussion of Brown's responsibility for his own despair, see Thomas F. Walsh, Jr., "The Bedeviling of Young Goodman Brown," *Modern Language Quarterly*, 19 (Dec. 1958): 331-36.

22. For a discussion of Chillingworth's diabolism, especially as seen in relation to Milton's Satan, see Darrel Abel, "The Devil in Boston," *Philological Quarterly*, 32 (Oct. 1953): 366-81. Cf. Stein, *Hawthorne's Faust*, pp. 104-13. Stein sees Chillingworth and other such characters not primarily as devils but as Faust figures.

23. Another but perhaps not so effective devil figure is Westervelt in *The Blithedale Romance* (1852). See, for example, *Works*, 3: 92, 158, 188, where he is associated with devil imagery.

24. Hawthorne writes of "the hollow prison-house of the fire" (11: 89). For the hell imagery, see pp. 162-63 above.

25. For a good discussion of this, see John W. Shroeder, "'That Inward Sphere': Notes on Hawthorne's Heart Imagery and Symbolism," *PMLA*, 65 (March 1950): 106-19.

26. Washington Irving had used a similar image in *Tales of a Traveller*, where "St. Peter's dome" is viewed as a "monument . . . over the grave of ancient Rome." See his *Works*, 7: 315.

27. See Mark 5:1-20 and corresponding passages in Matthew and Luke.

28. Tower imagery in *The Marble Faun* has been discussed in Gene A. Barnett, "Hawthorne's Italian Towers," *Studies in Romanticism*, 3 (Summer 1964): 252-56.

29. For a good discussion of the contrast between England and America in this novel, see Cushing Strout, "Hawthorne's International Novel," *Nineteenth-Century Fiction*, 24 (Sept. 1969): 169-81. Similar ideas may also be found in Gary J. Scrimgeour, "*The Marble Faun*: Hawthorne's Faery Land," *American Literature*, 36 (Nov. 1964): 271-87; and Clare R. Goldfarb, "*The Marble Faun* and Emersonian Self-Reliance," *American Transcendental Quarterly*, no. 1 (1st Quart. 1969): 19-23.

NINE: Conclusion

1. According to Randall Stewart, the British edition of *The Marble Faun*, called *Transformation*, was published on February 28, the American edition "a few days later." See *Hawthorne*, pp. 210-11.

2. Henry James, *Hawthorne* (Ithaca, N.Y., 1966), p. 34.

3. Ibid., pp. 34-35.

4. Ibid., pp. 52, 90, 98, 108, 131, 134.

5. Originally published as *Tales of Soldiers and Civilians*. Though dated 1891, it actually appeared in 1892.

6. See also Melville's short tale "The Bell-Tower," *Putnam's Monthly Magazine,* 6 (Aug. 1855): 123-30, and his satire on the Gothic tale, "The Apple-Tree Table; or, Original Spiritual Manifestations," idem, 7 (May 1856): 465-75.

7. For the early history of mesmerism in eighteenth-century France, see Robert Darnton, *Mesmerism and the End of the Enlightenment in France* (Cambridge, Mass., 1968), pp. 3-10, 47-72. For the influence of mesmerism on nineteenth-century literature, including the works of Poe, Hawthorne, and James, see Maria M. Tatar, *Spellbound: Studies on Mesmerism and Literature* (Princeton, N.J., 1978).

8. A good discussion of the development of spiritualism and its influence on American literature is Howard Kerr, *Mediums, and Spirit-Rappers, and Roaring Radicals: Spiritualism in American Literature, 1850-1900* (Urbana, Ill., 1972).

9. William Dean Howells, *The Undiscovered Country* (Boston, 1880), pp. 155-57.

10. Henry James, *The Bostonians,* introduction by Leon Edel, in *The Bodley Head Henry James* (London, 1967), 3: 107-10.

11. Ibid., p. 15.

12. For a good discussion of these developments, see Martha Banta, *Henry James and the Occult: The Great Extension* (Bloomington, Ind., 1972), pp. 9-36.

13. See the treatment of Bierce's style in Carey McWilliams, *Ambrose Bierce: A Biography* (New York, 1929), pp. 224-25.

14. William Dean Howells, *The Shadow of a Dream,* ed. Martha Banta, Ronald Gottesman, and David J.Nordloh, in *A Selected Edition of W.D. Howells,* 17 (Bloomington, Ind., 1970): 113-14.

15. William Dean Howells, *Questionable Shapes* (New York, 1903), pp. 36, 151-52, 218.

16. See *The Collected Works of Ambrose Bierce* (New York, 1966), 2: 294-95; 3: 48, 113-15.

17. Cf. M.E. Grenander, *Ambrose Bierce* (Boston, 1971), pp. 106-14. Grenander overinterprets, I believe, in trying to make all the events of the story rationally explainable. See also William Bysshe Stein, "Bierce's 'The Death of Halpin Frayser': The Poetics of Gothic Consciousness," *ESQ,* 18 (1st Quart. 1972): 115-22.

18. See especially James's discussion of "The Turn of the Screw" in the preface to volume 12 of the New York edition of his works. It may conveniently be found in Henry James, *The Art of the Novel,* introduction by R.P. Blackmur (New York, 1962), pp. 175-76.

19. Ibid., pp. 169, 174-75.

20. Leon Edel, introduction to *The Ghostly Tales of Henry James* (New Brunswick, N.J., 1948), pp. x-xi.

21. *Ghostly Tales of Henry James,* pp. 519-20, 457. The second reference is, of course, to Charlotte Brontë's *Jane Eyre* (1847).

22. It seems clear from his notebooks, however, that James intended his ghosts to be taken as real. See *The Notebooks of Henry James,* ed. F.O. Matthiessen and Kenneth B. Murdock (New York, 1947), pp. 178-79, 299. Cf. James's preface to the story in *Art of the Novel,* pp. 175-76.

23. Henry James, *The Portrait of a Lady,* New York edition (New York, 1908). The ghost may be found on 3: 62-65, and 4: 418; the enclosure imagery on 4: 190, 199, 358, and 393. James's projected full-length Gothic romance, *The Sense of the Past,* was never completed. The fragment was published posthumously in 1917.

INDEX

MAIN
SEP 2 6 1986